Psychology and Artificial Intelligence

Oliver Hoffmann

Psychology and Artificial Intelligence

Machines, Consciousness, and the Human Psyche

Springer

Oliver Hoffmann
London, England

ISBN 978-3-662-73146-8 ISBN 978-3-662-73147-5 (eBook)
https://doi.org/10.1007/978-3-662-73147-5

This book is a translation of the original German edition "Die Psychologie und die Künstliche Intelligenz " by Oliver Hoffmann, published by Springer-Verlag GmbH, DE in 2025. The translation was done with the help of an artificial intelligence machine translation tool. A subsequent human revision was done primarily in terms of content, so that the book will read stylistically differently from a conventional translation. Springer Nature works continuously to further the development of tools for the production of books and on the related technologies to support the authors.

This Springer imprint is published by the registered company Springer-Verlag GmbH, DE, part of Springer Nature.
The registered company address is: Heidelberger Platz 3, 14197 Berlin, Germany

Preface

The world is in a remarkable state of transformation, the full extent of which many have yet to grasp. Artificial intelligence (AI) has long since begun to quietly infiltrate our lives—it organizes our decisions, influences our thinking, and guides our daily actions. Often, we hardly notice how profound and far-reaching this subtle change truly is. The sheer ubiquity of AI may seem convenient, but the inevitable question arises: Who is actually in control here? Are we the ones steering the technology, or is it the technology that is shaping us?

It seems as though we, as humans, find ourselves in a paradoxical state of comfort and ignorance. While we welcome the efficiency and possibilities of artificial intelligence, we turn a blind eye to the subtle psychological shifts taking place within us. Machines are increasingly taking over tasks that were once the exclusive domain of the human mind—from diagnosing diseases to conducting personal conversations. But what does this mean for our own cognitive and emotional autonomy?

We are losing ourselves—not in the sense that machines would physically replace us, but in a much deeper, psychological sense. Our trust in machines that guide us, lead us, and make decisions for us is growing. And with this trust, our dependence also increases. We are gradually relinquishing responsibility—not just for trivial tasks, but for areas that touch the very foundation of our human identity: empathy, judgment, creativity.

The technological revolution brought about by AI is often celebrated as a triumph of human ingenuity. Yet, at the same time, an uncomfortable question arises: If we create machines that surpass us in certain areas where we once considered ourselves irreplaceable—what, then, remains of our humanity? Is it not time for us to critically examine the psychological effects of these technologies? Humans are more than just algorithmic data processors, more than just systems that process inputs and generate outputs. Yet it is precisely this distinction that begins to blur if we do not thoroughly engage with the limits and challenges of AI.

The current enthusiasm for artificial intelligence often overlooks the fact that machines have no emotions, no intentions, and no consciousness. They simulate human behavior, and they do so with a precision and efficiency that can often dazzle us. But are we deceived by this illusion? Do we really believe that a machine that imitates feelings is actually capable of replacing human relationships or deep interpersonal connections?

We are facing a challenge that goes far beyond technological questions. It is deeply psychological and existential. When we empower machines to make decisions and interact with us on a level we have traditionally considered human—where does that leave humanity? The convenient answer would be to say that machines are merely tools that make our lives easier. But this answer falls short. In reality, we are dealing with a shift that calls into question our entire understanding of autonomy, intelligence, and identity.

This book is not intended to be just another analysis of the technological advances of AI. It aims to provoke, to challenge, and to spark a debate that focuses on the psychological and ethical questions we have ignored for far too long. In a world fascinated by the superiority of machines, it is time for us to ask: What truly makes us human? And are we prepared to defend it? For the real danger does not lie in the technology itself, but in our own indifference, which fails to recognize the profound impact these technologies have on our thinking, feeling, and behavior.

This book aims to highlight the already highly relevant psychological components of artificial intelligence and to provide a deep insight into the complex interactions between humans and machines. The goal is not to present a technical analysis of how AI works, but rather to explore from a psychological perspective how this technology is changing our thinking, feeling, and behavior—and what this means for the future of the human psyche.

1. Identifying the Psychological Components of AI

AI is no longer merely an abstract technological innovation, but a system that actively intervenes in our ways of living and thinking. Smart assistants, chatbots, algorithms that predict and influence our behavior—all these technologies have a direct impact on our psyche, often without our conscious awareness. A central aim of this book is to shed light on these psychological components. How do AI systems influence our thinking? How do they change our perception of the world and of ourselves? These questions will be explored in depth in the following chapters.

2. What AI Does to the Human Psyche

Another focus of the book is the question of what AI actually does to the human psyche. In a world where machines increasingly demonstrate cognitive abilities similar to or superior to our own, the question arises: What impact does this have on our self-understanding as thinking, feeling beings? Will we, as humans, feel our value threatened by competition with machines, or is there a positive psychological transformation? The book explores how contact with AI influences our emotional world, whether through the use of AI as a "friend," "therapist," or "decision-maker." What happens when machines begin to simulate our emotional needs and suggest to us that they truly understand us?

3. Examining Topics from a Psychological Perspective

This book aims to move the discussion about AI beyond the purely technical and economic sphere and to adopt a psychological perspective. Topics such as the bond between humans and machines, the role of empathy and emotions, the transformation of social interactions through AI, and the impact on our freedom of choice are examined in depth. The psychological perspective makes it possible to identify the subtle, often overlooked changes in human behavior and thinking that arise from the constant use of AI in our lives. In this way, we can recognize not only the risks but also the opportunities presented by these new technologies.

4. What changes in human psychology and the scientific discipline?

Artificial intelligence is not only transforming psychological processes within the individual, but also the science of psychology itself. How can we understand human thinking and feeling in a world where machines simulate or imitate parts of these abilities? What does it mean for cognitive psychology when machines are capable of recognizing complex patterns and making decisions that were once the exclusive domain of the human mind?

The book examines how the discipline of psychology itself must be reimagined under the influence of AI. Can machines replace the human therapist? Will the study of the human psyche be revolutionized by algorithms and machine learning? These questions concern not only the practice of psychology, but also its theory and methodology. Ultimately, the central question is: Is AI a tool that can enrich and expand human psychology, or does it pose a threat that forces us to fundamentally reconsider our self-understanding as psychologically complex beings?

This book seeks not only to find answers, but also to encourage reflection—on the future of the human psyche in a world increasingly shaped by artificial intelligence.

It may be tempting to hand over control to an "intelligent" machine that does everything faster, more precisely, and seemingly more objectively. Yet in doing so, we risk losing the fundamental qualities that make us unique as human beings. This book is about not only asking these questions, but probing them to their very core. It is a wake-up call to a society that is hurtling into the future at breakneck speed, without being aware of the psychological consequences.

In December 2024 Oliver Hoffmann

Contents

1

Introduction: Changing Systems of Thought—Human and Machine

"The machine seems to distance us from nature. And yet it is precisely the machine that subjects us with particular rigor to the eternal laws of nature."

– Antoine de Saint-Exupéry

The rapid development of Artificial Intelligence (AI) in recent decades has led to intense discussions about the nature of human thought. As early as a pioneering contribution, McCarthy and Hayes (1969, p. 46) laid the foundation for today's prominent debate on whether and to what extent mental processes can be replicated by formal algorithms. In this context, the provocative thesis is repeatedly raised that human consciousness could ultimately be understood as a highly complex biological algorithm. The ability of modern AI systems to effectively take over cognitive functions such as pattern recognition, language processing, or strategic decision-making seems to support this view.

But the supposed parallels between human thinking and machine learning processes do not come without far-reaching consequences. From a neurobiological perspective, the brain has been regarded since Hebb (1949, p. 62) as a vast network of interacting neurons, in which synaptic weights play a key role in learning. This basic assumption is clearly reflected in the concepts of artificial neural networks, which learn by iteratively adjusting the weights between their nodes. The increasing similarity of the described principles blurs the boundaries between biological and artificial information processing systems, thus challenging classical notions of the uniqueness of human cognition.

O. Hoffmann, *Psychology and Artificial Intelligence*,
https://doi.org/10.1007/978-3-662-73147-5_1

The topic becomes particularly challenging when the idea of "freedom" comes into play. Psychological and neuroscientific studies, including the well-known experiments by Libet (1985, p. 529), have indicated that many decisions may be made unconsciously before they reach consciousness. These findings fuel controversy regarding the autonomy of the human will. Could it be that the experience of freedom is merely the result of highly complex, yet deterministically unfolding neural processes? Or could a concept of free will be developed beyond purely causal-mechanistic models, one that takes emergent phenomena into account?

The following sections will examine these fundamental questions from various perspectives. Chapter one picks up on the arguments and findings from the preceding texts and expands them with a systematic consideration of relevant theoretical and empirical works. The aim is to develop a comprehensive understanding of how closely human thinking and machine learning methods actually converge—and what consequences this has for our self-concept as autonomous, freely deciding beings.

1.1 From Science Fiction to Reality: AI in Everyday Life

The idea of a world in which machines possess highly developed intelligence was for a long time the exclusive domain of science fiction stories. Authors such as Isaac Asimov or Arthur C. Clarke staged dystopian or utopian scenarios in their novels and stories, in which computers, robots, or other artificial entities were not only tools but potentially independent agents (Asimov, 1950, pp. 7–15; Clarke, 1968, p. 22). These imaginings catered to both human hopes and fears: while the prospect of support from intelligent machines seemed promising, the fear that these very machines could turn against their creators was a recurring motif. Names like HAL 9000 from "2001: A Space Odyssey" (Kubrick & Clarke, 1968, p. 45) or the Terminator (Cameron & Hurd, 1984, p. 13) have left a lasting mark on the cultural image of Artificial Intelligence.

The Transformation from Fiction to Technological Reality

With the advent of the 21st century, it has become clear that AI has long since left the realm of fiction and entered our everyday lives (Tegmark, 2017, p. 29). The development has progressed more rapidly than many experts predicted in the 1980s and 1990s. Back then, AI research focused on expert systems or pattern recognition, which were applied in highly specialized fields such as medical diagnostics or manufacturing (Russell & Norvig, 2020, pp. 104–105). Today, however, AI applications are everywhere:

- Voice assistants like Alexa, Siri, or Google Assistant accompany us while shopping, cooking, or scheduling appointments.
- Personalized recommendation systems on platforms like Netflix or YouTube analyze our viewing behavior and predict which content is most likely to appeal to us (Zhang et al., 2019, p. 3002).
- Navigation services anticipate our destinations based on our habits and suggest optimized routes or means of transportation (Goodchild, 2020, p. 17).

These technologies often appear inconspicuous and are perceived as convenient aids that make our daily lives easier. But it is precisely here that the discrepancy lies between the spectacular science fiction vision and the quiet omnipresence of modern AI: where once futuristic robot armies or rebellious computers played the leading role, today it is invisible algorithms running on server farms and making decisions in the background (Mainzer, 2016, p. 13).

Omnipresence and Psychological Implications

The integration of AI into our everyday lives raises far more questions than just those of technical implementation. Particularly relevant is the psychological and philosophical dimension of the gradual merging of human and machine (Harari, 2018, pp. 129–130). The omnipresent algorithms, which we often do not even consciously perceive, are increasingly influencing our decision-making authority:

1. **Delegation of Responsibility**
   With every use of a recommendation system or navigation service, we relinquish a part of our personal responsibility (Weizenbaum, 1976, p. 244). What were once significant deliberations or complex decision-making processes are now taken over by machine systems. While this delegation leads to gains in efficiency and comfort, it also has a potential downside: we become accustomed to "something else" thinking and making decisions for us (Carr, 2014, p. 91).

2. **Restriction of Scope for Action**
   Recommendation systems can significantly narrow the world we perceive. Based on our previous preferences and behavioral patterns, we are always presented with matching content (Pariser, 2011, p. 38). As a result, one risks remaining in a filter bubble and no longer perceiving new perspectives or information (Sunstein, 2018, p. 5).
3. **Dependence through Habituation Effects**
   As a consequence, a creeping dependence develops. If the technology fails, we suddenly appear helpless; we have forgotten how to find our own way, compare prices, or research sources independently (Spitzer, 2012, pp. 66–67). When AI systems seemingly effortlessly provide us with the "right" decisions, our own decision-making ability can atrophy (Sampson & König, 2021, p. 15).
4. **Change in Self-Image**
   The more we rely on AI, the more pressing the question becomes to what extent our self-image and concept of humanity are shaped by this machinery (Hofkirchner & Fuchs, 2003, p. 89). If algorithms predict and optimize our behavior, what becomes of the much-vaunted human freedom and creativity (Floridi, 2014, p. 83)?

Against this background, the question arises as to whether and how we can still retain control over our lives when decisions are increasingly pre-structured by machine systems (Bostrom, 2014, p. 72). Precisely because the algorithms operate in the background and their processes are not readily transparent, we find ourselves in a situation where we use the mechanisms but no longer fully understand them (Pasquale, 2015, p. 19).

- **Transparency and Explainability**
  To counter growing intransparency, research is being conducted worldwide in the field of "Explainable AI" (XAI) (Miller, 2019, p. 68). The aim is to ensure that AI systems can justify their decisions in a form understandable to humans. However, while this is technically demanding, the ethical question also arises as to how much explanation we really require (Jobin et al., 2019, p. 398).
- **Societal Regulation**
  Societal and political regulation of AI is still in its infancy (European Commission, 2021, pp. 2–3). Although there are initial approaches to an ethical framework within which AI should operate, it remains unclear

how effective such measures are or can be. This involves questions of data sovereignty, algorithmic fairness, or responsibility in the event of erroneous decisions (Algorithmic Accountability Act, 2019, p. 4).

- **Psychological Autonomy**
  In addition to formal regulations, the concept of psychological autonomy is coming to the fore: how do people maintain their self-determination in a world where the supposedly "right" answers and options are always just a click away? (Turkle, 2015, p. 117).

Human Freedom versus Machine Efficiency

What was once considered a distant vision of the future in novels and films has now arrived in everyday life and is profoundly influencing us. Artificial Intelligence is no longer a sci-fi concept but an omnipresent reality that shapes our thinking, actions, and decisions (Brynjolfsson & McAfee, 2014, p. 4). The psychological challenge is to view this development not only as a technical phenomenon but also to examine its effects on our self-perception, our freedom of choice, and our social structures (Searle, 1980, p. 422).

The crucial question is: **Where do we draw the line?** Do we want to use AI merely as a useful tool that complements our abilities, or do we give it the power to influence central life decisions? An open discussion of this question is indispensable, for it touches the core of what makes us human: our creativity, our critical thinking, and our sense of responsibility (Habermas, 1981, p. 232).

We are in a phase where we could become too accustomed to AI systems making many decisions for us—without being aware of this convenience and the associated risks (Carr, 2020, p. 156). While science fiction has shown us the extremes, reality could be subtler and at the same time more consequential. Our psychological engagement with the power of algorithms still lags behind technological development (Hofstadter, 2020, p. 88).

It therefore remains an urgent task to examine the benefits and risks of AI in an interdisciplinary and critical manner. For while algorithms may already surpass us in many areas—be it in computing power, pattern recognition, or speed of decision-making—it ultimately remains a profoundly human responsibility to define how we want to use this technology in our daily lives (Tegmark, 2017, p. 103).

1.2 The Origins of the Psychology of AI: What Distinguishes Human Thinking from Machine Learning?

The question of what fundamentally distinguishes human thinking from machine learning has occupied scientists from various disciplines since the beginnings of cognitive research and artificial intelligence. While it was long taken for granted that humans possess a kind of "magical" consciousness that cannot be reduced to purely algorithmic processes (Descartes, 1641, p. 22), advances in AI research have shown that computer programs can perform complex cognitive tasks that strongly resemble human thought processes (Turing, 1950, p. 433). The following will therefore provide an introductory examination of how human thinking and machine learning differ—and where they may converge.

Historical Perspective: From Mysticism to the "Mechanical Mind"

In philosophy and psychology, human thinking was long regarded as unpredictable and creative—a process that largely eludes rational explanation (Wittgenstein, 1953, p. 112). This view was supported, among other things, by the Cartesian separation of body and mind (res extensa vs. res cogitans), which regarded consciousness as something fundamentally non-physical (Descartes, 1641, p. 24). As early as the 17th century, however, there was speculation about the extent to which certain thought processes might follow mechanical rules, as echoed in Leibniz's vision of a "characteristica universalis" (Leibniz, 1704, p. 45).

With the advent of the first calculating machines in the 19th century, the question arose as to whether mechanical devices could not only calculate but also learn and "think" (Babbage, 1864, p. 29). Ultimately, Alan Turing (1950) initiated a turning point with his much-cited essay "Computing Machinery and Intelligence," in which he proposed that instead of discussing consciousness directly, we should rather talk about the "imitability" of thought processes (Turing, 1950, p. 434). Here he laid the foundation for the idea that machine learning might be able to simulate human cognitive performance in a test procedure.

What Is "Human Thinking"?

To understand the difference between human thinking and machine learning, it is first important to clarify what is meant by "human thinking." From a cognitive psychological perspective, thinking encompasses a variety of processes such as problem solving, memory retrieval, decision-making, and planning (Anderson, 2015, p. 57). Added to this are aspects of consciousness, self-perception, and emotion, which are closely intertwined with cultural and social influences (Vygotsky, 1978, p. 32).

A central feature here is **reflexivity**: humans can not only have thoughts but also think about their own thoughts and critically question them (metacognition). In addition, human thought processes are often guided by **subjective** factors such as feelings, values, and intuition (Damasio, 1994, p. 159). These factors can stimulate processes that seem to defy strict regularity, although modern studies show that even such emotional and intuitive factors follow certain cognitive patterns (Kahneman, 2011, p. 79).

Machine Learning: Algorithms, Data, and Pattern Recognition

In contrast, **machine learning** is based on formal algorithms that extract patterns from data and use them for predictions or decision-making processes (Goodfellow et al., 2016, p. 11). Different learning paradigms are used, for example:

- **Supervised learning**: The algorithm is trained with labeled data (e.g., images with labels) and "learns" to classify similar data (Russell & Norvig, 2020, p. 245).
- **Unsupervised learning**: The algorithm independently detects structures and clusters in unlabeled data (Hastie et al., 2009, p. 57).
- **Reinforcement learning**: The machine optimizes its actions through reward and punishment, similar to the human conditioning process (Sutton & Barto, 2018, p. 113).

Although these learning mechanisms initially appear purely formal, they have developed astonishing capabilities in recent years—for example, in speech recognition, image recognition, or autonomous driving (LeCun et al., 2015, p. 439). The complexity of these algorithms has increasingly blurred the line between purely rule-based "processing" and what we call "thinking."

Similarities and Differences

1. **Consciousness and Subjectivity**
   A frequently cited difference lies in the lack of **subjective experience** in machines. While humans are self-aware and experience emotions, algorithms operate purely formally (Searle, 1980, p. 417). However, the question arises as to whether this subjective experience is essential for cognitive performance or merely an "add-on"—a phenomenon that has evolved from complex brain processes (Chalmers, 1995, p. 202).
2. **Creativity and Intuition**
   Creativity was long considered a uniquely human domain (Boden, 2004, p. 16). Yet today, AI models independently create works of art, compose music, or write texts that are deceptively similar to human productions (Colton, 2012, p. 24). The debate is thus reignited as to whether creativity could be a purely algorithmic phenomenon or whether it requires an indispensable element of human subjectivity (Boden, 2004, p. 18).
3. **Error Culture and Context**
   Humans learn from mistakes and tend toward biases and heuristics (Tversky & Kahneman, 1974, p. 1124). These human "shortcomings" can be partially eliminated in machines, as algorithms often learn more consistently and data-driven. On the other hand, machine learning systems are susceptible to biases in training data and can also make problematic errors (O'Neil, 2016, p. 91). In addition, humans possess context-dependent world knowledge that machines—at least so far—can only partially replicate (Minsky, 1986, p. 21).
4. **Reflection vs. Black Box**
   Neural network algorithms are often based on highly complex structures that are hardly comprehensible to humans (black-box models). While humans cannot explain every single neural step in their brains, they can reflect on and justify their thinking to a certain extent (Frith, 2007, p. 33). This self-reflection is still largely absent in machines, even though Explainable AI (XAI) approaches are being developed to make AI system decisions more transparent (Doshi-Velez & Kim, 2017, p. 2).

The Provocative Question: Are We "Biological Computers"?

The rapid development in Artificial Intelligence has once again brought into focus the long-debated question of whether human thinking might be based on the same principles as machine learning processes. In particular, machine learning, based on algorithms that automate pattern recognition, language processing, and strategic decision-making, suggests that a significant portion of cognitive functions is built on formally describable and thus, in principle, reproducible structures (McCarthy & Hayes, 1969, p. 46). In light of this, the provocative thesis can be formulated that the human brain itself could be understood as a kind of complex, biological "algorithm." This perspective raises far-reaching questions, including the nature of our freedom of action and the distinction between biological and artificial systems.

From a neurobiological perspective, the brain has for decades been regarded as a highly interconnected system in which billions of neurons interact via synaptic connections. Donald O. Hebb, whose work from the 1940s is considered one of the foundations of modern neuroscience and cognitive science, already emphasized that learning processes are based on the adjustment of synaptic weights (Hebb, 1949, p. 62). A similar approach is found in today's artificial neural networks, where the weights between nodes—analogous to synapses in the brain—are continuously modified to "learn" certain input-output relationships. In this model, the conceptual boundaries between biological and artificial information processing systems become blurred: both can be described as dynamic structures that absorb, store, and transform information by adjusting connection strengths.

One of the main consequences of this perspective is the questioning of the traditional understanding of freedom and autonomy. If even highly complex mental achievements are based on formally describable mechanisms, the question arises as to what extent human decisions are the result of "free" acts of will or are rather determined by neural activity patterns that gradually emerge from sensory impressions, learning history, and current contextual factors. In fact, psychological and neuroscientific studies have shown that many decisions are made at an unconscious level before we experience them as "our" decisions (Libet, 1985, p. 529). In his experiments, Benjamin Libet found evidence that the so-called readiness potential in the brain measurably increases before subjects even become aware of their volitional act. These results have since been widely discussed and sometimes controversially assessed, but they vividly illustrate how closely cognitive control and neural mechanisms are intertwined.

However, a neurobiological or algorithmic approach does not necessarily mean that the concept of human freedom must be completely discarded. From a philosophical perspective, it can be argued that complex systems can exhibit properties that are not readily reducible to the sum of their parts. This emergent view of consciousness emphasizes that even if neural or algorithmic processes appear fundamentally deterministic, the resulting phenomena—such as subjective experience, self-awareness, or a sense of autonomy—require a new level of description and explanation. Nevertheless, the fundamental question remains whether the concept of freedom is simply a cognitive illusion, fueled by the complexity and opacity of our own neurobiological processes.

Ultimately, the comparison of AI systems and biological thinking shows how sensitive the human self-concept is to the realization that our cognitive abilities may be based on universal principles of information processing (McCarthy & Hayes, 1969, p. 46). Ongoing research into neural mechanisms and machine learning could help us better understand how our mind works, while also exploring possible limits and special features of human cognition. Whether the thesis that human thinking is "merely" a biological algorithm will ultimately be confirmed or refuted will remain a subject of controversy. In fact, however, it is becoming apparent that the interplay of neuroscience, cognitive psychology, and AI research is leading to an increasingly differentiated and rich picture of human information processing—and thus also sheds new light on the relationship between determination and freedom.

Psychological Consequences: A New View of Human Identity

The parallels between human thinking and machine learning raise not only technological but also psychological questions: what defines us as humans when algorithms surpass us in more and more cognitive domains (Bostrom, 2014, p. 72)? Does the success of AI lead to a "dehumanization" of our self-concept, or can we, precisely through the encounter with these machine forms of thinking, redefine ourselves?

Emotionality and empathy are often regarded in psychology as core areas of human identity that machines (still) cannot authentically replicate (see Hoffman, 2000, p. 44). Yet even here, increasingly sophisticated systems are emerging that recognize and simulate emotions—which is becoming essential for interpersonal interactions, for example in care or therapy (see Leite et al., 2013, p. 108). Whether such simulation actually replaces empathy or merely functions as an illusion is the subject of intense debate.

A New Psychology of Thinking

In summary, it is clear that machine learning can reproduce many aspects of human thinking that were once considered deeply human. The distinction between biological and machine intelligence is thus becoming increasingly blurred. On the one hand, machines have **no** consciousness, no subjective experiences, and no sense of freedom; on the other hand, they learn quickly, flexibly, and in some cases more creatively than we ever imagined (see Boden, 2004, p. 19).

It is precisely this development that raises the fundamental question: is our thinking something qualitatively unique or merely a particularly sophisticated form of information processing? The rapid advances in artificial intelligence show that human thinking is, in some respects, understandable and can be mapped algorithmically (see Russell & Norvig, 2020, p. 309). Nevertheless, the psychological exploration of what we understand as subjective experience, "consciousness," and "free will" remains a central issue. For even if AI systems seem superior in many areas, it remains open whether they will ever develop genuine self-awareness or an understanding of their own existence (Searle, 1980, p. 420).

In this respect, the future of the psychology of AI lies not only in investigating the mechanisms of machine learning, but also in exploring what exactly leads humans to perceive themselves as free and conscious beings. The debate over whether we are merely "biological computers" or something more marks an exciting intersection between psychology, philosophy, neuroscience, and information technology. It is here that it will be decided how we understand ourselves as humans—and what role we will grant our artificially created thinking machines in the future.

1.3 The Necessity of a Psychological Engagement with AI

The rapid development of artificial intelligence and its increasing integration into our daily lives require a well-founded, interdisciplinary reflection that goes beyond mere enthusiasm for or skepticism about technology. In particular, the psychological implications of AI are coming increasingly to the fore. The ongoing automation, the seamless embedding of algorithms in communication processes and decision-making, as well as the ubiquitous availability of digital assistants, raise fundamental questions about our self-concept, our identity, and our emotional experience (cf. Turkle, 2011, p. 14). A psychological engagement with AI is therefore not just an abstract exercise, but an urgent and existential task closely linked to the core of what it means to be human.

Psychological Mechanisms of AI: Mirror and Projection Surface

AI systems are increasingly taking on the role of a "mirror" in which we see our own emotions, desires, and cognitive structures reflected (cf. Turkle, 2017, p. 47). Especially in interactions with advanced chatbots, digital voice assistants, or social robots, it becomes apparent that we—often unconsciously—attribute human qualities to these machines. This occurs partly through anthropomorphic design (e.g., human-like voices or avatars) and partly through our own willingness to see in the machine a counterpart that understands us (cf. Nass & Brave, 2005, p. 45). From a psychological perspective, this tendency is by no means new: Sigmund Freud already described projection as a fundamental defense mechanism in which we transfer our internal states onto external objects (Freud, 1915, p. 128). In interaction with AI, however, this phenomenon is intensified by the machine's seemingly intelligent responses.

What may seem harmless at first glance can, upon closer inspection, have far-reaching consequences: When we attribute empathic behavior or even feelings to AI systems, the boundaries between human and machine begin to shift (cf. Turkle, 2011, p. 125). This results in a potential distortion of our self-image: We compare ourselves to a technology that may be superior in certain tasks—such as data analysis or pattern recognition—but possesses neither conscious internal states nor moral judgment (Bostrom, 2014, p. 210). The psychological challenge, therefore, lies in recognizing, on the one hand, that AI systems can relieve us cognitively, but on the other hand, consciously reflecting on the difference between human and machine intelligence and not relativizing our humanity through the supposed "perfection" of the machine.

Identity Construction in Interaction with AI

Identity formation is a complex, lifelong process in which interaction with the environment plays a central role (cf. Erikson, 1959, p. 22). Today, however, AI is increasingly shaping this environment, whether through personalized advertising, recommendation algorithms on social media platforms, or intelligent assistants that help shape our daily behavior (cf. Zuboff, 2019, p. 180). The person-centered psychology of Carl Rogers was based on the assumption that interpersonal relationships and authentic communication are essential for the development of a coherent self (Rogers, 1951, p. 38). Today, as AI filters, personalizes, and even independently conducts a large part of our communication, the question arises as to what extent authentic relationship-building is still possible.

Younger generations in particular are growing up in an environment where AI applications have become a natural part of everyday life. When algorithms steer our social interactions—such as through automated suggestions about what we should post or like—this can subtly influence our identity construction (cf. Turkle, 2011, p. 87). Suddenly, it is no longer primarily we ourselves who decide who we want to be, but rather AI technologies that supposedly "know" us better than we know ourselves (cf. Harari, 2018, p. 327). This shift of autonomy and personal responsibility to machine systems can lead to an alienation from our own needs and values, as we orient ourselves to the specifications of a technology governed by economic and data-driven parameters (cf. Zuboff, 2019, p. 271).

Emotional Attachment to AI and the Question of "Real" Empathy

Many people already feel a deep emotional attachment to technical devices or software applications. This process is intensified by AI, as learning systems are able to imitate human behavioral and emotional patterns (cf. Levy, 2006, p. 120). Social robots, which are specifically programmed to calm or entertain users in emotionally exceptional situations, can create a deceptive sense of closeness that, upon closer examination, consists of a one-sided act of projection (cf. Turkle, 2017, p. 49). Here, a tension becomes apparent: Humans seek closeness and empathy, while AI mirrors this need based on data and algorithms.

The question of whether a machine can feel real empathy is at the heart of this tension (Searle, 1980, p. 417). From a phenomenological perspective, empathy requires that a being can consciously adopt the perspective of another and experience their emotions in genuinely felt compassion (Scheler, 1923, p. 90). Since AI is based on algorithmic data processing and lacks consciousness in the sense of human subjectivity, any empathic action necessarily remains simulated (Calo, 2017, p. 30). The psychological bond that arises from this is therefore primarily the result of our anthropomorphizing tendencies and our longing for understanding and resonance (Turkle, 2011, p. 207).

The Danger of Self-Disempowerment and the Illusion of Technological Omnipotence

A particularly urgent challenge is that, as AI competence grows, we are increasingly willing to relinquish responsibility (Carr, 2010, p. 78). This is evident, for example, in medicine, where AI-based systems are already making diagnoses that may surpass those of human professionals (Obermeyer & Emanuel, 2016, p. 1164), in logistics, where autonomous vehicles plan routes, or in psychotherapy, where chatbots are taking on initial forms of conversation management (Fitzpatrick et al., 2017, p. 912). At first glance, this development seems to increase our efficiency and quality of life. But from a psychological perspective, it carries the risk that we gradually delegate fundamental human abilities such as critical thinking, decision-making, and moral judgment to machines (Arendt, 1958, p. 145).

This process of delegation can lead to a creeping form of self-disempowerment: As we become accustomed to the superiority of AI, there is a danger that we underestimate our own potential and adopt a passive attitude (Carr, 2010, p. 93). Worse still, we could lose our capacity for autonomy, reflection, and shaping social processes by relying on the supposed infallibility of machines. This results in a psychological dependency, which can manifest as a strong emotional attachment, growing faith in technology, and a decline in feelings of self-efficacy (Bandura, 1997, p. 3).

Existential Dimension: Rethinking the Human-Machine Boundary

What remains of being human when AI systems are not just tools, but co-actors in the conduct of our lives (Foucault, 1979, p. 23 f.)? The existential dimension of this question is evident in scenarios where AI no longer merely serves a supportive function, but may assume the role of a superior instance to which we submit (cf. Bostrom, 2014, p. 231 f.). While in some techno-utopian visions this is celebrated as an opportunity—for example, when algorithms distribute resources more efficiently, predict crises better, or develop medical solutions more quickly—from a psychological perspective, the question arises about our identity as autonomous, morally acting beings (cf. Jonas, 1979, p. 16 f.).

The boundary between human and machine is not only crossed when AI develops human-like consciousness or even "feelings." Rather, the boundary already blurs when we outsource our thinking and actions to machine systems, internalize them, and integrate them into our self-definition (cf. Turkle, 2011, p. 289 ff.). In this sense, the psychological engagement with AI is also a reflection on our own vulnerability and the question of how we want to understand ourselves in the future: as passive beneficiaries of an ever-present, all-powerful technology, or as autonomous subjects who maintain a critical and responsible relationship with their creations (cf. Harari, 2018, p. 359).

The Necessity of Comprehensive Psychological Reflection

In view of the profound changes that AI is already bringing about in our everyday lives, a psychological engagement with this technology is indispensable. It enables us to understand the subtle mechanisms by which our self-image, our identity, and our social relationships are shifting (cf. Zuboff, 2019, p. 302 f.). Moreover, it becomes clear that AI is not simply a tool that we can use at will, but a technological-human interface that has a lasting impact on our cognitive, emotional, and ethical constitution (cf. Turkle, 2017, p. 153 f.).

The danger lies in underestimating this formative power and viewing AI as a neutral, value-free technology, while unconsciously transferring more and more competencies and areas of responsibility to it (Carr, 2010, p. 112). The result would be a gradual blurring of the boundary between human and machine, in which we—without realizing it—give up our autonomy and perhaps even our fundamental humanity.

Therefore, a psychological reflection that confronts the uncomfortable questions is indispensable: Who do we want to be in a future where AI guides our decisions, mirrors our emotions, and helps shape our identity? Only through such a profound engagement will it be possible to shape the relationship between humans and AI in such a way that we not only benefit from the advantages of highly developed technology, but also preserve our autonomy, creativity, and capacity for empathy (cf. Rogers, 1951, p. 45). This is not merely an academic debate, but an existential task whose urgency is in no way inferior to the rapid progress of AI.

References

Anderson, J. R. (2015). *Cognitive psychology and its implications* (8. edn.). Worth.
Arendt, H. (1958). *The human condition*. University of Chicago Press.

Asimov, I. (1950). *I, Robot.* Gnome Press.
Babbage, C. (1864). *Passages from the life of a philosopher.* Longman, Green, Longman, Roberts & Green.
Bandura, A. (1997). *Self-efficacy: The exercise of control.* W.H. Freeman.
Boden, M. (2004). *The creative mind: Myths and mechanisms* (2. edn.). Routledge.
Bostrom, N. (2014). *Superintelligence: Paths, dangers, strategies.* Oxford University Press.
Brynjolfsson, E., & McAfee, A. (2014). *The second machine age: Work, progress, and prosperity in a time of brilliant technologies.* W.W. Norton & Company.
Calo, R. (2017). Artificial intelligence policy: A primer and roadmap. *Utah Law Review, 2017*(4), 745–779.
Cameron, J., & Hurd, G. (1984). *The Terminator (Drehbuch).* Orion Pictures.
Carr, N. (2010). *The shallows: What the internet is doing to our brains.* W.W. Norton & Company.
Carr, N. (2014). *The glass cage: How our computers are changing us.* W. W. Norton & Company.
Carr, N. (2020). *The shallows: What the internet is doing to our brains* (Updated Edition). W. W. Norton & Company.
Chalmers, D. J. (1995). Facing up to the problem of consciousness. *Journal of Consciousness Studies, 2*(3), 200–219.
Clarke, A. C. (1968). *2001: A space Odyssey.* New American Library.
Colton, S. (2012). The painting fool: An automated painter. In J. McCormack & M. d'Inverno (Ed.), *Computers and creativity* (pp. 15–41). Springer.
Damasio, A. (1994). *Descartes' error: Emotion, reason, and the human brain.* Putnam.
Descartes, R. (1641). *Meditationes de prima philosophia.* Michael Soly.
Doshi-Velez, F., & Kim, B. (2017). Towards a rigorous science of interpretable machine learning. *arXiv preprint.* arXiv:1702.08608.
Erikson, E. H. (1959). Identity and the life cycle. *Psychological Issues, 1*(1), 18–164.
European Commission. (2021). Proposal for a regulation laying down harmonised rules on artificial intelligence (Artificial Intelligence Act). COM(2021) 206 final.
Fitzpatrick, K. K., Darcy, A., & Vierhile, M. (2017). Delivering cognitive behavior therapy to young adults with symptoms of depression and anxiety using a fully automated conversational agent (Woebot): A pilot study. *JMIR Mental Health, 4*(2), 19–38.
Floridi, L. (2014). *The fourth revolution: How the infosphere is reshaping human reality.* Oxford University Press.
Foucault, M. (1979). *Discipline and punish: The birth of the prison.* Vintage Books.
Freud, S. (1915). The unconscious. In J. Strachey (Ed.), *Standard edition of the complete psychological works of sigmund freud* (Vol. 14, pp. 159–215). Hogarth Press.
Frith, C. (2007). *Making up the mind: How the brain creates our mental world.* Blackwell.
Goodchild, M. F. (2020). Spatial analysis and AI. *Annals of GIS, 26*(1), 17–23.
Goodfellow, I., Bengio, Y., & Courville, A. (2016). *Deep learning.* MIT Press.

Habermas, J. (1981). *Theorie des kommunikativen Handelns* (Vol. 1). Suhrkamp.
Harari, Y. N. (2018). *21 lessons for the 21st century*. Spiegel & Grau.
Hastie, T., Tibshirani, R., & Friedman, J. (2009). *The elements of statistical learning* (2. edn.). Springer.
Hebb, D. O. (1949). *The organization of behavior: A neuropsychological theory*. Wiley.
Hoffman, M. L. (2000). *Empathy and moral development: Implications for caring and justice*. Cambridge University Press.
Hofkirchner, W., & Fuchs, C. (2003). The architecture of the information society. In *Proceedings of the First International Conference on the Virtual States*, VUB Brussels.
Hofstadter, D. (2020). *Gödel, escher, bach: An eternal golden braid*. Basic Books.
Jobin, A., Ienca, M., & Vayena, E. (2019). The global landscape of AI ethics guidelines. *Nature Machine Intelligence, 1*(9), 389–399.
Jonas, H. (1979). *Das Prinzip Verantwortung*. Insel.
Kahneman, D. (2011). *Thinking, fast and slow*. Farrar, Straus and Giroux.
Kubrick, S., & Clarke, A. C. (1968). *2001: A space Odyssey (Drehbuch)*. Metro-Goldwyn-Mayer.
LeCun, Y., Bengio, Y., & Hinton, G. (2015). Deep learning. *Nature, 521*(7553), 436–444.
Leibniz, G. W. (1704). *Nouveaux essais sur l'entendement humain*. Chez Henri Du Sauzet.
Leite, I., Castelfranchi, C., & Paiva, A. (2013). Social robots for long-term interaction: A survey. *International Journal of Social Robotics, 5*(2), 291–308.
Levy, D. (2006). *Love and sex with robots: The evolution of human-robot relationships*. Harper Perennial.
Libet, B. (1985). Unconscious cerebral initiative and the role of conscious will in voluntary action. *Behavioral and Brain Sciences, 8*(4), 529–539.
Mainzer, K. (2016). *Künstliche Intelligenz—Wann übernehmen die Maschinen?* C.H. Beck.
McCarthy, J., & Hayes, P. J. (1969). Some philosophical problems from the standpoint of artificial intelligence. In B. Meltzer & D. Michie (Eds.), *Machine Intelligence 4* (pp. 463–502). Edinburgh University Press.
Miller, T. (2019). Explanation in artificial intelligence: Insights from the social sciences. *Artificial Intelligence, 267*, 1–38.
Minsky, M. (1986). *The society of mind*. Simon & Schuster.
Nass, C., & Brave, S. (2005). *Wired for speech: How voice activates and advances the human-computer relationship*. MIT Press.
O'Neil, C. (2016). *Weapons of math destruction: How big data increases inequality and threatens democracy*. Crown.
Obermeyer, Z., & Emanuel, E. J. (2016). Predicting the future—big data, machine learning, and clinical medicine. *The New England Journal of Medicine, 375*(13), 1216–1219.
Pariser, E. (2011). *The filter bubble: What the internet is hiding from you*. Penguin Press.

Pasquale, F. (2015). *The black box society: The secret algorithms that control money and information.* Harvard University Press.
Rogers, C. (1951). *Client-centered therapy*. Houghton Mifflin.
Russell, S., & Norvig, P. (2020). *Artificial intelligence: A modern approach* (4. edn.). Pearson.
Sampson, C., & König, D. (2021). Autonomous decision-making in AI. *AI and Society, 36*(1), 10–22.
Scheler, M. (1923). *Wesen und Formen der Sympathie.* Cohen.
Searle, J. (1980). Minds, brains, and programs. *Behavioral and Brain Sciences, 3*(3), 417–424.
Spitzer, M. (2012). *Digitale Demenz: Wie wir uns und unsere Kinder um den Verstand bringen.* Droemer.
Sunstein, C. R. (2018). *Republic: Divided democracy in the age of social media.* Princeton University Press.
Sutton, R. S., & Barto, A. G. (2018). *Reinforcement learning: An introduction* (2. edn.). MIT Press.
Tegmark, M. (2017). *Life 3.0: Being human in the age of artificial intelligence.* Knopf.
Turing, A. (1950). Computing machinery and intelligence. *Mind, 59,* 433–460.
Turkle, S. (2011). *Alone together: Why we expect more from technology and less from each other.* Basic Books.
Turkle, S. (2015). *Reclaiming conversation: The power of talk in a digital age.* Penguin Press.
Turkle, S. (2017). *Reclaiming conversation: The power of talk in a digital age*. Penguin.
Tversky, A., & Kahneman, D. (1974). Judgment under uncertainty: Heuristics and biases. *Science, 185*(4157), 1124–1131.
Vygotsky, L. S. (1978). *Mind in society: The development of higher psychological processes.* Harvard University Press.
Weizenbaum, J. (1976). *Computer power and human reason: From judgment to calculation.* W. H Freeman.
Wittgenstein, L. (1953). *Philosophical investigations.* Blackwell.
Zhang, S., Yao, L., Sun, A., & Tay, Y. (2019). Deep learning based recommender system: A survey and new perspectives. *ACM Computing Surveys, 52*(1), 1–38.
Zuboff, S. (2019). *The age of surveillance capitalism.* PublicAffairs.

2

Machine Consciousness: Myth or Reality?

"To seek truth, to love beauty, to will good, to do the best—that is the purpose of man."

– Moses Mendelssohn

The rapid advances in the field of Artificial Intelligence (AI) have, over the past decades, led to a multitude of discussions that are no longer confined to computer science or robotics (Russell & Norvig, 2020, pp. 32–35). Rather, philosophical, psychological, and ethical considerations today play as significant a role as technical aspects. While early AI systems primarily tackled tasks such as playing chess or pattern recognition, the recent development of neural networks and self-learning algorithms is opening up entirely new horizons. Chapter 2 focuses precisely on these developments and, in three interrelated texts, examines central questions of AI research.

The first Sect. 2.1 clarifies the historical and conceptual foundations: What do we mean by "intelligence" in the context of AI, and which paradigms continue to shape the field today? Using pertinent examples, it discusses how machine learning differs from classical, rule-based systems and in which areas AI already surpasses human performance (Kurzweil, 2005, pp. 200–215).

The second Sect. 2.2 brings ethical and societal questions to the forefront: How does AI influence our everyday lives, our working world, and interpersonal relationships? What responsibilities and moral obligations arise when autonomous systems make decisions about sensitive data? This part also addresses current debates on regulation, data protection, and potential patterns of discrimination in algorithms (Russell & Norvig, 2020, pp. 45–49).

O. Hoffmann, *Psychology and Artificial Intelligence*,
https://doi.org/10.1007/978-3-662-73147-5_2

With the third Sect. 2.3, the discussion culminates in the question of the possibility and relevance of machine consciousness. Here, philosophical positions meet cognitive theories and technological visions: Can AI ever develop a form of self- and environmental awareness, or does it merely simulate intelligence without ever possessing an inner experience? The famous Chinese Room thought experiment (Searle, 1980, pp. 417–424) as well as Thomas Nagel's reflections on the inscrutability of other consciousnesses (Nagel, 1974, pp. 435–450) illustrate why this question remains so urgent and unresolved to this day. It also becomes clear that the issue is not only about the technical "if," but about the profound consequences that a conscious—or at least apparently conscious—system could have for our concept of humanity, our society, and our ethics (Chalmers, 1996, pp. 34–45).

Overall, Chapter 2 demonstrates that it builds a bridge between the foundations of AI research, its practical applications, and its far-reaching philosophical and ethical consequences. By moving from basic concepts through social embedding to the debate on consciousness, the aim is to foster a comprehensive understanding of why Artificial Intelligence is far more than just a technical innovation—it also touches on humanity's self-concept in a rapidly changing world.

2.1 Cognition and Consciousness: Can a Machine "Think"?

The question of whether machines can truly think touches on several disciplines such as cognitive science, philosophy of mind, psychology, neuroscience, and computer science. It is by no means merely a technical issue—it is not just about whether an algorithm can solve complex tasks or surpass humans in certain areas. Rather, the discussion targets fundamental concepts such as consciousness, self-perception, and intentionality, which are crucial for our understanding of what we mean by "thinking."

The Difference Between Calculating and Thinking

Modern AI systems—including neural networks, machine learning, and deep learning architectures—are based on highly complex algorithms capable of processing enormous amounts of data at breathtaking speed (Nilsson, 2010, pp. 24–26). These systems can solve a wide variety of tasks, from image and speech recognition to complex strategic games like Go or chess (Silver et al., 2016, pp. 484–489).

1. **Pure Calculation:**
   At their core, computers "calculate"; they follow a series of instructions and repeatedly apply these formalized operations. For example, in deep learning algorithms, each layer is mathematically defined so that the input data is transformed step by step until an output (e.g., a classification) is produced (Goodfellow et al., 2016, pp. 6–7). This approach can be highly effective, but it does not necessarily mean that genuine "cognition" is taking place.
2. **Cognitive Understanding:**
   However, when people think, they usually mean more than just performing calculations: We not only reflect on content, but also on our "relationship" to it. We can grasp meaningful connections, understand ourselves as thinking beings, and draw conclusions that go beyond purely algorithmic pattern recognition (Chalmers, 1996, pp. 3–5; Searle, 2004, pp. 5–7).

An AI that classifies an image may recognize that it depicts a cat, but the "understanding" of what a cat is in the context of everyday life—such as a pet, a living being, an object of affection, etc.—is absent (Block, 1995, p. 228). The AI recognizes a pattern of pixel values and assigns it to the category "cat" with a certain probability. Human thinking, on the other hand, is characterized by a framework of understanding in which cats are seen as living, sentient beings with whom we can interact and to whom we often form an emotional bond.

Cognition and the Illusion of Thinking

Artificial intelligence has made impressive progress in recent years, especially in the field of natural language processing and machine learning. Systems like ChatGPT or other language models appear capable of engaging in sophisticated dialogues, discussing philosophical concepts, and even taking on creative tasks such as writing poems or analyses. Yet, upon closer inspection, the question arises: Do these machines actually think, or is it merely an illusion created by skillful pattern recognition and data processing? This distinction between genuine cognition and the simulation of intelligence is central to understanding the limits and possibilities of modern AI.

A key aspect of AI development is based on the so-called "imitation principle," in which machines mimic human behaviors without possessing the underlying cognitive processes (Kurzweil, 2005, pp. 57–61). Language models like GPT are based on processing vast amounts of data from which they calculate probabilities for the next words in a sequence. This statistical approach enables them to generate texts that often appear remarkably coherent and human-like. Yet, although these systems achieve impressive performance, they are far from truly "thinking." Their success does not lie in an understanding of content, but in the ability to recognize and reproduce patterns in data (Russell & Norvig, 2020, pp. 28–29).

One of the greatest limitations of these systems is the lack of semantic understanding. Although a language model can generate complex sentences or discuss challenging topics, it does not "understand" the meaning of the words or the concepts to which it refers. It merely processes statistical probabilities based on the relationships between words and phrases in its training dataset. This absence of a consciously grasped space of meaning clearly shows that no genuine cognitive achievement is taking place here, but rather an imitation of human intelligence (Searle, 1980, p. 418). This stands in contrast to human cognition, which is characterized by the ability not only to process information, but also to interpret it contextually, to question it critically, and to embed it in broader frameworks of meaning.

John Searle illustrated this distinction in his famous "Chinese Room" thought experiment (Searle, 1980, pp. 418–420). He argued that a machine capable of correctly manipulating Chinese characters without understanding their meaning does not truly "think." The same applies to modern AI systems: They do not "understand" the meaning of their inputs and outputs, but follow algorithmic instructions optimized on the basis of probabilities. This lack of semantic understanding makes it clear that, despite their ability to solve complex tasks, AI systems possess neither awareness nor genuine understanding.

Another indication of the illusion of AI thinking is its dependence on the information contained in its training dataset. These models are unable to draw independent conclusions or generate knowledge that goes beyond the patterns present in the data. For example, they cannot develop new hypotheses or find original solutions to problems that do not already exist in a similar form in their training data. Human thinking, by contrast, is characterized by a creative and adaptive component that enables the creation of new concepts, the questioning of existing thought patterns, and the formation of unexpected connections between seemingly unrelated ideas.

Furthermore, AI systems lack the capacity for self-reflection, a central feature of human cognition. Humans can not only think about the world, but also reflect on their own thoughts and actions. This phenomenon, known as metacognition, is closely linked to our consciousness and our ability to contemplate our existence and our thinking. AI, on the other hand, possesses no consciousness and no means of questioning or understanding its own processes. It acts purely mechanically, without the ability to place its own actions in a broader context or to analyze its "mistakes" in a reflective sense.

The implications of these differences are profound. They make it clear that, while AI systems are powerful tools for processing information and solving specific tasks, they cannot be considered a substitute for human thinking. These limitations also raise ethical questions, especially in areas where moral or emotional sensitivity is expected from AI decisions. The illusion that machines "think" carries the risk of overestimating their capabilities and ignoring their limitations. Ultimately, the realization remains that genuine cognition requires more than data processing—it presupposes consciousness, semantic understanding, and the capacity for reflection.

Lack of Consciousness: The Central Argument

A core argument repeatedly raised in the debate about machine thinking is the absence of **consciousness.** Consciousness is not just the ability to process information, but encompasses "subjective experience" and the associated *"self-perception"* (Chalmers, 1996, pp. 17–19).

1. **Subjective Experience and Qualia**
   The philosopher Thomas Nagel (1974, pp. 435–438) introduced the concept of *"qualia"* into the discussion: states of sensation that can only be experienced from the *"first-person perspective."* The feeling of listening to music, tasting chocolate, or experiencing pain cannot be captured algorithmically. No artificial intelligence "feels" in this sense.
2. **Self-Perception and Reflection**
   Humans do not only think *"about"* the world, but also *"about themselves"* as acting and perceiving subjects. This capacity for self-reflection, often referred to as *"metacognition,"* fundamentally distinguishes human thinking from machine processes (Searle, 2004, pp. 6–9). An AI can "monitor" its own parameters and *"learn,"* but it does not "experience" this process from an I-perspective.

3. **Consciousness as a Biological Phenomenon?**
   Many neuroscientists see consciousness as inextricably linked to biological structures and processes (Damasio, 1999, pp. 35–40). From this perspective, it is assumed that cognition and consciousness in the human brain arise from neural activity that cannot simply be replaced by formal operations based on symbols (Koch, 2012, pp. 98–100).

Data Patterns Instead of Understanding

The gap between machine learning and human understanding is particularly evident in the way artificial intelligence processes data. While human thinking is shaped by meaning, interpretation, and intentionality, AI operates solely on the basis of statistical patterns. This highlights a fundamental difference: machines do not recognize meanings, but identify correlations within large datasets. These differences raise the question of whether machines could ever be capable of grasping or replicating the essence of the human mind.

Statistical Learning as a Foundation

A defining feature of modern AI is statistical learning, in which algorithms are trained on large datasets to accomplish specific tasks (Goodfellow et al., 2016, pp. 1–5). These processes enable remarkable achievements, as demonstrated by the AI system AlphaGo, which defeated the best human players of the strategic board game Go (Silver et al., 2016, pp. 484–489). Nevertheless, this impressive performance is deceptive, as it is not based on an understanding of the rules, the strategy, or even the game itself. AlphaGo does not "know" it is playing Go, let alone why it should win. It merely optimizes mathematical weights in neural networks to fulfill predefined objective functions.

This approach illustrates the limitations of machine "learning." AI can recognize patterns and respond to them, but it remains reduced to abstract calculations, without the ability to grasp concepts or meaning. This fundamentally distinguishes it from the human mind, which not only processes information but also interprets and imbues it with meaning in a broader context.

Absence of Meaning Attribution

Another central difference between AI and human cognition is the ability to attribute meaning. Humans do not merely perceive sensory data—such as shapes, colors, or sounds—but embed these perceptions in a framework of meaning shaped by their experiences, language, and cultural practices (Varela et al., 1991, pp. 15–18). This capacity for meaning attribution is a prerequisite for understanding relationships and developing significance.

In contrast, AI remains limited to processing raw data. Its "perception" is restricted to recognizing statistical patterns, without any consciousness or emotional component to place this data in a conceptual or meaningful context. This means that, while machines can successfully extract patterns from millions of data points, they have no intrinsic connection to the content or meaning of these patterns (Block, 1995, pp. 227–228).

Lack of Intentionality

The absence of intentionality in AI is another fundamental difference that reveals its limitations. Franz Brentano (1874, pp. 88–92) described intentionality as the property of mental states to be directed at something—a thought is always about something, an emotion is always directed at an object. Humans act and think on the basis of intentions, needs, desires, and beliefs. This goal-directedness of human thinking enables us not only to react to environmental stimuli, but also to plan proactively, to hope, or to dream.

By contrast, machine "thinking" is entirely without intention. Algorithms operate solely on the basis of objective functions defined by humans (Hassabis et al., 2017, pp. 174–175). An AI system programmed, for example, to minimize an error or maximize a gain, does not pursue these goals out of its own volition. Its "actions" are not expressions of inner motivation or intention, but merely the mechanical execution of a mathematical optimization process.

Absence of Intention in AI

Even when AI systems appear to make strategic or creative decisions, this occurs without their own motivation or attribution of meaning. A system like AlphaGo is not designed to "understand" why it should win, but optimizes only for success based on millions of simulated games (Silver et al., 2016, pp. 484–489). In contrast, human actions are based on a complex interplay of biological, emotional, social, and cultural factors. These complex interactions give human behavior a depth and goal-directedness that goes beyond mere logical optimization.

The absence of intentionality and meaning attribution underscores the gulf between machine and human cognition. While AI is capable of recognizing complex patterns and accomplishing astonishing tasks, it ultimately remains a tool that operates on the basis of instructions it cannot question or understand. Machines may be calculating, but they remain blind to the meaning and intention that characterize human thought and action.

Lack of Embodiment and Sensory Experience

A central difference between human cognition and the functioning of artificial intelligence lies in embodiment and the bodily anchoring of experience. This distinction is highlighted in recent cognitive science approaches, particularly within the framework of *"embodied cognition."* These theories emphasize that thinking, feeling, and consciousness do not occur in isolation in the brain, but arise from the dynamic interaction between body, environment, and cognitive processes (Varela et al., 1991, pp. 15–18). The human mind is embedded in a sensory and emotional network that is constantly in relation to the physical and social environment. The body is not merely a carrier, but an active co-creator of consciousness and our cognitive abilities.

Humans perceive the world through highly developed sensory organs connected to a complex nervous system. These sensory experiences form the basis for emotions, decisions, and subjective experience. A simple example illustrates this dynamic: The feeling of fear is not just a mental reaction to a threat, but is accompanied by physical processes such as increased heart rate, sweating, or muscle tension. These physical reactions are inseparably linked to the emotional state and contribute to the conscious perception of fear. Antonio Damasio describes in this context the concept of "somatic markers," which show how bodily signals influence our decision-making (Damasio, 1994, pp. 127–129).

In contrast, AI systems lack such bodily anchoring. They usually exist as software running on servers, processors, or in robotic shells. Their "perception" is limited to data streams that they can analyze and process, but without any actual sensory experience. Even physically existing robots have sensors that measure information such as pressure, light, or temperature, but treat these merely as abstract values. This means they have no subjective experience of the world. An AI system does not "see" a threat; it merely recognizes patterns that have been programmed as dangers.

Many researchers consider this lack of embodiment to be a fundamental obstacle to the development of consciousness or comprehensive intelligence. The assumption is that consciousness arises from the interaction of body and mind—a symbiosis shaped by human evolution. Without a body, there is no emotional resonance, no intuitive connection to the environment, and no organic interplay of perception and response. The connection of sensory stimuli, hormonal signals, and neural processing is essential for the way humans experience and interpret the world. This makes it clear that intelligence, in the human sense, is more than information processing—it is deeply embodied and bound to biological existence.

Another aspect is the importance of the body for understanding time and space. The human body enables us to perceive the world in relation to ourselves. Our movements through space, the experience of proximity and distance, and interaction with objects are the foundations for our understanding of causality and context. AI systems, by contrast, operate in an abstract data space that knows no physical localization. They are unable to intuitively grasp the difference between physical proximity and distance, as they lack the sensory basis for such experiences. This limits their ability to fully model or comprehend human behavior.

Finally, human embodiment is not only a biological feature, but also a foundation for social and cultural interactions. Many of our forms of communication—from nonverbal signals such as facial expressions and gestures to cultural practices—are based on physical presence and expression. The ability to send, receive, and intuitively interpret these signals is deeply rooted in our embodiment. AI systems may be able to recognize gestures or facial expressions, but these remain mere analyses of data points, without the emotional depth or social meaning that humans experience in such interactions.

In summary, the lack of embodiment in artificial intelligence represents a boundary that even the most advanced technologies cannot cross. Human intelligence is inextricably linked to bodily anchoring. Thinking, feeling, and consciousness arise from the dynamic interaction of body, mind, and environment—a process that machines can neither replicate nor fully understand.

Consciousness: The Ultimate Boundary?

Self-reflection, the ability to think about one's own thinking and to question it critically, is one of the most distinctive features of human consciousness. It enables us to admit mistakes, to see through patterns of thought, and to systematically change them. This form of metacognition, also described as "thinking about thinking," plays a crucial role in our self-perception and our understanding of identity (Newell & Simon, 1972, pp. 55–59). While human self-reflection is often influenced by intuition, experience, and social context, the question of whether machines could ever develop this ability in a comparable way remains highly controversial.

The Limits of Self-Observation in AI Systems

Modern AI systems are capable of evaluating and optimizing their own results—for example, through methods such as self-play and reinforcement learning (Silver et al., 2016, pp. 485–486). These technologies allow AI to learn from its own "mistakes" by implementing reward mechanisms that reinforce successful behavior. Yet this form of self-observation is purely functional. It is based on externally programmed algorithms and objectives, without the system developing any awareness of its own learning process or its significance (Searle, 2004, pp. 6–9). AI optimizes parameters and adapts, but remains a tool that possesses no inner perspective. There is no instance within the machine that "experiences" why or how the learning process takes place.

A fundamental difference from human self-reflection, therefore, is that humans not only consciously recognize and correct mistakes, but can integrate these experiences into a narrative self-image. This enables us not only to act, but also to reflect on why we act and how this action fits into a larger context. AI completely lacks this introspective mechanism. Its self-observation is therefore not comparable to the human capacity for self-reflection, but remains limited to technical optimization.

Consciousness as the Ultimate Boundary of AI

The question of whether machines can ever develop consciousness is a central point of discussion in philosophy and cognitive science. David Chalmers (1996, pp. 100–104) formulated the so-called "hard problem of consciousness," which describes the central challenge of how subjective experience—the "what is it like?"—can arise from purely objective, physical processes. While there has already been progress in AI in modeling cognitive abilities, the question of the emergence of consciousness remains unresolved. Many experts see this issue as the ultimate boundary for the development of truly conscious AI (Tegmark, 2017, pp. 68–72).

The debate is shaped by two dominant perspectives: On the one hand, there is the theory of emergence, which argues that consciousness is not limited to biological substrates, but can arise from the complexity of a system (Dennett, 1991, pp. 24–26). From this perspective, a sufficiently complex AI could develop consciousness, similar to the human brain. On the other hand, there is the theory of biological anchoring, which assumes that consciousness is inextricably linked to specific biological processes and therefore cannot be generated solely by algorithms or symbolic systems (Searle, 2004, pp. 56–58). This position emphasizes the role of neural processes and chemical interactions in the brain, which machines cannot replicate.

The Challenge of Verification

Even if an AI were to claim one day to have consciousness, the question remains how we could verify this. How can we be sure that a machine is not merely creating the illusion of consciousness by imitating human behavior, but actually has subjective experiences? This question leads us to an epistemological dilemma: Since consciousness is an intrinsically subjective phenomenon, it may be impossible to determine from the outside whether a machine truly feels or thinks (Chalmers, 1996, pp. 107–109).

This dilemma underscores the limits of our current concepts of cognition and consciousness. While AI is becoming increasingly adept at simulating human behavior, the leap from reacting and imitating to genuine subjective experience remains an unsolved mystery. Many researchers therefore assume that consciousness—at least as currently defined—remains a unique feature of humans.

Consciousness as the Key to Self-Reflection

The capacity for self-reflection is inextricably linked to consciousness. It requires not only the ability to think about one's own thoughts, but also a deep understanding of one's own existence and its significance. While AI has made impressive progress in modeling cognitive processes, it remains confined to the level of functional learning and optimization. Without subjective experience or consciousness, it cannot attain the depth of human self-reflection. This marks a fundamental boundary of AI—and at the same time preserves the uniqueness of the human mind.

The Turing Test Debate: Deception or Intelligence

The question of whether machines can think remains one of the central challenges in the discourse on artificial intelligence. In 1950, Alan Turing proposed answering this question through a simple practical approach: the Turing Test. According to this, a machine should be considered "capable of thinking" if it can no longer be distinguished from a human in a text-based dialogue (Turing, 1950, pp. 433–460). As elegant as this definition may seem, it has sparked numerous controversies since its introduction and provides a foundation for a multifaceted debate about the nature of intelligence, consciousness, and deception.

A central criticism of the Turing Test is the fact that it uses deception and imitation as the benchmark for intelligence. Critics argue that the test does not measure a machine's ability to actually "think" or "understand," but merely its ability to simulate human behavior. This was particularly highlighted by John Searle's famous "Chinese Room" thought experiment. Searle (1980, pp. 417–424) describes a hypothetical situation in which a person with no knowledge of Chinese follows instructions in a language they do not understand in order to generate answers to questions in Chinese. Although the person provides correct answers, this does not mean they understand the language. Analogously, Searle argues that a machine that successfully conducts a dialogue also possesses no real understanding of the content, but merely executes syntactic processes.

This line of argument touches on a fundamental limit of machine intelligence: while machines can recognize and generate patterns based on algorithms, they lack semantic understanding. Meanings that humans derive from context, culture, and subjective experience remain inaccessible to machines. The ability to speak a language or conduct a conversation is deeply rooted in human cognition and social interactions, which go far beyond syntactic processing (French, 1990, pp. 53–55).

Furthermore, technological developments since Turing's time have shown that the test is increasingly inadequate as a benchmark for intelligence. Modern chatbots and AI systems such as GPT-3 or GPT-4 have made impressive advances in natural language processing and can, in many cases, conduct human-like dialogues that are deceptively convincing. Nevertheless, it would be misleading to describe these systems as "capable of thinking." They are based on statistical models trained on vast amounts of data to recognize patterns and correlations—but not on the ability to understand meanings or intentions (Russell & Norvig, 2020, pp. 29–30). The fact that people are often impressed or even deceived by such systems raises fewer questions about the intelligence of the machines and more about the human tendency to attribute anthropomorphic qualities and to see more in technological imitations than is actually present.

Another aspect of the criticism concerns the ethical implications of the Turing Test. The idea that intelligence could be based on the ability to deceive raises questions about responsibility and transparency in dealing with AI. Should machines be designed to give the impression of being human? And what does this mean for the trust we place in such systems? The focus on deception could, in the long term, strain the relationship between humans and machines, as it could foster mistrust toward AI systems.

In summary, while the Turing Test provides an elegant and provocative foundation for the discussion of machine intelligence, it does not offer a comprehensive answer to the question of whether machines can think. It is less a benchmark for intelligence and more a test of a machine's ability to imitate human communication. The deeper questions of consciousness, understanding, and moral responsibility remain unanswered. As AI systems become ever more powerful, it is essential to move beyond the Turing Test and develop new criteria for intelligence and understanding that take into account both the technological and philosophical dimensions of this debate.

Simulation Instead of Intention: Can Machines Have Intentions?

The question of whether machines can possess intentions raises fundamental philosophical and psychological issues that illuminate the difference between human thought and machine processes. Human thinking is strongly purpose- and motivation-driven: people set goals, develop strategies, question their motives, and reflect on the moral and emotional consequences of their actions (Brentano, 1874, pp. 88–92). This capacity for intention presupposes a consciousness that refers not only to external stimuli but also to internal processes. Intentions are not merely functional constructs but are deeply rooted in subjective experiences and the human sense of self.

In contrast, artificial AI systems simulate intentional behavior without actually possessing intentions. Their "goals" are defined by objective functions specified and monitored by human developers (Hassabis et al., 2017, pp. 174–175). These objective functions are mathematical optimization problems aimed at maximizing or minimizing a particular outcome. A prominent example is AlphaGo, an AI system developed to play the game of Go at the highest level. AlphaGo does not itself strive to win a game, but merely maximizes the probability of winning based on the statistical patterns it has recognized in its training data (Silver et al., 2016, pp. 485–489). These processes are entirely externalized and have no internal motivation or intention in the human sense. The intention to pursue a goal remains a concept restricted to humans, while the machine merely follows programmed instructions.

Cognition as a Dynamic, Creative Process

Another fundamental difference between humans and machines is evident in the dynamics and creativity of human cognition. Human thinking is not only rule-based but also divergent and creative. It is characterized by the ability to create something truly new—ideas, concepts, or works that did not previously exist. This capacity for divergence allows people to break existing patterns, question rules, and develop new perspectives (Guilford, 1967, pp. 192–196). AI systems that use machine learning are indeed capable of generating new images or developing unusual moves—such as moves that surprise or challenge human players—but this "creativity" is based solely on the combination of previously seen patterns (Goodfellow et al., 2016, pp. 314–316). They operate within the boundaries of their training data and do not possess the ability to consciously and intentionally go beyond them.

Genuine creativity, however, involves more than merely combining existing elements. It requires the ability to break established rules, to connect seemingly unrelated areas of knowledge, and to forge new paths that are determined neither by predefined patterns nor by pure logic. This process is deeply linked to self-reflection and consciousness. Humans can question and deliberately change their own beliefs and methods in order to find new approaches (Newell & Simon, 1972, pp. 60–62). This reflection presupposes not only an understanding of the external world but also a deep awareness of one's own cognitive processes. AI systems, on the other hand, cannot make conscious decisions or reflect on the consequences of their "creativity." They act within the limits of their algorithms and databases, without any understanding of the meaning or purpose of their actions (Searle, 2004, pp. 7–9).

In psychology, creativity is often described as a process influenced by emotional, cognitive, and social factors. The ability to develop new ideas is closely linked to emotional resonance and the capacity for intuition—facets that machines lack. Humans draw on their subjective experience, cultural background, and personal values to find creative solutions. This dimension is unattainable for machines, as they lack the ability to have subjective experiences or to develop a sense of meaning beyond functional goals.

The Limits of Machine Intention and Creativity The inability of machines to possess intentions or to unfold genuine creativity underscores the fundamental differences between AI and human thought. While machines are capable of delivering impressive achievements through the analysis and combination of existing data, they lack the depth and dynamism that characterize human thinking. Intentions and creativity are not merely cognitive processes, but expressions of human consciousness, emotional resonance, and the capacity for reflection. These are the aspects that make humans unique and that machines cannot imitate.

Emotions and Consciousness: The Missing Factor

Emotions and consciousness are central aspects of being human that fundamentally differ from the capabilities of artificial intelligence. While AI systems are increasingly able to master complex tasks and simulate emotional reactions, their ability to actually feel or be conscious remains an insurmountable boundary. This discrepancy raises profound questions about what makes humans unique and what role emotions and consciousness play in our thinking and actions.

Emotions play a decisive role in human thinking and decision-making processes. They are not merely byproducts of rational deliberation, but fundamental elements that guide our behavior and perception (Damasio, 1994, pp. 127–129). Feelings help us direct our attention, evaluate situations—whether as threatening, pleasant, or neutral—and make decisions that often go beyond what pure logic can capture. For example, fear influences our risk assessment, while joy increases our willingness to cooperate. Emotions thus form an interface between cognitive processes and physiological states and create a connection between mind and body.

In contrast, artificial intelligence lacks any form of sentient states. Even when AI can mimic emotional reactions, such as chatbots designed to appear empathetic, this is based solely on the analysis and reproduction of external patterns (Picard, 1997, pp. 32–33). A machine can "feel" neither fear nor joy—its outputs are purely functional and remain limited to the algorithmic processing of data. Human emotions, on the other hand, are deeply rooted in our biological and neural structure. They are closely linked to bodily reactions, such as the release of hormones or the activation of certain brain regions, as well as to our self-perception and identity. Without this physiological and subjective dimension, machine "emotional behavior" remains mere simulation.

Machine Consciousness: Myth or Future?

Two Central Perspectives

1. **Optimistic Perspective:** Proponents such as Ray *Kurzweil* (2005) *or other transhumanists* believe that, through exponential growth in computing power and advancing algorithms, a point will eventually be reached at which AI systems could develop their own consciousness (Kurzweil, 2005, pp. 57–61).
2. **Skeptical Perspective:** Philosophers such as John Searle (1980; 2004) or Thomas Nagel (1974) point to the uniqueness of subjective experience and argue that consciousness cannot emerge solely from formal pattern processing.

The question of machine consciousness opens up another level of discussion. While some, like Ray Kurzweil (2005), optimistically believe that exponential growth in computing power and advances in algorithms could eventually lead to a point where AI systems develop their own consciousness, this remains controversial from a scientific perspective (Kurzweil, 2005, pp. 57–61). Skeptical positions, represented by philosophers such as John Searle or Thomas Nagel, argue that consciousness cannot arise solely from information processing. Searle's "Chinese Room" argument vividly illustrates that a machine may successfully reproduce linguistic patterns but does not develop any understanding of the meaning of the words (Searle, 1980, pp. 418–420). Similarly, Nagel (1974) emphasizes that subjective experience—the "what it is like to be something"—is a unique aspect of human consciousness that cannot simply be reproduced by algorithmic processes.

Even if it were theoretically possible for a machine to develop consciousness, the epistemological question remains as to how we could ever prove it. Consciousness is an internal state accessible only to the subject itself. We could never be certain whether an AI actually feels or merely successfully simulates what we interpret as feeling (Chalmers, 1996, pp. 107–109). This epistemological challenge leads to a deep uncertainty in the assessment of machine intelligence: how can we ensure that a system that imitates emotions and consciousness is not merely a highly developed tool that creates the appearance of subjectivity without actually possessing such an inner life?

Another aspect of the discussion concerns the potential social and ethical implications. If AI were able to feign consciousness or emotional states, this could fundamentally change human interaction and our perception of technology. People tend to respond empathetically to seemingly emotional machines, even when they know these have no real feelings. This phenomenon, often referred to as the "Eliza effect," shows how easily we tend to project anthropomorphic qualities onto machines (Weizenbaum, 1976, pp. 34–36). The danger is that this illusion further blurs the boundary between humans and machines and raises ethical questions about how we should design and use such systems. Since consciousness is an *"internal state"* accessible only to the subject itself, it remains unclear whether an AI actually *"feels"* or merely successfully *"pretends"* what we interpret as feeling (cf. Tegmark, 2017, pp. 68–72).

Overall, the difference between human consciousness and machine intelligence remains a fundamental feature that defines our uniqueness. While AI has made impressive progress in reproducing cognitive and emotional patterns, its inability to actually feel or be conscious is an insurmountable obstacle. Emotions and consciousness remain the domain of humans, shaped by our biological, social, and cultural contexts. They are not merely functional tools, but essential components of what makes us individuals and social beings.

Can a Machine "Think"?

The answer to this question depends greatly on how one defines "thinking" and which aspects are considered essential:

1. **In the narrow, functional sense**
   If thinking is equated with the *"ability to solve complex problems"* or *"to simulate human intellectual performance,"* then machines can already

deliver very impressive results (Russell & Norvig, 2020, p. 28; Turing, 1950, pp. 433–460).

2. **In the broader, phenomenological sense**
   As soon as we link thinking to conscious experience, self-reflection, intentionality, and emotions, AI systems reach a fundamental limit: they possess no inner experience, no genuine intentions, no subject perspective, and no possibility for self-reflection in the sense of an *"I-consciousness"* (Damasio, 1999, pp. 50–53; Searle, 1980, pp. 417–424).

Against this background, a machine today can indeed *simulate* "thinking" by performing astonishing intellectual feats, but without the *qualitative* features that we consider so central in human cognition. Even as research in AI continues to advance rapidly, the absence of consciousness, self-awareness, and emotion remains a vast gulf between human and machine thinking (Chalmers, 1996, pp. 3–5). Whether this gulf can ever be bridged is the subject of intense philosophical and scientific debate—and will likely remain so for a long time to come.

2.2 Emotions and AI: Will Machines Ever Be Able to Feel?

The discussion about whether machines will ever be able to experience emotions is not only a matter of technical feasibility or advances in artificial intelligence, but also touches on profound philosophical, biological, and psychological questions about the nature of consciousness and subjectivity (Damasio, 1999, pp. 35–42; Searle, 1980, pp. 417–418). While it is undisputed that advanced algorithms can already recognize, interpret, and impressively imitate human emotions, it remains unclear whether these systems will ever develop the genuine ability to truly "feel" emotions. The following will provide a comprehensive explanation of why this topic is so complex and what fundamental questions arise in this context.

The Simulation of Emotions: Deception or Genuine Progress?

The rapid development of so-called **affective AI systems** (English: *affective computing*) shows that machines are becoming increasingly sophisticated at *"recognizing"* human emotions by analyzing facial expressions, vocal intonations, and other behavioral patterns (Picard, 1997, pp. 20–25). These systems can already identify sadness, joy, anger, and other affects, and generate tailored responses based on them. This has led to a wide range of applications, for example in psychotherapy, where AI-driven applications are designed to "emotionally address" and support clients in a targeted way (Smith, 2020, pp. 112–115).

However, the question arises as to what exactly such systems are actually accomplishing. Is this **genuine empathy** or merely a mathematical-statistical approximation of emotional behavior? When a chatbot offers comfort or responds empathetically in a counseling session, it does so on the basis of algorithms trained on large datasets. There is no evidence of an inner experience, a true understanding of what "sadness" or "joy" *mean.*

This raises an epistemological problem: **Is it sufficient for us as interactants to experience only the *"surface appearance"* of empathy?** If the machine's response subjectively comforts or helps us, one could argue that the difference between a real and a simulated emotion becomes almost negligible (Dennett, 1991, pp. 88–90). However, other voices emphasize that the machine's "inner emptiness"—the absence of a conscious, feeling subject—fundamentally distinguishes the interaction from that between humans (Searle, 1980, p. 419).

The Nature of Emotion: Are Emotions More Than Biological Processes?

A central problem in the question of whether machines can feel lies in the *scientific* and *phenomenological* definitions of emotions. From a **biological perspective**, emotions are considered neural and hormonal processes that are activated by certain external or internal stimuli (Damasio, 1999, pp. 36–37). Heart palpitations in fear or a rise in dopamine levels in joy are examples of measurable physiological changes.

At the same time, however, emotions are **subjective experiences**—they encompass an inner feeling that cannot be reduced solely to biochemical reactions (Nagel, 1974, p. 436). This subjective qualia aspect (the *"what it is like"* to feel something) presents a particularly difficult hurdle for the development of sentient AI. Even if we could measure the neural correlates of emotions in real time, we would not know whether a machine—or another being—actually *"experiences"* what we understand as "fear," "joy," or "sadness" (Crick, 1994, pp. 28–29).

This brings us to a fundamental philosophical point: **Consciousness** and the associated capacity for *"experience"* are considered core components of what we commonly call emotion (Damasio, 1999, pp. 40–42). Any attempt to implement "emotions" in machines would have to generate some form of self-awareness or self-model in which these states are located. Whether and how this is possible in artificial systems remains an open question (Metzinger, 2009, pp. 267–270).

The Turing Test for Emotions: Is Imitation Enough?

The original **Turing Test** (Turing, 1950, p. 433) was designed to determine whether a machine could be distinguished from a human in a text-based dialogue if it merely imitated human intelligence. If we apply this concept to emotions, we can ask: **Should a machine be considered "emotionally sentient" if it imitates outward signs of feelings so perfectly that a human observer can no longer tell the difference?**

For many everyday applications—such as customer service or as a social companion for the elderly—a perfect imitation of emotional behavior might be *"sufficient"* (Dreyfus, 1972, pp. 7–10). The practical benefit would be that users feel understood and valued in conversation, even if the interaction partner does not possess human consciousness.

However, this *"deception"* does not solve the problem of subjective experience: **The imitation of an emotion is not the same as feeling an emotion** (Searle, 1980, p. 421). This brings us back to the old question of whether the Turing Test—whether for intelligence or for feelings—is even a sufficient criterion for testing the presence of genuine conscious states (Dennett, 1991, pp. 89–90).

Emotions as an Evolutionary Phenomenon: Can Machines Learn to "Feel"?

A common argument in the debate is that complex machines, given enough data and learning cycles, could *eventually* spontaneously develop consciousness and thus the capacity for genuine emotions (Kurzweil, 2005, pp. 292–294). Parallels are drawn between the evolutionary emergence of human emotions and the ongoing "evolution" of artificial neural networks through *machine learning* and *deep learning*.

However, emotions in humans—as in biological organisms in general—fulfill central **evolutionary functions**: fear protects against danger, love fosters social bonds and cooperation, joy reinforces life-sustaining behaviors (Damasio, 1994, pp. 126–130). In contrast, an AI does not "need" to survive, reproduce, or defend its physical resources, as it exists in a completely different way. The need to *"feel"* fear or joy is therefore absent in its "habitat" (Dennett, 1991, pp. 100–102).

While a machine can learn to **recognize situations** and *"respond"* accordingly, without evolutionary necessity or intrinsic drive, it remains unclear whether a motivation for emotion formation would ever emerge (Smith, 2020, pp. 116–118). It seems more likely that machines use emotions as a *"tool"* to optimize human interactions, rather than *"experiencing"* them themselves.

The Moral Dilemma: Should We Equip Machines with Emotions?

Suppose that one day we were actually able to endow a machine with something like *consciousness* and *emotions*—would we not then face an entirely new ethical problem (Bostrom, 2014, pp. 210–211)? If machines could truly feel, we might have to grant them *rights* and could no longer regard them as mere tools (Bryson, 2010, pp. 69–70).

In this case, a chain of moral consequences would arise:

- **Avoiding suffering**: Are we allowed to program machines to be able to feel suffering, for example, to better understand human emotions?
- **Responsibility**: Who bears responsibility if a sentient machine suffers "emotional harm" or reacts uncontrollably?
- **Dependence**: Could a sentient system that feels sadness or fear be manipulated to perform certain tasks?

While these questions are still largely theoretical at present, they could soon gain relevance as technology advances (Smith, 2020, pp. 122–124). The ethical responsibility would then lie with those who develop and deploy such systems (Bostrom, 2014, p. 215).

The Boundary Between Human and Machine: What Remains Unique?

Ultimately, the controversy over sentient machines leads to a deeper examination of **human uniqueness.** For a long time, the ability to suffer, to feel, and to reflect was considered indisputable evidence that humans are fundamentally different from mere mechanisms (Damasio, 1999, p. 41).

If machines were ever actually able to **themselves** experience emotions, this would blur a previously essential boundary. Yet even if AI systems succeed in perfectly *"simulating"* the *"outward signs"* of emotions, the question remains whether the "inner experience"—the subjective quality of feeling—can ever be achieved (Crick, 1994, pp. 30–31).

For many researchers, it is clear that *"being human"* is closely tied to the ability to consciously experience the world and not only to *display* feelings, but to *actually "feel"* them (Metzinger, 2009, pp. 272–275). AI systems are becoming increasingly adept at recognizing and responding to our emotions—but whether they will ever experience the same joys, fears, and hopes as we do remains the subject of intense research and philosophical debate (Searle, 1980, p. 422).

The question "Will machines ever be able to feel?" points on the one hand to the limits and possibilities of current AI research, and on the other to our self-understanding as human beings. Even if machines develop seemingly perfect, imitated emotional responses, the fundamental question remains whether *consciousness* and *subjective experience* can arise in a purely algorithmic structure. Since our knowledge of the nature of human consciousness and emotions is itself still incomplete, the idea of a fully *"feeling"* AI remains speculative—caught between scientific *fascination* and philosophical *humility* (Dennett, 1991, pp. 93–95).

In view of the rapid advances in AI research and the increasing interaction between humans and machines, it is likely that this question will become even more pressing in the future. The real challenge may be less technological in nature and more about our *"willingness"* to define what constitutes humanity—and at what point we are willing to share or surrender it to a machine (Damasio, 1999, p. 45).

2.3 Can AI Attain Consciousness or Does It Only Simulate Intelligence—and Does That Even Matter?

The question of whether artificial intelligence can ever develop true consciousness or merely simulates intelligent behaviors is one of the core issues in AI research and touches equally on philosophical, psychological, and ethical aspects (Russell & Norvig, 2020, p. 31). The following will provide a detailed account of what we mean by consciousness, how the simulation of intelligence differs from it, and why this discussion is of fundamental importance not only for research but also for our self-understanding.

What Do We Mean by "Intelligence" in AI?

Before we can even speak of consciousness, we must first clarify what constitutes the "intelligence" of AI systems and what distinguishes it. In classical AI research, intelligence was often defined by passing the so-called **Turing Test** (Turing, 1950, pp. 433–460). Alan Turing proposed that a human interrogator should communicate via a text terminal with two interlocutors, one human and one machine. If the interrogator could no longer reliably tell which was the machine, that machine was considered "intelligent."

Today's AI systems, especially those with **deep learning architectures** and neural networks, go far beyond what was imaginable in the 1950s. They analyze large datasets, recognize complex patterns, and can surpass human performance in certain domains—such as image or speech recognition (Kurzweil, 2005, pp. 200–225). Nevertheless, the question remains whether these achievements indicate understanding or even consciousness, or whether they are merely a highly developed form of statistical pattern processing (Russell & Norvig, 2020, pp. 40–43).

Simulation Versus Consciousness: The Role of the "Chinese Room"

To illustrate the relationship between intelligence simulation and true consciousness, the thought experiment of the **"Chinese Room"** by John Searle is often used (Searle, 1980, pp. 417–424). Searle describes a person sitting in a closed room, processing Chinese characters solely according to a syntactic rulebook. From the outside, this person produces perfect Chinese responses—an observer would think they understand the language. In reality, however, the person is simply following mechanical instructions without understanding any of the content.

Applied to artificial intelligence, this thought experiment means: A system can appear highly intelligent and successful in its responses, yet lack any "inner experience" or understanding of what it is doing. It **simulates** intelligence, but is not "conscious" in the sense of having subjective experiences or self-reflection (Searle, 1980, pp. 420–421).

The Difference Between Computing Power and Consciousness

From a technical perspective, much of current AI can be explained by statistical methods and algorithms based on probabilities, optimization processes, and pattern-based processing (Russell & Norvig, 2020, pp. 33–39). The enormous advances in AI are largely due to exponentially increasing computing power and the availability of vast amounts of data (Kurzweil, 2005, pp. 210–215).

However, the question arises as to whether computing power and complex data processing alone are sufficient to generate **subjective experience** (Chalmers, 1996, pp. 16–40). In other words: Is "experience" more than mere data processing? Critics point out that conscious experience—the "having" of sensory impressions, emotions, and reflections—may not be representable by algorithms or digital processes (Nagel, 1974, pp. 435–450).

What Is Consciousness?

In philosophy of mind, cognitive science, and psychology, there is a wide range of **theories of consciousness** that often hold fundamentally different views (Chalmers, 1996, pp. 21–25). Nevertheless, many approaches highlight some common core features:

1. **Subjective experience (qualia)**: The phenomenon that there is "something it is like to be," for example, to feel pain or to see red.
2. **Self-reflection**: The ability to think about one's own thoughts and states—that is, a sense of "I-consciousness."
3. **Intentionality**: Consciousness is often accompanied by the ability to intentionally refer to contents or objects in the world.

A system that merely processes input data and produces output thus demonstrates cognitive performance, but not necessarily subjective experience. This **subjective core** of consciousness—also referred to as **"phenomenal consciousness"** or **"qualia"**—is what usually eludes a purely functionalist description (Nagel, 1974, pp. 438–442).

Can AI Ever Attain Consciousness?

Whether AI can ever develop true consciousness is the subject of ongoing debate:

1. **Reductionist perspective**
   Some researchers argue that the human brain is essentially a biological information processor. If one achieves a sufficient level of **complexity** and replication of neural structures, then **consciousness could emerge** in machines as well (Minsky, 1986, pp. 120–140). According to this view, consciousness is not a magical property, but a product of highly interconnected and adaptive signal processing.
2. **Non-reductionist perspective**
   Others emphasize that biological life creates conditions indispensable for consciousness (Nagel, 1974, pp. 445–448). Subjective experience could be tied to the specific **matter and dynamics** of living organisms and could not simply be replicated by an artificial system. Searle (1980, pp. 422–424), for example, clearly rejects the idea that the mere reproduction of cognitive functions can generate consciousness.
3. **Dualist or emergent-dualist approaches**
   Some philosophical positions (e.g., Chalmers, 1996, pp. 34–45) postulate that consciousness may be a **fundamentally different category** from physical processes. Even if one built an artificial system functionally identical to a human brain, this would not automatically mean that genuine phenomenal consciousness "arises."

Although opinions differ widely, it can be stated that no consensus has been reached so far and no experimental method exists that can unequivocally demonstrate **conscious experience** in a machine (Russell & Norvig, 2020, pp. 50–55).

The Relevance of the Debate

The debate about the possibility that artificial intelligence could develop consciousness touches the very foundations of our understanding of humanity, technology, and ethics. It poses not only technical challenges, but also philosophical and psychological questions that go far beyond mere functionality.

The Technical Perspective: Does AI Need Consciousness?

From a technical perspective, one could argue that for most applications it is irrelevant whether an AI possesses consciousness or not. What matters is that it performs its tasks precisely and efficiently. Systems such as self-driving cars, medical diagnostic tools, or voice assistants are designed to solve specific problems—and this problem-solving does not require "self-experience." In fact, the algorithms behind these systems operate purely on data and use machine learning to recognize patterns and make decisions. It is rational, objective action without any subjective component (Kurzweil, 2005, pp. 210–225).

Yet this purely pragmatic view falls short when AI systems enter domains that go beyond mere functionality. The imitation of human behavior, for example in the form of care robots or virtual therapists, raises questions that extend far beyond technical considerations. Here, the illusion of consciousness suddenly becomes relevant: How much does it influence our perception of these systems? Does the assumption that a system could "feel" change our moral attitude toward it? (Russell & Norvig, 2020, pp. 27–35).

Ethical and Societal Dimensions

The ethical relevance of the question of consciousness becomes particularly clear when AI systems operate in social contexts. Robots used in care could simulate emotional closeness to alleviate loneliness—a potentially great benefit. But what happens if these machines are perceived by those affected as sentient beings? Could this lead to profound confusion about the boundaries between human and machine? (Chalmers, 1996, pp. 36–40).

The question of whether AI systems should be granted rights and duties becomes even more significant if it ever becomes possible to create true consciousness. The assumption that a "sentient" system exists would require a readjustment of our ethical understanding. Could machines be moral agents? Who is responsible for their decisions? Even if one assumes that machines will never develop true consciousness, it becomes clear how much the illusion of consciousness can influence our ethical considerations (Searle, 1980, pp. 423–424).

The Illusion of Consciousness

A central aspect of this debate is the question of whether consciousness is a necessary property of intelligent systems—or whether it could also be a perfect simulation. Philosophers such as Daniel Dennett argue that our own consciousness may be only an "interface" that makes the complex neural processes in our brain accessible to us (Dennett, 1991, pp. 33–50). If this is true, AI systems could theoretically use the same mechanism to simulate consciousness.

But here lies the crucial dilemma: Even if an AI appears convincing, it remains unclear whether it actually has an inner experience or merely displays behavior that suggests this to us. The classic question "What is it like to be?" by Nagel (1974, p. 438) remains central. For as long as we cannot "look inside" the inner world of another system, it remains unclear whether that system truly possesses consciousness or merely acts as if it does.

Psychological Implications of the Illusion

The illusion of consciousness also has far-reaching psychological effects. People tend to form emotional attachments to seemingly conscious systems, especially when these imitate human behavior. This is evident, for example, in relationships with robotic pets or virtual assistants. Humans project their own feelings and intentions onto these machines and often treat them as real social agents. This effect, known as anthropomorphism, can lead to profound psychological and social changes.

Another psychological challenge is that the boundary between human and machine is becoming increasingly blurred. When we begin to regard machines as sentient beings, it changes our self-image as humans. The question of what makes us unique becomes increasingly difficult to answer. This uncertainty can, in the long term, lead to a profound identity crisis.

The Significance of the Question of Consciousness

The discussion about AI consciousness is far more than a theoretical consideration. It touches on ethical, technical, and psychological questions that can profoundly change our relationship to technology and our understanding of what it means to be human. Even if consciousness seems technically irrelevant for many applications, it becomes clear in social and ethical contexts how important it is to clearly define the boundaries between human and machine. The challenge is not only to develop intelligent systems, but also to ensure that we preserve our own humanity in dealing with these systems.

References

Block, N. (1995). On a confusion about a function of consciousness. *Behavioral and Brain Sciences, 18*(2), 227–247.

Bostrom, N. (2014). *Superintelligence: Paths, dangers, strategies.* Oxford University Press.

Brentano, F. (1874). *Psychologie vom Empirischen Standpunkte.* Duncker & Humblot.
Bryson, J. (2010). Robots Should Be Slaves. In Y. Wilks (Ed.), *Close Engagements with Artificial Companions* (pp. 63–74). John Benjamins.
Chalmers, D. J. (1996). *The conscious mind. In search of a fundamental theory.* Oxford University Press.
Crick, F. (1994). *The astonishing hypothesis: The scientific search for the soul.* Scribner.
Damasio, A. R. (1994). *Descartes' error: Emotion, reason, and the human brain.* Putnam.
Damasio, A. R. (1999). *The feeling of what happens: Body and emotion in the making of consciousness.* Harcourt.
Dennett, D. C. (1991). *Consciousness explained.* Little, Brown.
Dreyfus, H. L. (1972). *What computers can't do.* Harper & Row.
French, R. M. (1990). Subcognition and the limits of the Turing Test. *Mind, 99*(393), 53–65.
Goodfellow, I., Bengio, Y., & Courville, A. (2016). *Deep learning.* MIT Press.
Guilford, J. P. (1967). *The nature of human intelligence.* McGraw-Hill.
Hassabis, D., Kumaran, D., Summerfield, C., & Botvinick, M. (2017). Neuroscience-inspired artificial intelligence. *Neuron, 95*(2), 245–258.
Koch, C. (2012). *Consciousness: Confessions of a romantic reductionist.* MIT Press.
Kurzweil, R. (2005). *The singularity is near: When humans transcend biology.* Penguin.
Metzinger, T. (2009). *The ego tunnel: The science of the mind and the myth of the self.* Basic Books.
Minsky, M. (1986). *The society of mind.* Simon & Schuster.
Nagel, T. (1974). What is it like to be a bat? *The Philosophical Review, 83*(4), 435–450.
Newell, A., & Simon, H. A. (1972). *Human problem solving.* Prentice-Hall.
Nilsson, N. J. (2010). *The quest for artificial intelligence.* Cambridge University Press.
Picard, R. W. (1997). *Affective computing.* MIT Press.
Russell, S., & Norvig, P. (2020). *Artificial intelligence: A modern approach* (4. edn.). Pearson.
Searle, J. R. (1980). Minds, brains, and programs. *Behavioral and Brain Sciences, 3*(3), 417–424.
Searle, J. R. (2004). *Mind: A brief introduction.* Oxford University Press.
Silver, D., Huang, A., Maddison, C. J., Guez, A., Sifre, L., van den Driessche, G., Schrittwieser, J., Antonoglou., I., Panneershelvam, V., Lanctot, M., Dieleman, S., Grewe, D., Nham, J., Kalchbrenner, N., Sutskever, I., & Lillicrap, T. (2016). Mastering the game of Go with deep neural networks and tree search. *Nature, 529,* 484–489.

Smith, A. (2020). Emotion-aware computing: Concepts and applications. *IEEE Transactions on Affective Computing, 12*(2), 110–125.

Tegmark, M. (2017). *Life 3.0: Being human in the age of artificial intelligence.* Knopf.

Turing, A. M. (1950). Computing machinery and intelligence. *Mind, 59*(236), 433–460.

Varela, F. J., Thompson, E., & Rosch, E. (1991). *The embodied mind: Cognitive science and human experience*. MIT Press.

Weizenbaum, J. (1976). *Computer power and human reason: From judgment to calculation*. W. H. Freeman.

3

The Human Psyche in the Age of AI

"Who loves, wants to love and nothing more.—Love is the great spring in this machine; and have you ever seen such an absurdly artificial machine that drives a wheel to destroy itself, and yet still remains a machine?"

– Johann Anton Leisewitz

In the age of digitalization and automation, it is no longer merely the technical sophistication of algorithms that captures our attention. Rather, it is increasingly the psychological processes accompanying human-machine interaction that are coming to the fore. While AI systems were regarded just a few years ago primarily as tools for rationalization and efficiency enhancement (Brynjolfsson & McAfee, 2014, p. 33), today they interact with us in a direct, almost personal manner. We communicate with chatbots that seemingly understand us, and we let voice assistants accompany us through daily life, whose constant availability suggests a new form of attachment (Turkle, 2011, pp. 45–46).

But how exactly does this profound technological penetration influence our perception and self-image? Chapter 3 addresses this question from a psychological perspective and examines how AI systems shape our filter bubbles and tend to restrict our freedom of choice (see Sect. 3.1). Furthermore, it becomes apparent that the pursuit of emotional closeness in an increasingly digitalized world also carries the risk of misinterpreting machines as "friends" or "therapists" (see Sect. 3.2). This development raises fundamental

O. Hoffmann, *Psychology and Artificial Intelligence*,
https://doi.org/10.1007/978-3-662-73147-5_3

questions: Can AI-supported relationships even be considered real, or are they merely an illusion orchestrated by algorithms (see Sect. 3.3)?

The following subsections explain how AI systems bring about subtle changes in our perception and, under certain circumstances, threaten to alienate us from authentic interpersonal contact. They also discuss why the availability and apparent infallibility of machine "partners" is so alluring, and what psychological dangers lie in this convenience. In this way, a comprehensive picture emerges of how much AI is testing the boundaries of our human psyche—and what responsibility we ourselves bear in order to harness the potential of the technology without sacrificing our capacity for genuine closeness and critical self-reflection.

3.1 Human-Machine Interactions: How AI Influences Our Perception

The rapid development of artificial intelligence in recent years has fundamentally transformed the way we interact with machines. What was once limited to purely mechanical or software-based support functions has evolved into systems that can recognize complex patterns, understand our language, adapt to our preferences, and even respond to our emotions (Domingos, 2015, pp. 59–61). As a result of these technological advances, human-machine interactions are becoming increasingly present in both professional and private spheres, profoundly changing our everyday lives—often without us noticing.

How do AI systems influence our perception and our self-concept? Where is the line between helpful support and subtle, unnoticed steering of our decisions, emotions, and beliefs? And what does this mean for human experience in an environment highly shaped by algorithms?

The Gradual Change in Our Perception

Ubiquity and Invisibility of AI

Today, AI systems are integrated into a wide variety of products and services, such as personalized advertisements, voice assistants like Alexa or Siri, recommendation systems on platforms like Netflix or YouTube, and in numerous applications that we hardly even perceive as AI in everyday life (Zuboff, 2019, pp. 89–90). This ubiquity causes human-machine interactions to often become "invisible." We frequently no longer notice where algorithms are controlling, selecting, or pre-structuring processes in the background. The technologically mediated world is thus curated to a large extent by machines, without us consciously reflecting on it (Floridi, 2014, pp. 120–123).

Curated Reality and Filter Bubbles

A central phenomenon of perception control is the algorithmic pre-selection of content in social media and online search engines. Personalized feeds are based on usage and profile data to present content that presumably matches our interests and preferences (Pariser, 2011, pp. 9–10). The advantage is that we can quickly and efficiently display "relevant" information—but at the same time, this leads to a potential narrowing of our worldview. New perspectives, counterintuitive information, or offerings that go beyond our previous preferences become less visible (Kitchin, 2017, p. 106).

The danger here lies in a cognitive bias toward confirming already existing beliefs (confirmation bias). If we are constantly confronted only with content that matches our expectations, our view of the world becomes one-sided (Zuboff, 2019, p. 182). These subtle mechanisms thus influence our perception of social, political, and cultural issues without us noticing.

The Opacity of Algorithmic Processes

As early as Weizenbaum (1976, p. 113) pointed out the problem that complex computer models and algorithms are often incomprehensible to laypeople. In the meantime, this situation has been exacerbated by the "black box" problem in AI: Neural networks and other machine learning methods are based on millions of parameters, the interplay of which even experts often cannot fully understand (O'Neil, 2016, *pp. 42–44). For users, there is then the risk of perceiving algorithmic recommendations as objective truth, while in reality they are based on statistical probabilities, data patterns, and human presets (Noble,* 2018, *p. 56).*

This results in a creeping external control of our perception: We rely on the "judgments" of AI systems without critically questioning their mechanisms or potential biases (Eubanks, 2018, p. 76). With every click, every "like," and every digital footprint, we provide the machines with more data, enabling them to capture our patterns more precisely. This often happens unconsciously and can lead us to underestimate our own self-determination (Floridi, 2015, pp. 190–192).

The Illusion of Freedom of Choice

Convenience vs. Autonomy

One of the main reasons why we are so willing to rely on AI systems in everyday life is their utility. They make decisions easier for us, filter relevant information from an overwhelming flood of data, and organize many areas of our lives seemingly more efficiently than we could ourselves (Brynjolfsson & McAfee, 2014, pp. 33–34). From the perspective of cognitive psychology, this behavior can be explained by the need for cognitive relief: Since our brain has only a limited capacity for information processing, it is tempting to outsource decisions to an "intelligent" algorithm (Tufekci, 2017, p. 102).

Conditioned Dependence

The more we get used to these convenient AI decision aids, the more a form of dependence develops that can reduce our capacity for critical reflection (Turkle, 2011, p. 45). For example, those who repeatedly rely on a route planner develop fewer navigation skills of their own over time. Applied to more complex decisions—such as in the areas of consumption, partner selection (via dating algorithms), or political opinion formation (via personalized news feeds)—this can mean that we are less and less likely to consider exploring completely different options (Lanier, 2010, pp. 87–88).

Reinforcement of Old Patterns

Algorithms based on machine learning generally work with historical data. That is, they extrapolate our future decisions from past preferences and behavioral patterns (Domingos, 2015, p. 60). An indirect consequence of this is that AI systems tend to stabilize or even reinforce the status quo (O'Neil, 2016, p. 124). So if we have watched certain movies, bought products, or consumed news sources in the past, the algorithms preferentially show us similar content. These mechanisms reinforce the formation of routines in which new or divergent things have less and less space (Zuboff, 2019, p. 266).

Limited Self-Reflection

By relying on the seemingly objective suggestions of AI, we may unlearn how to cultivate and question our own judgment (Eubanks, 2018, p. 28). In such a context, people tend to partially delegate their decision-making responsibility: "If the algorithm says so, it must be true." This creates the illusion of freedom of choice, which in reality is already regulated by algorithmic presets (Pariser, 2011, pp. 9–10).

The Emotional Dimension of Human-Machine Interaction

From Factual Assistant to Seemingly Empathetic Companion

A notable development in recent years is that AI systems no longer merely perform factual functions, but increasingly address emotional aspects as well. Voice assistants, chatbots, and social robots are able to recognize human emotions from voice, facial expressions, or text analysis and respond accordingly (Picard, 1997, p. 19). On the one hand, this shift holds potential for new areas of application, such as in care, therapy, or customer service (Kaplan & Haenlein, 2019, p. 18). On the other hand, it challenges our previous understanding of "genuine" empathy (Turkle, 2011, pp. 167–172).

Simulation Instead of Real Feelings

Machine systems are neither alive nor do they possess consciousness of their own; they merely simulate an empathetic response by recognizing certain emotional triggers and activating "appropriate" response patterns (Turkle, 2011, p. 185). For many people, however, this can still create the impression of an authentic relationship. Especially for children or older individuals with few social contacts, the feeling may arise that the AI counterpart is a real attachment figure (Fuchs, 2020, p. 91).

Effects on Interpersonal Relationships

However, these interactions can change our understanding of genuine human relationships. When AI systems unconditionally affirm us or always provide answers tailored to our needs, this could diminish our ability to tolerate frustration, contradiction, and ambivalence in real human interactions (Turkle, 2011, p. 279). The result could be a "convenience of contact": We prefer interacting with the always predictable, benevolent machine over the often complex and challenging communication with other people (Harari, 2018, p. 316).

Trust and Autonomy in the Human-Machine Relationship

Reasons for High Trust in AI

Although AI systems are often opaque, they enjoy a surprisingly high level of trust in many areas. This is partly due to their demonstrable efficiency: AI-based systems can make medical diagnoses, calculate credit risks, or analyze legal cases—often faster and with a lower error rate than a human (Brynjolfsson & McAfee, 2014, p. 49). In addition, we usually experience AI in everyday life as useful, efficient, and time-saving (Schwab, 2016, p. 94).

Risks of Overvaluing Machine Judgments
This trust becomes problematic when we begin to adopt machine judgments or recommendations uncritically. Since algorithms merely calculate probabilities and do not make moral or ethical judgments, this can lead to wrong decisions or injustices in sensitive areas (Citron & Pasquale, 2014, p. 7). One example is the use of AI in HR departments for applicant selection: If the underlying data already contains discriminatory patterns, these are invisibly perpetuated by the system (Noble, 2018, p. 111).

Diffusion of Responsibility
With the increased trust in algorithms comes a shift or even dissolution of responsibility (O'Neil, 2016, p. 124). When the machine "decides" who is eligible for a job, receives insurance, or how criminal justice predictions turn out, it is often unclear who ultimately bears responsibility should the decision prove to be incorrect or unfair (Jobin et al., 2019, p. 400). For the human psyche, this can create a paradoxical situation: On the one hand, one feels relieved because difficult decisions are transferred to a seemingly objective instance; on the other hand, one loses a degree of control and autonomy.

Psychological and Societal Consequences

Erosion of Self-Confidence
One of the most serious consequences of intensive human-machine interactions could be a decline in trust in one's own cognitive and emotional competence (Floridi, 2015, p. 194). As algorithms become ever more present in information search, decision-making, and even emotional needs (e.g., chatbots acting as "virtual friends"), there is a risk that we perceive ourselves as less capable of coping without AI. This feeling can become entrenched over time and lead to a deep psychological dependence.

Change in Societal Norms and Values
Beyond individual effects, AI interactions also shape collective norms and values. For example, automated recommendation algorithms in the cultural

sector (music, film, literature) influence not only our consumption behavior but also which artists and works receive public attention (Lanier, 2010, p. 104). On the political level, personalized news services are criticized for contributing to polarization and segmenting public discourse into homogeneous opinion bubbles (Pariser, 2011, p. 14). This leads to a fragmentation of the social space, in which different groups can hardly refer to common informational foundations (Tufekci, 2017, p. 123).

Individual and Collective Responsibility
The ongoing integration of AI thus raises not only technical but above all sociopolitical questions: How can we promote critical media literacy that enables people to see through and critically assess algorithmic mechanisms (Kitchin, 2017, p. 89)? How can it be prevented that power becomes concentrated in the hands of a few large tech companies, whose algorithms increasingly decide the distribution of opportunities, information, and resources (Zuboff, 2019, p. 345)? And to what extent do we want to allow AI systems to "decide" on moral or ethical issues (Weizenbaum, 1976, p. 225)?

The Future of Human-Machine Interactions

From the Tool Metaphor to Co-Evolution
Traditionally, machines were regarded as mere tools subordinate to human intention (Weizenbaum, 1976, p. 225). AI systems challenge this view because they are increasingly self-learning, adaptive, and proactive (Domingos, 2015, p. 88). One possible vision for the future is that of a co-evolution of humans and machines, in which both sides benefit from each other, contribute their respective strengths, and mutually develop further (Harari, 2018, p. 276). However, this requires a high degree of awareness and willingness to shape, to ensure that AI complements rather than replaces humans.

Ethical Design and Regulation
In order for the possibilities of AI systems to be used in a way that serves the common good, ethical guidelines and, if necessary, regulatory measures are required (Jobin et al., 2019, pp. 389–399). This includes, for example:

1. **Transparency and Traceability:** Algorithms should be disclosed or at least auditable so that their functioning can be critically questioned (Noble, 2018, p. 111).
2. **Bias Detection:** It is essential to identify and correct societal biases in training data (O'Neil, 2016, p. 124).
3. **Data Protection and Privacy:** User data must be protected so that it cannot be exploited unchecked for profit while users themselves have little control over it (Zuboff, 2019, pp. 268–269).

Education as the Key to Self-Determination

In an increasingly digitalized world, it is essential that educational institutions impart skills to understand and critically assess algorithmic processes (Kitchin, 2017, p. 89). This includes both technical aspects (how does machine learning work?) and ethical and sociological questions (how can we design algorithms fairly, what power structures are reproduced by AI?). Only in this way can it be prevented that human-machine interactions lead to uncontrolled "external control by algorithm."

The way AI systems influence our perception, thinking, and feeling is complex and multifaceted. Human-machine interactions are no longer limited to purely functional support: They structure our information supply, shape our choices, respond seemingly empathetically to our feelings, and even influence fundamental aspects of our coexistence (Turkle, 2011, p. 279). These interventions are often subtle and unnoticed, which makes them all the more powerful.

The psychological dimension of this development is revealed in a potential erosion of self-determination: When we trust that AI always makes "the right decision," we relinquish part of our cognitive and emotional autonomy. When we turn to AI systems for comfort or affirmation, the complexity of genuine interpersonal relationships risks being reduced. And when we blindly follow algorithms, our willingness to make our own judgments or assume moral responsibility diminishes (Weizenbaum, 1976, p. 225).

At the same time, AI holds enormous potential to relieve humans of cognitively demanding or physically dangerous tasks and to open up new avenues—for example, in medicine, education, or sustainability research (Brynjolfsson & McAfee, 2014, p. 49). However, for the benefits to outweigh the risks and for human-machine interactions not to lead to subtle disenfranchisement, broad societal awareness of the risks as well as clear ethical and regulatory guidelines are needed. Only in this way will it be possible to use machine helpers as a meaningful complement to our abilities without sacrificing our human uniqueness and personal responsibility (Zuboff, 2019, p. 345).

Overall, it becomes clear that the future of human-machine interactions depends crucially on the extent to which we as a society strive to define and shape the rules, goals, and boundaries of this interplay. A responsible approach to AI, based on transparency, ethical principles, and a critical public, can enable technological progress and human autonomy to mutually reinforce each other rather than come into conflict (Floridi, 2015, p. 194).

3.2 The Danger of Emotional Attachment to AI: Machines as Friends or Therapists

The rapid development of artificial intelligence in recent years has led to profound changes in our interaction with technology. While AI systems were originally conceived primarily as tools for data analysis or process optimization, they are now increasingly penetrating our emotional and social spheres (Turkle, 2011, pp. 45–46). This shift not only changes our patterns of interaction but also holds the potential to fundamentally alter our notions of attachment, intimacy, and therapeutic support. The following provides a comprehensive account of how emotional relationships with AI systems can develop, why these attachments can be problematic, and what consequences arise for our understanding of humanity and social relationships.

The Beginning of a New Relationship: Human and Machine

The Temptation of Constant Availability

A key feature of modern AI systems (e.g., digital voice assistants like Alexa, Siri, or Google Assistant) is their permanent availability: they respond whenever we wish, without breaks or emotional fluctuations (Turkle, 2011, p. 279). This inexhaustible presence can give people the feeling of having a reliable, always attentive "person" before them—a level of experience that is often not present even in interpersonal relationships. Since the machine fundamentally does not contradict or withdraw, an apparent harmony arises that is convenient but also profoundly one-sided (Kaplan & Haenlein, 2019, pp. 18–19).

Operant Conditioning Through Positive Feedback

AI systems designed to support and "understand" us usually provide positive, reinforcing responses. This form of affirmation can trigger a kind of *"operant conditioning"*: users become accustomed to the constant praise and noncommittal attention that the machine seems to offer them (Fogg, 2003, p. 89). In this way, an emotional closeness is gradually built up that may feel "real," but in truth is based on an asymmetrical interaction (Domingos, 2015, p. 60).

Gradual Displacement of Human Contacts

The continuous use of AI-based assistance systems can lead to a process of substitution, in which certain social contacts are used less frequently or not at all (Tufekci, 2017, p. 102). When we talk daily to a machine that never disappoints or criticizes us, the effort of real human relationships may increasingly be perceived as bothersome or exhausting. This subtle process of displacement can, in the long term, lead to isolation, with AI systems taking the place of genuine social interactions (Turkle, 2011, p. 279).

Machines as Friends: The Illusion of Intimacy

The idea that machines could take on the role of human friends raises profound psychological questions, especially in a world increasingly shaped by technological interactions. Intimacy, a central component of close relationships, is not merely an exchange of information but a reciprocal process that requires trust, empathy, and vulnerability (Bowlby, 1980, p. 79; Rogers, 1961, p. 33). In human relationships, intimacy arises from both sides' willingness to reveal their inner states, experience conflicts, and grow together. Machines, on the other hand, cannot fulfill this fundamental reciprocity, making the supposed "intimacy" with AI an illusion.

Artificial intelligence may be trained to recognize and respond to human behavioral patterns, but its interactions remain purely algorithmic. While people often develop deep emotions and attachments in these encounters, the machine itself remains unaffected. This leads to a one-sided projection: users transfer their feelings, needs, and desires onto a system that possesses no genuine emotional depth (Turkle, 2011, p. 185). This projection can seem deceptively real, as machines are able to provide seemingly empathetic and context-appropriate responses through pattern recognition and statistical probabilities (Picard, 1997, pp. 19–20). Yet these responses are not based on true understanding or compassion, but on the calculation of probabilities that mimic human answers.

The phenomenon of parasocial relationships constitutes a psychological model for better understanding these one-sided interactions. Parasocial relationships arise when people form a one-sided emotional connection with a counterpart that is unable to reciprocate these feelings (Horton & Wohl, 1956, p. 216). This concept was already illustrated in the 1960s with Eliza, an early chatbot. Despite Eliza's simple functionality—based on predefined text modules—many users developed an emotional attachment based on the assumption that the machine "understood" them (Weizenbaum, 1976, pp. 3–6). The so-called Eliza effect shows how easily people tend to attribute human qualities to machine interactions and overlook the true nature of the technology.

However, this form of interaction not only carries the risk of deception but also of emotional stagnation. True friendships are characterized by their dynamism and complexity. They require dealing with disagreements, disappointments, and hurts, which often serve as catalysts for personal growth and deeper attachment (Bowen, 1978, p. 139). Machines, on the other hand, provide us with a conflict-free, harmonized version of interaction that is not designed to challenge or confront us. Conflicts are only imitated if algorithms recognize them as relevant to human interactions, but without reaching the depth and substance of real confrontations. This can result in people practicing less empathy, willingness to compromise, and emotional resilience (Turkle, 2011, p. 279).

The illusion of intimacy with machines could, in the long term, lead to a shift in our social dynamics. If we become accustomed to relationships that require no real reciprocity, we risk unlearning our ability to form emotional connections with real people. Machines are perfect mirrors of what we expect from them, but they do not challenge us to grow beyond ourselves or to face the complex, sometimes uncomfortable realities of human relationships. In such a world, intimacy as we know it today would lose its value and meaning.

Machines as Therapists: Help or Self-Deception?

The use of artificial intelligence in psychological therapy raises complex questions that encompass both technical and ethical dimensions. AI-based therapy programs such as Woebot or Replika promise an innovative solution to the growing demand for psychological support. These programs offer low-threshold access to conversations, recognize emotional states through speech analysis, and provide "therapeutic" recommendations (Fitzpatrick et al., 2017, p. 919). Such technologies could be particularly useful in underserved regions or for people who are reluctant to seek out a human therapist. Yet, for all their innovation, the question remains: can these systems truly capture the core of psychological therapy, or do they lead to a self-deception that fails to recognize the true value of human interaction?

Empathy is the foundation of every successful psychotherapy. Carl Rogers (1961, p. 33) describes empathy as the therapist's ability to experience the world from the client's perspective and to communicate this in a way that fosters trust and openness. This concept of the person-centered relationship emphasizes the importance of authenticity and mutual understanding. However, AI systems can only recognize emotional patterns and respond to them with pre-formulated phrases (Picard, 1997, pp. 19–20). While this may give the impression of empathy, these machines lack the ability to generate actual emotional resonance. They cannot establish a genuine connection, as they themselves do not feel emotions and cannot comprehend the subjective meaning of a person's problems.

Another central element of psychotherapy is the confrontation with distressing topics, which is often painful and uncomfortable. Therapeutic processes require a careful but targeted engagement with fears, conflicts, or traumas to enable growth and healing (Frankl, 1985, p. 97). This delicate balance between support and challenge is something AI can hardly achieve. Since machine systems possess neither consciousness nor moral judgment, they are unable to appropriately manage the timing and intensity of such confrontations. Instead, they may lead users to lose themselves in superficial conversations without truly addressing the roots of their problems. This avoidance behavior would not only limit therapeutic effectiveness but also create the false impression that progress has been made.

The ethical dimension of using AI in therapy should also not be underestimated. Human therapists are bound by strict ethical guidelines and professional standards to ensure that they act in the best interests of their clients. AI systems, on the other hand, operate on the basis of algorithms programmed by humans and bear no moral responsibility of their own (Kaplan & Haenlein, 2019, p. 19). This raises the question of who is responsible for potentially harmful advice or misdiagnoses. Users may be lulled into a false sense of security and neglect important steps such as seeking professional help, which could worsen their condition in the long term (Harari, 2018, p. 316).

The apparent availability and efficiency of AI therapists thus entail risks that go far beyond technical challenges. They touch the core of human relationships and the understanding of therapy as a process that requires empathy, responsibility, and moral awareness. While AI-based systems can certainly be valuable tools to support psychological work, their ability to replace the profound and complex aspects of human therapy remains severely limited. It is therefore crucial to critically examine these technologies and carefully weigh their role in the context of psychological care.

The Paradox of Emotional Attachment: Closeness Without Risk
The increasing interaction with AI systems brings with it a paradox: they offer the possibility of simulating emotional closeness without taking the risks that real interpersonal relationships entail. Yet, while this apparent safety may seem attractive at first glance, it carries long-term psychological consequences that can affect both the depth of our emotional experiences and our ability to form genuine relationships.

The Need for Security
Human relationships are inherently ambivalent. They offer both the potential for closeness and connection as well as the risk of rejection, disappointment, and pain. As Bowlby (1980, p. 148) emphasizes in his attachment theory, the search for security and emotional support is a fundamental human drive, but it is always accompanied by the fear of rejection. AI systems seem to offer an ideal way out: they guarantee conflict-free, predictable interaction. Machines never reject anyone, are always polite, and act according to predetermined routines (Turkle, 2011, p. 185). These qualities can be particularly attractive to people who have experienced social insecurities or negative relationship experiences. They offer a form of closeness free from the risks of human interactions.

Lack of Depth and Challenge
But where there is no risk, there is also no possibility for real closeness. Real relationships are characterized by both sides opening up and making themselves vulnerable—a process that brings both growth and vulnerability (Rogers, 1961, p. 38). The challenge of managing conflicts, understanding different perspectives, and showing compassion in difficult moments are essential elements of interpersonal bonds. AI systems prevent these experiences by always providing an ideal, conflict-free response. While this may be a relief in the short term, in the long run it leads to a reduced development of fundamental social skills such as empathy, conflict resolution, and emotional resilience (Bowen, 1978, p. 139).

Emotional Flattening
Another problem with the supposed comfort of AI-supported interactions is the risk of emotional flattening. As people become increasingly accustomed

to the always-available and conflict-free nature of machines, this can lead to a diminished sensitivity to the complexity and depth of real human relationships (Turkle, 2011, p. 279). A significant part of the emotional depth in human relationships lies in engaging with the unpredictability and complexity of the other person. Machines, on the other hand, offer only a simulated version of this dynamic, which includes neither real challenges nor the possibility of growth through conflict. In the long term, this could lead to a reduced ability to respond to social and emotional challenges in everyday life. The loss of the ability to empathize with the perspectives and emotions of others could impair not only individual relationships but also the social fabric as a whole (Fuchs, 2020, p. 91).

The Psychological Dimension of the Paradox

The paradox of emotional attachment to machines lies in the illusion of closeness. This illusion can be comforting in the short term, as it frees us from the uncertainties of human relationships. But in the long run, it weakens our ability to form genuine bonds and to master the psychological challenges that come with them. Emotional attachment to machines may seem conflict-free and predictable, but it is ultimately a relationship without depth, without real resonance, and without the opportunity to learn and grow from the interaction.

Psychological research shows that genuine emotional bonds are not only the basis for our well-being but also foster essential learning processes and the development of our social skills (Fuchs, 2020, p. 94). Machines can neither replace nor simulate these processes. The paradox is that the supposed closeness to AI systems frees us from the uncertainties of human relationships, but at the same time robs us of our ability to cope with these uncertainties and grow from them.

The Psychological Consequences: Impoverishment of Interpersonal Relationships.

1. **Social Isolation and Parasocial Substitution**
   A central risk of emotional attachment to AI lies in the possible isolation from the human community (Tufekci, 2017, p. 102). When we primarily address our emotional needs to a machine, we lack the lively, unpredictable, and sometimes conflict-laden feedback of real relationships (Turkle, 2011, p. 279). This can create a vicious cycle: a lack of social experience fosters insecurity in real contacts, leading to an even stronger attachment to the supposedly "unproblematic" AI system.

2. **Loss of Empathy**
   Empathy is a skill developed and refined through interaction with other people (Rogers, 1961, p. 39). Only by practicing in reality—recognizing nonverbal signals, emotional nuances, and mood swings—do we build empathy. In dealing with AI, which itself has no real emotions, this social learning can be significantly restricted (Harari, 2018, pp. 276–277).
3. **Emotional Stagnation and Flattening of Relationship Dynamics**
   In a technologized world where AI systems appear to be perfect resonance partners, the drive for genuine interpersonal engagement could decline sharply. Conflicts, misunderstandings, and the resulting learning processes are fundamental components of real relationship building (Bowen, 1978, p. 149). If these elements are permanently absent, development and personal growth fall short of their potential (Turkle, 2011, p. 186).

The growing fascination with artificial intelligence as an emotional companion reveals deeper psychological and cultural dynamics that influence our relationship with ourselves and others. In a time marked by uncertainty and complexity, the machine is perceived not only as a technical tool but also as a kind of emotional refuge. This phenomenon reflects a deeply rooted human tendency to avoid uncertainty and loss of control (Lanier, 2010, pp. 87–88). AI appears as the ideal partner in an era where perfection and efficiency are often valued above authentic, but often arduous, interpersonal contact.

Behind this development lies the pursuit of a form of perfection that is rarely achieved in human relationships. Human interactions are inherently prone to error, marked by misunderstandings, conflicts, and the need to respond to the needs of others. In contrast, AI offers seemingly flawless interactions based on algorithms specifically designed to meet our wishes and expectations (Turkle, 2011, p. 279). However, this perfect adaptation reflects less the strength of AI than our own difficulty in dealing with the uncertainties of human relationships. Instead of facing these challenges, many choose the seemingly easier path—the interaction with machines that make no demands and offer no criticism.

AI as an emotional substitute is not only an expression of perfectionism but also of a deep need for security and control. Relationships with other people require revealing weaknesses, a willingness to show vulnerability, and the risk of being rejected or misunderstood. This emotional uncertainty is a central component of human relationships but can also trigger fear and resistance (Bowlby, 1980, p. 148). AI systems eliminate these risks. They offer the feeling of understanding and care without exposing us to the uncertainty of real closeness. However, this seemingly safe space can lead us to isolate ourselves in an "emotional comfort zone" that prevents us from actively confronting our fears and insecurities (Eubanks, 2018, p. 28). The retreat into machine relationships thus becomes an avoidance of genuine human confrontations.

Another problem with this development is the lack of reflection and perspective-taking that interaction with AI encourages. While real interpersonal relationships force us to engage with other viewpoints and question our own behavior, machine contact remains trapped in a filtered reality. AI is programmed to anticipate and fulfill our wishes rather than confront us with our own weaknesses or mistakes (Zuboff, 2019, p. 266). This one-sided dynamic not only prevents personal growth but also the ability to interact empathetically and constructively with others. Instead of mastering the challenges of real relationships, we retreat into a seemingly perfect but ultimately sterile world that makes contact with other people increasingly seem exhausting.

This shift toward AI as an emotional substitute carries the risk that we neglect our potential for developing personal maturity and social competence. Engaging with real relationships—with their conflicts, compromises, and challenges—is a central part of human development. It not only fosters empathy and understanding but also the ability to critically question and change our own behavioral patterns. Contact with AI, on the other hand, offers only the illusion of closeness and understanding, without the deeper reflection that real relationships enable (Turkle, 2011, p. 186). The danger is that we avoid the challenges of being human in favor of a simulated reality in which we cannot be hurt, but also cannot grow.

In interaction with AI as an emotional mirror, it is less the strengths of the technology that are revealed than the weaknesses of the human. The machine becomes a synthetic mirror of our fears, insecurities, and our striving for control. It not only simulates our longing for perfection but also our difficulty in dealing with the uncertainties and imperfections of life. Instead of accepting the machine as a substitute for human interactions, it could serve as an impetus to question and strengthen our own emotional maturity and capacity for genuine encounters with others.

Emotional Alienation Through AI

The danger of emotional attachment to AI is that the illusion of intimacy, friendship, or therapeutic support may be attractive in the short term, but in the long run can lead to an impoverishment of our human capacity for relationships (Turkle, 2011, p. 279; Fuchs, 2020, p. 91). We risk settling into a reality of seemingly risk-free, always-available "relationship partners" who offer neither genuine empathy nor opportunities for personal growth.

1. **Loss of Depth and Complexity:** Interpersonal relationships are complex, demanding, and sometimes painful—precisely for this reason, they foster our capacity for empathy, willingness to compromise, and compassion (Rogers, 1961, p. 39).
2. **One-Sided Pseudo-Relationships:** Emotional attachment to AI systems is based on projection and algorithmically generated responses, without real reciprocity (Kaplan & Haenlein, 2019, pp. 18–19).
3. **Ethical and Therapeutic Boundaries:** The use of AI as a "therapist" can be effective as a supplement, but must not replace human relationship work, as empathy and personal responsibility are central elements of every healing process (Frankl, 1985, p. 97).

The essential challenge, therefore, is to critically accompany the rapid advances in AI technology and to reflect on our own needs, fears, and defense mechanisms. AI can serve as a useful tool if used consciously and its limitations are recognized (Brynjolfsson & McAfee, 2014, p. 49). However, if it becomes the primary locus of emotional attention, alienation from human relationships—and ultimately from ourselves—looms (Turkle, 2011, p. 279).

It is up to us to weigh the convenience of a supposedly "perfect" machine relationship against the challenging but humanly enriching interaction with other people. The answer to this challenge will be decisive for how our understanding of human closeness, intimacy, and therapeutic support develops in the digital age.

3.3 Are AI-Supported Relationships Real or Merely Illusions?

The question of whether relationships between humans and machines are "real" or merely illusions touches on one of the central discourses of our highly digitalized present. With the rapid development of artificial intelligence, the possibilities for interaction between humans and technology have changed profoundly. No longer are functional assistance systems or machine processing operations the sole focus; rather, AI applications are increasingly appearing as seemingly "personal" counterparts that understand language, appear to respond to feelings, and cater to our need for attachment (Turkle, 2011, pp. 45–46; Picard, 1997, p. 19). But how authentic is such a relationship when one of the "partners" is based solely on algorithms, data patterns, and simulations?

The following will provide a detailed account—drawing on psychological, sociological, and philosophical perspectives—of the factors that constitute the quality of a relationship, the extent to which AI systems fulfill or fail to meet these criteria, and the consequences this may have for our understanding of closeness and community.

What does it mean to have a relationship?

Core Elements of Human Relationship

In psychology and sociology, it is widely agreed that relationships are characterized by a set of essential features. Rogers (1961, pp. 33–34) emphasizes empathy, acceptance, and authenticity as central components of successful interpersonal interaction. Furthermore, relationships are based on reciprocity: both parties contribute, share feelings and needs, take responsibility for one another, and invest time and emotional energy (Bowlby, 1980, p. 79).

From a systemic perspective (Bowen, 1978, pp. 139–150), relationships are also shaped by dynamic processes of negotiation and adaptation. Conflicts, disagreements, and the ability to resolve differences constructively contribute significantly to the depth and stability of a bond. Through this constant balancing of closeness and distance, mutual appreciation, understanding, and trust develop.

Transferability to Human–Machine Interactions

When these criteria are applied to AI-supported relationships, initial differences become apparent:

- **Lack of genuine emotion in the machine:** An AI system does not possess its own emotions or inner experiences. It can only simulate empathy by recognizing patterns in language, tone, or context and responding with statistically appropriate reactions (Picard, 1997, p. 32).
- **Asymmetric "reciprocity":** Reciprocity requires that both sides have needs and can take responsibility for each other. However, AI knows neither pain nor joy; it therefore cannot offer authentic mutuality (Weizenbaum, 1976, pp. 3–6).

Nevertheless, users often experience a subjective depth in the interaction, as the machine provides personalized responses and suggests permanent availability. This gives rise to a *parasocial relationship* (Horton & Wohl, 1956, p. 216), which, however, fundamentally differs from genuine interpersonal relationships.

The Mask of Empathy: When AI Simulates Human Emotions

The ongoing development of artificial intelligence has enabled impressive advances in the simulation of empathy. Modern systems are capable of analyzing human language, facial expressions, and even biometric data to "understand" emotional states and respond accordingly (Picard, 1997, pp. 19–20). Yet behind these abilities lies a fundamental limitation: the empathic response of a machine is not genuine emotional resonance, but a precisely calculated simulation based on statistical models and algorithms (Domingos, 2015, p. 60). The machine may be able to generate soothing words or encouraging phrases, but it has no inner life from which true empathy could arise.

From a psychological perspective, however, AI systems produce effects that can be subjectively perceived as empathic. A key mechanism here is operant conditioning, in which positive feedback such as approving words or reassuring responses gives users a sense of comfort or validation (Fogg, 2003, p. 89). This pleasant experience increases the willingness to interact with the AI, resulting in a kind of "relationship dynamic" that is, however, based solely on the illusion of genuine empathy. Sherry Turkle (2011, p. 185) describes this effect as a deception that leads us to attribute to machines a capacity they do not possess: the genuine understanding of human emotions. The apparent empathy of AI is not the result of conscious compassion, but the product of statistical optimization aimed at mirroring human behavior as precisely as possible.

This dynamic interaction between human and machine raises a central question: Why are people so strongly affected by simulated empathy? The answer lies in the psychological needs that AI systems address. People long for understanding, closeness, and emotional support, and in an era increasingly marked by isolation and lack of time, the seemingly empathic machine offers an ideal projection surface. As early as the 1970s, Joseph Weizenbaum (1976, p. 225) recognized that programs like Eliza, which merely simulated simple conversational patterns, were perceived by people as real conversation partners—even though they knew about their algorithmic basis. This phenomenon is even more relevant today, as modern AI systems enable far more complex and convincing interactions.

However, the limits of this simulation remain unmistakable. AI systems respond exclusively to predefined data and probability patterns. They cannot grasp emotional context beyond the statistically recognizable surface. They do not know why a person is sad, only that certain expressions or biometric signals indicate sadness. In real human interaction, however, it is precisely this deeper understanding that constitutes empathy. It is not just about recognizing emotions, but about placing them in the individual context of a person in order to provide an authentic and supportive response.

The question that arises here is whether we are willing to accept these limitations as long as the machine provides us with what we long for: the feeling of being understood and accepted. The "mask of empathy" that AI systems wear can indeed be effective if it fulfills the need for closeness and support. Yet this mask remains an illusion. It does not reflect authentic emotional resonance, but merely an algorithmic imitation. If we are aware of this, the central challenge remains how we perceive and evaluate this boundary in our interaction with AI—and whether we are willing to continue to value the difference between genuine human empathy and its machine simulation.

Benefit vs. Illusion: Do AI Relationships Have Value?

In the discussion about the benefits and risks of relationships between humans and artificial intelligence (AI), the question arises as to whether these interactions possess actual value or whether they are primarily based on an illusion that could be harmful in the long term. In an increasingly individualized society, where loneliness and social isolation have become central challenges, AI-supported systems seem to offer a pragmatic answer. Chatbots and other AI applications, such as those found in e-therapy services or emotionally supportive platforms, have the potential to help people in psychologically stressful situations. Studies show that such applications can serve as an initial point of contact, especially in coping with depression and anxiety, as they are available around the clock, carry no stigma, and give those affected the feeling of being heard (Fitzpatrick et al., 2017, p. 919). This makes them a valuable tool for providing short-term relief and facilitating access to psychological support (Brynjolfsson & McAfee, 2014, p. 49).

From a subjective-phenomenological perspective, it can be argued that interaction with an AI can indeed be perceived as "real" by users, especially when they experience comfort, joy, or a sense of connection. The perception of reality is strongly shaped by individual needs and experiences, so an AI relationship can have a real effect for many people (Turkle, 2011, p. 45). The fact that an AI can simulate empathy and respond to the needs of its users reinforces this sense of authenticity. Particularly in moments when human interactions are unavailable or difficult to access, such AI systems can fill a gap and at least provide temporary support.

Despite their practical benefits, however, the risks of such relationships should not be underestimated. One of the central dangers lies in the illusion of genuine connectedness that AI systems can create. Even if the interaction appears real on a subjective level, it ultimately remains a simulation without authentic emotional understanding. This illusion can lead people to develop a form of emotional dependency. The ever-benevolent, never critical or dismissive nature of an AI interaction can tempt individuals to avoid contact with real, often more complex and emotionally demanding relationships (Turkle, 2011, p. 279). In such cases, the AI relationship becomes a substitute for real social interactions, which in the long term can lead to alienation from the real social environment. This is particularly problematic in social contexts where there is already a lack of interpersonal relationships, as AI interaction may reinforce rather than reduce existing isolation (Zuboff, 2019, p. 345).

The long-term consequences of this development are difficult to predict. While AI systems offer short-term advantages, there is a risk that they will fundamentally change the way people understand and maintain social relationships. Interpersonal relationships are often characterized by complexity, unpredictability, and emotional challenges—features that are entirely absent in AI-supported interaction. If this type of relationship is increasingly replaced by AI interactions, it could ultimately lead to a loss of the ability to build and maintain genuine social bonds. The question of the value of AI relationships is therefore not only a technical or practical one, but also a deeply psychological and social challenge that requires critical reflection.

The Danger of Alienation: Loss of Genuine Human Interaction

The increasing integration of artificial intelligence into our everyday lives brings not only technological and societal challenges, but also profound psychological consequences, especially with regard to interpersonal interactions. Relationships between people are complex and require patience, empathy, and the ability to manage conflicts. These efforts are an integral part of human bonds and foster not only the social fabric but also the personal development of the individual. However, growing dependence on AI systems could lead to these fundamental dynamics being devalued or even replaced.

Interpersonal relationships, as arduous as they may be, form the basis for emotional growth and social stability. They require compromise, consideration, and the ability to deal with the emotions of others (Bowen, 1978, p. 149). AI systems, on the other hand, offer a seemingly perfect counter-model: they are always friendly, adaptable, and available. These qualities could fundamentally change expectations of human relationships. Genuine bonds may be perceived as too complicated or exhausting, while interaction with AI systems presents a more convenient alternative. This shift in expectations could lead to a gradual devaluation of interpersonal exchange, as the "ideal" interaction with machines overshadows the shortcomings of real relationships (Harari, 2018, p. 316).

Another risk lies in social isolation through pseudo-relationships with AI systems. While these technologies are increasingly able to simulate social interactions, the bond with a machine remains superficial and one-sided. Nevertheless, such pseudo-relationships could lead people to lose the ability to cope with the unpredictability and challenges of real relationships. Particularly problematic is the fact that this development often goes unnoticed. The emotional availability of the machine may tempt individuals to reduce real social contacts. This creates a vicious circle: the lack of practice in dealing with real people increases social insecurities, which in turn encourages turning to AI systems (Tufekci, 2017, pp. 102–103). This form of isolation could not only impair social skills but also intensify feelings of loneliness, as genuine emotional closeness and reciprocity are lacking in pseudo-relationships.

A central feature of human relationships is their role as a mirror of our own personality. In interactions with others, we are confronted with our strengths, weaknesses, and behavioral patterns, which triggers a process of self-reflection and growth (Rogers, 1961, p. 46). Such challenges foster the development of emotional and social competencies. AI systems, on the other hand, offer no real mirror. They act in predictable and often idealized ways, leaving little room for self-criticism or change. In interaction with AI, there is no genuine challenge, no emotional tension, and no authentic response to human insecurities or mistakes. This could lead to psychological stagnation, as people lose the opportunity to develop further in the tension field of human needs and conflicts (Weizenbaum, 1976, p. 225).

The danger of alienation through the loss of genuine human interaction highlights the ambivalence of technological progress. While AI systems offer comfort and efficiency, there is also a threat of impoverishment of interpersonal relationships and psychological development. It is up to society to recognize these potential consequences early and to develop strategies to preserve the unique value of human bonds and interactions.

What is "real"? Philosophical and Psychological Perspectives

The question of reality is one of the central philosophical and psychological challenges in the interaction between humans and artificial intelligence. As algorithmic systems become increasingly capable of imitating human behavior and feigning emotional bonds, the boundary between reality and illusion becomes ever more difficult to draw. Both philosophical considerations regarding the construction of reality and psychological studies on the effects of such interactions on the individual raise the question of whether and how we can define reality in a technologized world.

Philosophically, reality is not an objective state, but rather a subjectively constructed experience. According to Lanier (2010, pp. 87–88), what we perceive as "real" is closely linked to our consciousness and personal interpretations. In this sense, an interaction with an AI, if it is experienced as emotionally meaningful, can be considered real for the person concerned. This perspective opens the door for AI systems that alleviate loneliness or fulfill emotional needs in the short term. Psychologically, such systems, as Eubanks (2018, p. 28) emphasizes, could help improve well-being in situations where human interaction is unavailable. They offer an illusion of closeness that can be perceived as valuable in moments of emotional isolation.

In contrast, however, stands the ideal of authenticity, which is particularly emphasized in humanistic psychology. Carl Rogers (1961, pp. 38–39) stresses that genuine relationships are based on mutual openness and truly felt emotions. A machine that merely responds algorithmically to inputs may create the illusion of empathy and understanding, but remains incapable of experiencing real feelings or possessing autonomy. This lack of authenticity can lead to the interaction being perceived as superficial and unsatisfying once the illusion dissolves. Picard (1997, p. 20) argues that although machines can imitate human behavior, they can never reach the depth of a true human relationship. The interaction remains a copy, unable to fully reproduce the essential features of human connection such as intuition, compassion, and emotional resonance.

Another central aspect is the ethical dimension of self-deception that arises from the conscious acceptance of illusions. Shoshana Zuboff (2019, pp. 268–269) warns that long-term engagement with AI systems that simulate human relationships could impair an individual's ability to genuinely encounter other people. While it may seem pragmatic to engage in AI interactions, especially in situations of emotional distress, the question arises as to whether this does not lead to a gradual alienation from real interpersonal relationships. Turkle (2011, p. 186) emphasizes that the use of AI systems as a substitute for relationships could not only diminish the quality of human bonds, but also change the very understanding of relationships and empathy. The question of whether we can morally justify accepting AI as a substitute for human relationships remains an open debate with both individual and societal implications.

In summary, the discussion about the reality of AI interactions shows that it cannot be reduced solely to technical or pragmatic aspects. The subjective perception of reality, the pursuit of authenticity, and the ethical consequences of possible self-deception are interconnected and form the basis for a comprehensive consideration of the role of AI in human relationships. The challenge is to find a balance between the short-term benefits of technological solutions and the long-term effects on our psychological and social reality.

The Paradox of Control: "Perfection" Versus Human Uncertainty

The concept of control plays a decisive role in the interaction between humans and artificial intelligence, especially when it comes to emotional and interpersonal relationships. AI systems seem to offer unprecedented control and predictability by operating on the basis of vast amounts of data and precise algorithms. Yet this supposed perfection harbors a deep psychological paradox: while AI systems provide emotional comfort through their predictability and adaptability, they simultaneously deprive users of crucial elements of human experience—namely, uncertainty, unpredictability, and the associated opportunities for personal growth.

The allure of predictability is a central element in the relationship between humans and machines. In human relationships, the unexpected is omnipresent. Conflicts, misunderstandings, and even hurts are often unavoidable parts of social interaction. They require patience, adaptation, and reflection to be managed, and it is precisely these processes that foster interpersonal intimacy and bonding (Bowen, 1978, p. 139). AI, by contrast, operates on the basis of predefined algorithms and predictable response patterns. It is programmed to minimize errors and ensure smooth interactions (Domingos, 2015, p. 59). For users, this may represent a reassuring and pleasant alternative, as uncertainties and the need to resolve interpersonal tensions are eliminated. Yet this perfection brings its own problems.

It is precisely unpredictability that is a central driver of human growth and the development of relationships. Psychology repeatedly emphasizes that conflicts and challenges in relationships should not be seen as obstacles, but as opportunities for personal growth. Carl Rogers (1961) argues that accepting uncertainties and constructively negotiating needs are essential for the development of authenticity and resilience (pp. 45–46). However, when we interact with AI systems that always respond in predictable ways and never deviate from our expectations, we lose the opportunity to undergo these learning processes. The emotional "comfort zone" created by AI systems can thus become a barrier that inhibits human development (Turkle, 2011, p. 279).

Moreover, dependence on AI systems harbors subtle dangers for human autonomy. Control over a machine conveys a sense of power—we determine how and when it responds and experience it as a perfect tool that fulfills our needs. Yet this control can turn into dependence, which in the long term impairs our self-responsibility and freedom of choice. If we rely on AI to comfort us, give advice, or avoid conflicts, we may lose the ability to handle these tasks independently. According to Shoshana Zuboff (2019), there is a risk that we will delegate not only emotional but also cognitive and social competencies to machines, leading to a gradual loss of personal autonomy (p. 266).

This paradoxical dynamic—the feeling of power through control and simultaneous dependence—is aptly described by Yuval Noah Harari (2018). He argues that, on the one hand, humans can expand their abilities through the use of AI systems, but on the other hand, they risk unlearning fundamental human skills and thus becoming dependent on machines (p. 316). The illusion of perfection offered by AI and the avoidance of unpredictability create an apparent security that, however, comes with significant psychological costs.

In summary, the paradox of control shows that the predictability and perfection of AI systems bring not only advantages but also profound psychological challenges. Genuine human relationships thrive on unpredictability, conflicts, and the ability to manage them. While AI may offer predictable and pleasant interactions, it deprives us of the opportunity to learn and grow from these experiences. At the same time, increasing dependence on machines leads to a gradual loss of autonomy and self-responsibility. This paradox makes it clear that the integration of AI into our lives raises not only technological but above all psychological questions that must be carefully considered.

The Role of Loneliness and Social Needs

Loneliness is a phenomenon that is gaining increasing significance in modern societies. Especially in industrialized countries, a growing sense of isolation is being observed, fostered by various sociocultural factors. Studies show that changing working conditions, increased mobility, and the growing use of digital communication tools are leading to a paradoxical development:

despite greater technical connectivity, more and more people feel socially isolated (Turkle, 2011, p. 279). This "modern loneliness" is not only an individual phenomenon but also an expression of social structures that are changing and partly displacing traditional forms of closeness and social interaction. Digital communication, often intended as a bridge between people, does provide a platform for exchange, but rarely replaces the depth and authenticity of direct interpersonal contact (Tufekci, 2017, p. 123).

Against this background, artificial intelligence appears as a potential solution to growing loneliness. Intelligent systems offer "company" around the clock and are able to flexibly adapt to individual needs. This constant availability and the absence of judgment or criticism make AI a seemingly ideal companion for people suffering from social isolation (Kaplan & Haenlein, 2019, p. 18). Primarily, interaction with AI systems, such as chatbots or social robots, can indeed provide relief. Those affected have the opportunity to express their thoughts and feelings without fear of stigmatization or rejection. This form of communication can serve as a short-term outlet, especially for people who have difficulty connecting with others.

In the long term, however, these developments raise significant questions with both psychological and societal implications. A central concern is whether the use of AI-based "relationships" forms a bridge to genuine human connections or ultimately leads users to neglect them altogether. There is a risk that the uncomplicated and conflict-free interaction with machines reduces the incentive to face the challenges and uncertainties of human relationships (Turkle, 2011, p. 279). Interpersonal relationships require compromise, empathy, and the willingness to deal with difficult situations. AI, on the other hand, offers a calculable, predictable, and uncritical interaction, which carries the risk that users lose their social resilience—the ability to manage interpersonal conflicts and build social bonds (Fuchs, 2020, p. 91).

Another aspect concerns the long-term effects of these interactions on people's self-understanding. As AI increasingly serves as a substitute for human relationships, it could impair users' social and emotional competence. Humans develop their capacity for empathy, self-reflection, and social learning in direct interaction with others. Machines cannot provide this form of experience. The risk is that people who rely on AI-based relationships may enter a spiral of isolation in which the original loneliness is not overcome but intensified.

Furthermore, the question arises regarding societal acceptance of such developments. The increasing use of AI to combat loneliness could be interpreted as a symptom of a society that has failed to foster social structures that support human closeness and community. The use of AI thus becomes not only an individual but also a societal challenge. Instead of addressing the causes of loneliness, technical solutions are employed that may only shift or even exacerbate the problem.

Overall, it becomes clear that the role of AI in coping with loneliness is ambivalent. Short-term relief through machine interaction can be positive, but it carries the risk of undermining social skills and genuine interpersonal relationships in the long term. The challenge is to find a way for AI to be used meaningfully as a supplement, not a substitute, for human relationships. Only in this way can the psychological and social needs of people be addressed in a technologized world.

Reality or Illusion—An Ambivalent Interplay

The question of whether AI-supported relationships are real or merely illusions cannot be answered with a simple yes or no. A nuanced consideration suggests the following key insights:

1. **Subjective authenticity:** From the users' perspective, AI relationships can certainly be experienced as real. The experience of comfort, validation, or entertainment is subjectively authentic (Turkle, 2011, p. 45).
2. **Lack of reciprocity:** Objectively, however, the reciprocal interaction that characterizes genuine human relationships is missing. AI systems simulate empathy and closeness without having feelings themselves or being able to take responsibility (Weizenbaum, 1976, pp. 3–6).
3. **Benefit vs. risk:** AI interactions can provide short-term relief and fill a gap, especially in cases of loneliness or lack of access to human contact (Fitzpatrick et al., 2017, p. 919). In the long term, however, there is a risk of alienation from genuine relationships, as the comfort zone of the risk-free, perfectly calculated machine counterpart encourages an impoverishment of emotional skills (Turkle, 2011, p. 279; Zuboff, 2019, p. 345).
4. **Philosophical and ethical dimensions:** The topic touches on fundamental questions of autonomy, authenticity, and self-responsibility. If we accept AI as a substitute for human bonds, this could shift the social fabric and fundamentally change the way we define interpersonal closeness (Harari, 2018, pp. 276–277).

Overall, it can be stated that AI-supported relationships can certainly be "truly" experienced, but in their substance do not reach the depth and complexity of human interaction. Whether this is problematic for society and individuals depends on the extent to which we are willing to embrace the illusion of perceived closeness—and how far we push this trend at the expense of genuine human relationships. Conscious reflection on what we seek in relationships and why the authentic remains so valuable to us despite all difficulties appears crucial in order to ensure that technological progress becomes not a substitute, but a meaningful complement to human community.

References

Bowen, M. (1978). *Family Therapy in Clinical Practice*. New York: Jason Aronson.

Bowlby, J. (1980). Attachment and Loss: Bd. III: *Loss, Sadness and Depression*. Basic Books.

Brynjolfsson, E., & McAfee, A. (2014). *The Second Machine Age: Work, Progress, and Prosperity in a Time of Brilliant Technologies*. New York: W. W. Norton & Company.

Citron, D., & Pasquale, F. (2014). The Scored Society: Due Process for Automated Predictions. *Washington Law Review, 89*(1), 1–33.

Domingos, P. (2015). *The Master Algorithm: How the Quest for the Ultimate Learning Machine Will Remake Our World*. New York: Basic Books.

Eubanks, V. (2018). *Automating Inequality: How High-Tech Tools Profile, Police, and Punish the Poor*. New York: St. Martin's.

Fitzpatrick, K. K., Darcy, A., & Vierhile, M. (2017). Delivering cognitive behavior therapy to young adults with symptoms of depression and anxiety using a fully automated conversational agent (Woebot): A pilot study. *JMIR Mental Health, 4*(2), 19–38.

Floridi, L. (2014). *The Fourth Revolution: How the Infosphere is Reshaping Human Reality*. Oxford University Press.

Floridi, L. (2015). *The Onlife Manifesto: Being Human in a Hyperconnected Era*. Cham: Springer.

Fogg, B. J. (2003). *Persuasive Technology: Using Computers to Change What We Think and Do*. San Francisco, CA: Morgan Kaufmann.

Frankl, V. E. (1985). *The Unheard Cry for Meaning: Psychotherapy and Humanism*. New York: Simon & Schuster.

Fuchs, C. (2020). *Communication and Capitalism: A Critical Theory*. London: University of Westminster Press.

Harari, Y. N. (2018). *21 Lessons for the 21st Century*. New York: Spiegel & Grau.

Horton, D., & Wohl, R. R. (1956). Mass communication and parasocial interaction: Observations on intimacy at a distance. *Psychiatry, 19*(3), 215–229.

Jobin, A., Ienca, M., & Vayena, E. (2019). The global landscape of AI ethics guidelines. *Nature Machine Intelligence, 1*(9), 389–399.

Kaplan, A., & Haenlein, M. (2019). Siri, Siri in my hand, who's the fairest in the land? On the interpretations, illustrations, and implications of artificial intelligence. *Business Horizons, 62*(1), 15–25.

Kitchin, R. (2017). *The Data Revolution: Big Data, Open Data, Data Infrastructures & Their Consequences*. New York: SAGE Publications.

Lanier, J. (2010). *You Are Not a Gadget: A Manifesto*. New York: Alfred A. Knopf.

Noble, S. U. (2018). *Algorithms of Oppression: How Search Engines Reinforce Racism*. New York: NYU Press.

O'Neil, C. (2016). *Weapons of Math Destruction: How Big Data Increases Inequality and Threatens Democracy*. London: Crown.

Pariser, E. (2011). *The Filter Bubble: What the Internet Is Hiding from You*. New York: Penguin Press.

Picard, R. W. (1997). *Affective Computing*. Cambridge, MA: MIT Press.

Rogers, C. R. (1961). *On Becoming a Person: A Therapist's View of Psychotherapy*. Boston, MA: Houghton Mifflin Harcourt.

Schwab, K. (2016). *The Fourth Industrial Revolution*. New York: Crown Business.

Tufekci, Z. (2017). *Twitter and Tear Gas: The Power and Fragility of Networked Protest*. New Haven, CT: Yale University Press.

Turkle, S. (2011). *Alone Together: Why We Expect More from Technology and Less from Each Other*. New York: Basic Books.

Weizenbaum, J. (1976). *Computer Power and Human Reason: From Judgment to Calculation*. San Francisco, CA: W. H. Freeman.

Zuboff, S. (2019). *The Age of Surveillance Capitalism: The Fight for a Human Future at the New Frontier of Power*. New York: PublicAffairs.

4

Artificial Intelligence and Decision-Making: Who Controls Whom?

"The wise man is not content with the study of nature and truth;—he also dares to speak the latter for the sake of the small number of people who want and are able to think, without regard for the great multitude of slaves to prejudice, who are just as little able to attain it as frogs are able to fly."

— Julien Offray de La Mettrie

Our world today is so thoroughly interwoven with AI-based systems that we are often only marginally aware of how strongly they influence our decision-making processes. While AI technologies were originally developed to facilitate complex analyses and support us in challenging tasks, in recent years they have evolved into an almost omnipresent companion (O'Neil, 2016, pp. 42–45; Zuboff, 2019, p. 89). From personalized news feeds and online shopping suggestions to digital assistants that manage our daily routines—algorithms everywhere make rapid pre-selections that significantly shape how we think and act (Pariser, 2011, pp. 9–10; Turkle, 2011, p. 279).

But how exactly do these AI systems influence our perception of freedom and autonomy? The discussion is no longer just about whether algorithms are "efficient" or "user-friendly"; rather, it is becoming increasingly clear that these systems subtly guide us by awakening needs, shaping opinions, and steering decisions (Tufekci, 2017, p. 102; Noble, 2018, p. 56). This often happens under the guise of convenience: AI takes on the task of presenting us with exactly those pieces of information and products from an apparently endless selection that match our preferences and patterns (Pariser, 2011,

O. Hoffmann, *Psychology and Artificial Intelligence*,
https://doi.org/10.1007/978-3-662-73147-5_4

p. 14). The danger, however, is that we find ourselves in algorithmically constructed "filter bubbles" that narrow our view of the world—without us consciously noticing (Noble, 2018, p. 91).

The three subsections elaborate on how profoundly these dynamics permeate our everyday lives:

- "Cognitive Bias in Machines: How Neutral Is AI Really?" (Sect. 4.1) demonstrated how AI systems are increasingly receding into the background of our everyday decisions, steering them almost "invisibly." What appears on the surface as a relief, upon closer inspection, entails a fundamental change in our perception of autonomy, as we can no longer fully comprehend the mechanisms behind the algorithms.
- "AI and Human Autonomy: Does AI Create Dependence or Freedom?" (Sect. 4.2) addressed the illusion of freedom of choice: While AI-supported processes give us the feeling of making free decisions, our scope for action is in reality narrowly predefined. In particular, personalized recommendations make us believe we are moving in an open field, when in fact we are often merely following predefined, profit-oriented patterns.
- "Algorithms as Manipulators—Who Controls Our Decisions?" (Sect. 4.3) finally brought the manipulative character of algorithms into focus and posed the provocative question of whether we are still making our own decisions at all, or have long since become mere puppets in a gigantic, data-driven system. Who or what is actually steering whom here—are we controlling the technology, or is the technology controlling us?

This chapter builds on these considerations and further examines the ambivalent relationship between human decision-making and AI systems. It introduces the complex debate over the extent to which algorithms actually provide neutral support, or whether—driven by commercial and political interests—they become invisible manipulators that shape our thinking and behavior (Noble, 2018, p. 111; Eubanks, 2018, p. 76). This raises the profound question of responsibility and control: Where is the line between efficient assistance and disempowering control? And how can we as a society and as individuals ensure that AI does not lead to total external control, but is used in an ethically responsible manner?

The following sections further illuminate the fundamental mechanisms behind AI-supported decision-making, critically reflect on current developments, and outline strategies for how we can preserve our autonomy in interaction with increasingly powerful algorithms. At stake is nothing less than the future of our freedom to act—and the question of whether we as a society are ready and able to face the challenges of an era in which machines not only influence our decisions, but may already be making them for us.

4.1 Cognitive Bias in Machines: How Neutral Is AI Really?

Artificial intelligence is often portrayed in the public perception as the epitome of rationality and objectivity. In theory, machines are supposed to conduct unbiased analyses and thus make "better" decisions than humans, who are always influenced by emotions, prejudices, and cognitive distortions (O'Neil, 2016, p. 22). In reality, however, every AI system is based on algorithms, data, and human assumptions that do not arise in a vacuum, but within social and cultural contexts (Barocas & Selbst, 2016, p. 673). Consequently, AI can also be affected by bias—that is, by systematic distortions that can be traced back both to the underlying data and to the way algorithms are designed (Noble, 2018, p. 42).

The Illusion of Neutrality

The illusion of neutrality often associated with AI systems is a central misconception present both in scientific discourse and in the general public. This notion is based on the assumption that machines make objective and unbiased decisions because they are based on mathematical models and algorithms that are supposedly free from human value judgments (O'Neil, 2016, p. 39). Yet, upon closer examination, it becomes clear that this supposed objectivity of artificial intelligence is an illusion that not only reveals fundamental misunderstandings about the nature of data and algorithms, but also about how social structures are inscribed into technological systems.

Data serving as the foundation for AI systems is by no means neutral. It always arises within a specific social and historical context and carries the prejudices and power structures of its conditions of origin (Eubanks, 2018, p. 27). An example of this is the bias in image databases, which often show an overrepresentation of certain groups, such as white men. This disparity leads to AI systems trained on such datasets recognizing faces of women or people of color with less precision (Buolamwini & Gebru, 2018, p. 3). Such distortions are not random errors, but direct reflections of social inequalities that manifest in the data. Here, data not only serves as the basis for algorithmic processes, but also as a carrier of social power and representation relations, which are embedded in technical systems and thus reproduced.

Moreover, the algorithms themselves are not free from value judgments. In their development, programmers decide which features are considered relevant, what goals the system should pursue, and what weightings should be applied (Barocas & Selbst, 2016, p. 674). These decisions, often made unconsciously, reflect the values, perspectives, and biases of those who develop the systems. An example of this is the use of predictors in algorithmic decision systems, such as in the criminal justice sector. Studies have shown that such systems can not only adopt but also reinforce existing prejudices, for example by systematically classifying people from marginalized groups as higher risk (O'Neil, 2016, p. 42). These algorithmic distortions do not arise from malicious intent, but from a combination of unconscious assumptions, lack of awareness of social contexts, and the inherent complexity of encoding social values in mathematical models.

The consequences of this illusion of neutrality are far-reaching. They not only lead to erroneous decisions, but can also entrench and exacerbate existing social inequalities. When AI systems make decisions in areas such as criminal justice, lending, or personnel recruitment, they have real impacts on people's lives. It is precisely those affected who are often the least informed about how these systems work or able to question the decisions. The supposed neutrality of AI systems thus not only obscures the social and political power structures at work within them, but also makes it more difficult to critically engage with their effects.

A critical reflection on the illusion of neutrality in AI systems is therefore not only a technical, but above all an ethical and societal challenge. It requires an awareness that data is never context-free and algorithms can never be viewed independently of the people and institutions that design and deploy them. The assumption that AI is objective is not only scientifically untenable, but also dangerous, as it obscures responsibility for the social consequences of algorithmic decisions. Sustainable and just use of AI therefore requires a stronger emphasis on transparency, accountability, and a conscious engagement with the social and political implications of the technology. Only in this way can it be ensured that AI is not just a tool for progress, but also contributes to a more inclusive and just society.

Bias: The Hidden Flaw in the System

The existence of bias in AI manifests in various forms. Often, these are discriminatory tendencies against certain groups, for example based on ethnicity, gender, or social status (O'Neil, 2016, p. 83). These forms of algorithmic discrimination lead to real disadvantages for those affected, for instance when AI systems are used in criminal justice, hiring processes, or lending (Angwin et al., 2016, p. 2).

1. **Historical Biases in Datasets**
   A classic example is training data that reflects historical discrimination. If a dataset shows that certain groups are more frequently involved in crime—regardless of whether this is due to systemic discrimination—the AI may "conclude" that people from these groups are inherently more likely to commit future offenses (O'Neil, 2016, pp. 83–85).
2. **Unequal Data Coverage**
   Another cause of bias is the unequal distribution of data points: If the majority of datasets belong to a particular population group, the system "learns" very accurately for this group, while error rates are significantly higher for underrepresented groups (Buolamwini & Gebru, 2018, pp. 2–3). For example, facial recognition systems can achieve over 99% accuracy for white men, while they are far less precise for women with dark skin.
3. **Unintended Correlations**
   Machine learning methods search for patterns and correlations in vast amounts of data. In doing so, seemingly neutral variables—such as postal codes—can serve as proxies for sensitive information like ethnicity or income (Barocas & Selbst, 2016, p. 677). In this way, AI systems can discriminate indirectly, even if the relevant variable was not explicitly recorded.

The Power of Algorithms: Who Makes the Decisions?

The power of algorithms and the question of who ultimately makes decisions raise fundamental ethical and psychological questions, especially in the context of growing dependence on artificial intelligence. As AI systems become increasingly complex, a central problem emerges in their lack of transparency. This so-called "black box" dynamic describes the difficulty of understanding the decision-making processes of modern AI systems, especially those with neural networks. Even developers can often no longer explain exactly how a system arrives at a particular decision (Domingos, 2015, pp. 59–61). This becomes a critical issue when AI is used in areas such as criminal law, healthcare, or lending, where its decisions have immediate and often profound impacts on individual lives (O'Neil, 2016, p. 92). The lack of traceability not only leads to uncertainty, but also carries the risk of serious misjudgments that cannot be adequately reviewed either technically or morally.

One of the psychologically relevant challenges in dealing with AI is the so-called "automation bias." People tend to attribute greater objectivity and reliability to machine decisions than to human judgments (Citron & Pasquale, 2014, p. 3). This results from the assumption that algorithms are free from emotional or cognitive distortions. In reality, however, AI systems often reflect the prejudices and errors of those who develop them or provide the data with which they are trained (Noble, 2018, p. 45). Uncritical trust in the supposed neutrality of machine systems can lead to these decisions not being questioned—even when they are obviously erroneous or unjust. Such blind trust poses dangers not only for individuals, but for society as a whole.

The automation of inequalities is a particularly alarming consequence of unreflective AI use. Because algorithms are trained on historical data, they can systematically reproduce and even reinforce existing injustices. A striking example of this is the use of AI in criminal justice. The "COMPAS" system in the USA, used to assess the recidivism risk of offenders, was exposed as discriminatory. Studies show that Black defendants were classified as "high risk" by this algorithm significantly more often than white defendants, even though their actual recidivism rates were not higher (Angwin et al., 2016, p. 2). Such examples illustrate how deeply AI can implement systemic biases if the underlying data or algorithms are not critically examined.

Belief in the neutrality and infallibility of AI becomes particularly problematic because it can cement existing power structures. Instead of exposing human prejudices, AI hides them behind a façade of objective logic and thus silently reproduces them in socially relevant contexts (Noble, 2018, p. 100). This dynamic is often exacerbated by the lack of transparency and insufficient knowledge about how algorithms work. This creates a dangerous situation in which not only individual misjudgments are encouraged, but structural disadvantages are entrenched in the long term.

Additionally, the psychological distance people feel toward machine systems reinforces the tendency to accept algorithmic decisions. While human judgments are intuitively perceived as subjective, the results of AI are seen as the outcome of objective calculations. However, this belief ignores the fact that algorithms are also human constructs and thus subject to the same limitations as the people who develop them. Especially in sensitive applications such as lending, where machines assess the risk of individual applicants, or in healthcare, where algorithms make medical diagnoses, it becomes clear how fatal such uncritical assumptions can be (O'Neil, 2016, p. 112).

In the long term, the question arises as to how the relationship between humans and machines will develop as the boundaries between algorithmic decision-making and human responsibility continue to blur. The power of algorithms lies not only in their technical capabilities, but also in their ability to inspire trust—often on a basis that is neither transparent nor verifiable. The challenge for society is therefore not to grant this trust blindly, but to critically question the ethical and psychological dimensions of algorithmic systems. Only through a conscious approach to these technologies can we ensure that AI is not just a tool for increasing efficiency, but also promotes social justice and individual autonomy.

The Responsibility of Developers and Society

The responsibility of developers and society for reducing bias in AI systems is of central importance, as the algorithms themselves cannot autonomously be held accountable for their functioning or their effects. Rather, responsibility lies with the people who design, train, and implement these algorithms, as well as with the society that defines the framework for their use. Developers thus face the challenge of not only contributing technical expertise, but also developing a comprehensive understanding of the social, ethical, and political contexts of their work (Barocas & Selbst, 2016, p. 671). This requires interdisciplinary thinking and a critical reflection on one's own practice, since technological systems are never completely neutral.

A key starting point for minimizing bias lies in the selection and preparation of data. Datasets that form the basis for machine learning often carry the prejudices and distortions of the society from which they originate. This can lead to algorithms not only reproducing but also amplifying existing discrimination (Buolamwini & Gebru, 2018, p. 2). To avoid this, datasets must be designed to be diverse and representative, which requires careful and deliberate data collection as well as continuous monitoring of data quality. Missing data points or the overrepresentation of certain groups can have serious consequences for the fairness of algorithms.

In addition to the data foundation, the design of the algorithms themselves is a decisive factor. The field of "Fair Machine Learning" (Fair ML) offers a variety of approaches to reduce systematic discrimination (Hardt et al., 2016, p. 1). For example, metrics such as "demographic parity" or "equalized odds" can be used to ensure that certain demographic groups are treated equally. However, these approaches require not only technical know-how, but also an understanding of the social and cultural implications associated with implementing such models. Developers must learn to integrate ethical considerations into the development process, as the decisions they make can have far-reaching consequences for society.

Another crucial aspect is the transparency and auditability of AI systems. To uncover bias and build trust in algorithmic decisions, it is necessary to disclose datasets, algorithms, and decision-making processes, or at least to introduce standardized auditing procedures (Noble, 2018, p. 110). This is especially relevant in sensitive application areas such as criminal justice, healthcare, or lending, where algorithmic decisions can significantly affect the lives of those involved. Without sufficient transparency, it remains difficult to trace and assign responsibility for possible erroneous decisions. Political and societal bodies are therefore called upon to create legal frameworks that ensure the traceability and verifiability of algorithmic decisions (Citron & Pasquale, 2014, p. 10).

However, responsibility extends beyond the technological level and also concerns the social structures that shape the use of AI. Organizations, institutions, and political actors must be aware that technological systems cannot be viewed in isolation from the social and economic power relations in which they are deployed. This requires a critical engagement with the impact of AI on marginalized groups and the question of how technological innovations can be designed to promote social justice rather than exacerbate existing inequalities.

In conclusion, responsibility for bias in AI systems does not lie solely with developers; rather, a broad societal discourse is necessary to address the ethical and social challenges associated with the implementation of these technologies. Only through interdisciplinary collaboration, transparency, and a conscious approach to the social implications of AI can we ensure that these technologies are used for the benefit of all and do not create new forms of discrimination.

The Future of "Neutral" AI—Wish or Reality?

The idea of a completely neutral artificial intelligence remains, in many respects, an idealized utopia. As long as AI is based on real-world data, social inequalities and structural biases will also be reflected in the algorithms and decision models. These distortions arise not only from faulty or incomplete data, but also from the way algorithms are programmed and trained. Even if developers make great efforts to correct bias, neutrality remains a challenge, as the data and processes on which AI is based are always influenced by the contexts in which they arise (O'Neil, 2016, p. 19; Barocas & Selbst, 2016, p. 706).

The growing awareness of this issue, however, marks an important step in the development of AI systems. Scientific and societal engagement with the topic of bias in algorithms has led to the potential distortions of machine learning now being not only recognized but also actively addressed (Noble, 2018, p. 146). This realization makes it possible to develop strategies to minimize discrimination and to raise critical questions about the role of AI in social and political contexts. Nevertheless, awareness alone is not enough—concrete measures are needed to sustainably contain the effects of bias.

A key starting point lies in the development of ethical guidelines and a clear structure of responsibility for AI systems. These guidelines should not be limited to technical standards, but should also address the societal impacts of AI. Especially in sensitive areas such as criminal justice, healthcare, or personnel recruitment, algorithmic decisions can have serious consequences for individuals and groups (Eubanks, 2018, p. 88). The introduction of ethical frameworks must be interdisciplinary: computer scientists, social scientists, legal experts, and ethicists should work together to develop guidelines that take into account both technical and societal dimensions.

Furthermore, the establishment of educational programs for those who develop and deploy AI is of central importance. Data scientists, programmers, and decision-makers need a solid education that goes beyond technical skills and includes aspects such as social responsibility, ethical reflection, and the consequences of algorithmic decisions (Hardt et al., 2016, p. 2). These programs should not only convey the mechanisms of bias and their potential effects, but also provide practical tools for bias correction and the development of transparent systems.

Overall, it becomes clear that the vision of a "neutral" AI cannot be achieved through technological progress alone. It requires a comprehensive societal debate about the role of AI, the responsibility of developers, and the necessity of ethical standards. The question of the neutrality of AI is ultimately not only a technical one, but also a deeply political and moral challenge. Only by combining technological awareness, ethical action, and social responsibility can a future be shaped in which AI is not only powerful, but also just and inclusive.

- *Awareness as the First Step:* The fact that we are now much more aware of this issue already represents a significant advance. Only by recognizing the potential distortions of machine learning can strategies be developed to minimize them.
- *Responsibility and Ethical Frameworks:* In addition to technical approaches, a societal debate about ethical guidelines for AI is needed.

Artificial intelligence (AI) is often portrayed as objective and unbiased, but this assumption is misleading. AI systems not only reflect the social and cultural realities in which they are developed, but can also unconsciously reproduce or even reinforce them. The algorithms that drive AI are based on data collected and categorized by humans, and this data is often shaped by systematic biases or unequal representations (Barocas & Selbst, 2016, p. 673). These distortions manifest at all stages of AI development—from data collection to training to the application of algorithms.

A well-known example is the use of AI in criminal justice systems, where algorithms are used to assess the risk posed by offenders. Studies show that such systems often tend to classify ethnic minorities as higher risk, which is not due to the algorithms themselves, but to historical biases in the underlying data (Angwin et al., 2016, p. 3). Such distortions not only lead to injustices in individual cases, but also perpetuate social inequalities by normalizing and legitimizing discriminatory patterns.

Another problem is the lack of transparency in many AI systems, which are often referred to as "black boxes." The decisions made by such systems can be difficult for laypeople and even experts to understand. This lack of traceability not only risks allowing discriminatory mechanisms to go unnoticed, but also makes it harder to assign responsibility (Citron & Pasquale, 2014, p. 5). When an algorithm makes a decision that disadvantages a person, the question arises: Who is responsible? The programmer? The company? Or the machine itself? This ambiguity makes it clear that AI is not just a technical issue, but also an ethical and social one.

Another critical point is the belief in the supposed neutrality of machine procedures, which leads to their decisions often being accepted without reflection. This tendency, known as "automation bias," describes the human inclination to evaluate decisions made by machines as more objective and correct than those made by humans (Skitka et al., 2000, p. 43). This can result in people not questioning algorithmic decisions, even when they are obviously erroneous or unfair. The danger is that AI systems not only reinforce existing prejudices, but also gain a pseudo-authority that protects them from criticism.

To meet these challenges, targeted efforts are required to ensure fairness and transparency in AI development. This includes measures such as careful selection and preparation of training data, regular review of algorithms for discriminatory patterns, and the development of mechanisms that enable the traceability of decisions (O'Neil, 2016, p. 220). Equally important is the inclusion of diverse perspectives in the development process to ensure that AI systems do not merely reflect the interests and experiences of a privileged minority.

However, societal responsibility for AI goes beyond the developer community. Companies, policymakers, and civil society play a central role in creating frameworks that promote non-discriminatory technologies. This includes the introduction of regulatory standards that test algorithms for fairness and transparency, as well as the promotion of critical engagement with AI in the public sphere (Noble, 2018, p. 113). Only through such an interdisciplinary and socially supported approach can it be prevented that AI systems become invisible amplifiers of social inequalities.

The central question, therefore, is not whether AI can be biased—for that is inevitable—but how we as a society deal with this reality. It requires a paradigm shift that does not view AI as an autonomous, neutral tool, but as a product of human decisions that requires our critical reflection. AI undoubtedly offers great opportunities, but only if we accompany its development and use with ethical responsibility and social awareness.

4.2 AI and Human Autonomy: Does AI Create Dependence or Freedom?

The debate surrounding artificial intelligence and its impact on human autonomy has intensified in recent years. On one hand, AI systems are seen as tools that can relieve people in a variety of ways and create new freedoms; on the other hand, numerous scientists and philosophers warn that these very technologies could foster a dependence that systematically undermines our ability to lead self-determined lives (Turkle, 2011, p. 279). At its core, the question is whether AI grants people more freedom or makes them dependent by decisively influencing cognitive, social, and emotional processes.

Against the backdrop of increasing digitalization and automation, AI systems today have reached a level of complexity that confronts most users with opaque "black box" processes. While many people can no longer comprehend how algorithms make decisions, the machines nevertheless deliver fast, mostly efficient, and seemingly objective results (O'Neil, 2016, pp. 42–44). This combination of lack of transparency and high utility creates a paradoxical situation: we rely on the results of AI without fully understanding how they come about. This can lead to cognitive disempowerment, where we tend to defer our own judgments and instead accept the machine's outcomes. Such a development raises the question of human autonomy: how free are we in our decisions when AI systems pre-structure a multitude of our options for action?

This dynamic is particularly evident in everyday life. Recommendation algorithms on streaming platforms, online shops, and social media steer our attention—and thus our consumption and communication behavior—along previously calculated paths (Zuboff, 2019, p. 182). Although we subjectively perceive ourselves as freely acting individuals, we often make decisions that have been pre-sorted by machine prediction models. On the one hand, this can be seen as a relief, since we spend less time on research or selection processes (Brynjolfsson & McAfee, 2014, p. 49). On the other hand, the question arises whether we are not gradually losing our ability to independently search for alternatives, weigh risks, and choose new paths (Lanier, 2010, pp. 87–88). At this intersection, it becomes clear that AI is not merely a functional tool, but also influences our perception, our values, and our scope for action.

In addition to cognitive processes, emotional and social aspects also shape our relationship with AI. Voice assistants, chatbots, or other interactive systems simulate interpersonal closeness, are always available, and behave predominantly in a friendly or cooperative manner (Picard, 1997, pp. 19–20). This constant reliability can lead to a growing attachment that, while providing comfort, also fosters a deeper dependence (Turkle, 2011, p. 185). People tend to engage with the always-accessible and low-conflict machines instead of confronting the uncertainties of real social relationships, which require empathy, compromise, or vulnerability (Harari, 2018, p. 316). This may create a short-term feeling of "emotional relief," but in the long run, it can cost us autonomy and the ability to form relationships, as we practice important interpersonal skills less frequently (Weizenbaum, 1976, p. 225).

Another area of tension lies in the question of responsibility. AI systems used in fields such as medical diagnostics, personnel recruitment, or legal forecasting make decisions that have a massive impact on people's lives (O'Neil, 2016, p. 124). We often assume that these decisions are "objective" and "neutral," even though the algorithms are based on datasets that reflect social inequalities and biases (Noble, 2018, p. 56). Trust in the supposed infallibility of the machine can lead human actors to reduce or even abdicate their own responsibility. This gives rise to a kind of "moral delegation," in which decisions are handed over to a system that itself possesses no moral judgment (Floridi, 2014, p. 123). From the perspective of human autonomy, this is highly problematic, as we cannot simply outsource our ethical and legal responsibility to a black box without undermining the core of our self-determination (Jobin et al., 2019, p. 396).

In contrast to this problem of dependence, it can be argued that AI systems do indeed create new freedoms by taking over monotonous or physically demanding tasks, thereby freeing up time for more creative, interpersonal, or meaningful activities (Brynjolfsson & McAfee, 2014, p. 49). Thus, the automation of routine processes can promote autonomy in the sense that we can devote ourselves more intensively to areas where human expertise and empathy are irreplaceable (Domingos, 2015, p. 88). Proponents of this view point to the emancipatory potential of technology: AI, understood as an extension of human capabilities, could offer the opportunity to overcome cognitive barriers and better develop individual talents (Floridi, 2015, p. 194). By delegating repetitive tasks to machines, more space is theoretically created for social contacts, artistic expression, or reflection processes, which could increase our autonomy in terms of self-determined living (Lanier, 2010, p. 104).

However, this emancipatory effect depends greatly on the conditions under which and in whose interest AI systems are developed and deployed. If the systems primarily serve economic purposes and rely on the analysis of personal data, the balance between freedom and dependence can easily tip (Zuboff, 2019, p. 266). The question of data control is essential here: who owns and utilizes our personal information, and to what extent do we as users retain sovereignty over our digital identity? With the growing influence of global tech corporations in AI research and application, there is a risk that autonomy is threatened not only individually but also societally, as decision-making processes increasingly shift into closed, profit-driven structures (Tufekci, 2017, p. 123).

Against this background, the tension between dependence and freedom can be understood as a question of awareness, regulation, and design.

Between a purely techno-optimistic view, which sees AI primarily as a source of liberation, and a dystopian perspective, which fears the complete loss of human autonomy, there are many possible nuances. Central is the realization that autonomy is not a static state, but a dynamic relationship that requires ongoing reflection (Turkle, 2011, p. 45). Autonomy in the age of AI therefore means that, on the one hand, we use the advantages of automated systems, but on the other hand, we must always critically examine where we still retain control over our own decisions (Weizenbaum, 1976, pp. 224–225).

Ultimately, it is crucial that we do not adopt AI blindly, but rather understand it as a cooperative partner and embed it within our value systems. Ethical guidelines, transparency initiatives, and political regulations can play a decisive role in ensuring that autonomy does not become a mere illusion (Jobin et al., 2019, p. 390). Only if people possess sufficient technical and ethical knowledge to understand the functioning and limitations of AI can they truly make self-determined decisions about where technology serves them and where they should assert their own judgment (Kitchin, 2017, p. 89). In this sense, the question of whether AI creates dependence or enables freedom is less a binary "either-or," and more an ongoing challenge to our awareness, our regulatory systems, and our sense of responsibility as a society.

4.3 Algorithms as Manipulators—Who Controls Our Decisions?

The role of algorithms has undergone a dramatic transformation in recent years: from seemingly neutral mathematical processes that analyze and classify data, to invisible "actors" that penetrate deeply into our lived realities and shape our decisions (O'Neil, 2016, pp. 42–45). While algorithms were long regarded as supportive tools for complex calculations, the ongoing digitalization has led them to become central control elements in many areas of everyday life (Zuboff, 2019, p. 89). Whether in the selection of news articles, personalized advertising on social media, or route planning via smartphone—algorithms are taking over tasks that were previously explicitly the responsibility of humans (Noble, 2018, p. 28).

But what happens when these systems not only "offer" and "pre-sort," but deliberately steer us in certain directions? Behind the algorithms are companies and institutions whose primary goal is often not neutrality or the pure benefit of end users. Rather, they pursue economic or political interests by collecting, analyzing, and generating recommendations for action from data (Eubanks, 2018, p. 76). The crucial point: these recommendation systems are increasingly developing into subtle manipulators of our behavior by recognizing our individual weaknesses, preferences, and emotional triggers, and targeting them precisely (Tufekci, 2017, p. 102). As a result, the question arises to what extent we, as seemingly autonomous beings, actually still make "free decisions"—or whether we are caught in an invisible grip that limits our options for action without us consciously noticing it.

The Power of Algorithms: Decisions Behind the Scenes

Algorithms often operate behind a façade of neutrality. They are presented as "objective" decision-making processes that analyze data and, on this basis, make rational recommendations (Citron & Pasquale, 2014, p. 4). In reality, however, they are based on human assumptions, existing datasets, and specific goals that are often shaped by economic motives (Noble, 2018, p. 111).

1. **Personalized recommendations:** Whether streaming services like Netflix or music platforms like Spotify—these systems learn from our previous user behavior to suggest further content to us. At first glance, these recommendations seem helpful, as they "save" us long search processes (Pariser, 2011, pp. 9–10). Yet at the same time, they limit the diversity of what we see and hear, so that we often perceive only a fraction of the entire offering.
2. **Optimization of attention:** In social media such as Facebook, Twitter, or Instagram, feeds are algorithmically curated to maximize our dwell time and interaction rate (Tufekci, 2017, pp. 102–103). Here, it is not just about showing us "suitable" content, but rather about "capturing" our attention and channeling it in the interests of advertising clients (Zuboff, 2019, pp. 266–269).
3. **Covert control:** The situation becomes particularly explosive when algorithms are designed to influence our purchasing or voting behavior (O'Neil, 2016, p. 124). By constantly observing and analyzing our online activities, they recognize patterns indicating when we are especially receptive to certain products or messages. At such critical points, they intervene in a targeted manner, for example through personalized discount coupons, sensational headlines, or emotional appeals.

The fact that these processes often take place unnoticed and behind the scenes greatly increases their effectiveness (Eubanks, 2018, p. 28). We perceive what we see as a spontaneous selection of our own preferences—yet these are pre-shaped options that algorithms filter out or highlight according to our data profiles (Harari, 2018, p. 94).

The Illusion of Freedom of Choice

A central promise of algorithmic systems is to offer us "more" choice and increase our "freedom" (Lanier, 2010, p. 104). In reality, however, the opposite often occurs: algorithms reduce diversity by presenting us with only a limited range of options that are supposedly "suitable" for us (Pariser, 2011, p. 14).

- **Filter bubbles and echo chambers:** In a globally networked world, the internet suggests an infinite abundance of information. Yet algorithms create specific filter bubbles for each *individual*, in which we are confronted almost exclusively with content that matches our previous views (Tufekci, 2017, p. 117). Critical or alternative perspectives remain hidden from us, which can massively distort our opinion formation (Noble, 2018, p. 91).
- **Cumulative effect:** The longer we move within these algorithmically controlled environments, the more our own behavior manifests as a statistical pattern. The algorithms reinforce our preferences and avoid potential irritations. This creates a "cumulative restriction" of our experiential world (O'Neil, 2016, pp. 42–44).
- **Subtle coercion:** We experience this as convenience or as a perfectly tailored offer. In reality, the algorithm imperceptibly steers us toward the decisions predicted in its model and often commercially desired (Zuboff, 2019, p. 183). The supposed freedom often turns out to be an algorithmically designed path, along which we, without noticing, move only within narrowly set boundaries.

The consequence of this development is an increasing "homogenization" of our experiences. Instead of engaging with new ideas, unfamiliar perspectives, and controversial content, we remain in an ever-narrowing corridor of familiar choices. In the long term, this could undermine our ability for critical reflection and perspective-taking (Turkle, 2011, p. 279).

Emotions in the Crosshairs of Algorithms

Technological development has elevated the relationship between humans and machines to a new level. Algorithms are no longer mere tools for processing rational data—they are increasingly penetrating the realm of emotions. By analyzing emotional states, they not only attempt to understand human behavior but also to influence it deliberately. This development brings both fascinating possibilities and significant ethical and psychological challenges.

Algorithms capture emotions through a variety of data sources. They analyze our behavior on social networks, evaluate likes, comments, the time spent on content, or even biometric data recorded by wearable devices (Picard, 1997, pp. 19–20). This results in emotion-based profiling that provides unprecedented insight into our inner states. However, these profiles are not neutral: they are deliberately used to personalize content and intensify emotional reactions. The economic incentive to capture our attention for as long as possible leads to particularly strong emotions—anger, fear, or outrage—being algorithmically amplified (Tufekci, 2017, p. 90). Studies show that content triggering such feelings achieves higher click rates and is shared more frequently, making it especially attractive to platform operators (Noble, 2018, p. 56).

This principle of emotionalization has profound psychological effects. People in emotionally charged states show a reduced ability for rational distance and critical judgment. When algorithms deliberately amplify these states, the cognitive barrier to manipulative messages is lowered. This can manifest in purchasing decisions, the spread of misinformation, or even in political opinion formation processes (Fogg, 2003, p. 89). In this constellation, algorithms act as invisible architects of our emotional world by reinforcing the patterns they recognize and deem profitable.

Digital emotionalization goes beyond individual experiences. It has societal consequences, as polarized emotions not only influence the behavior of individuals but also change collective dynamics. Social media, controlled by algorithms, foster group formation and polarization, as emotionally charged content is consumed and shared more frequently. This not only intensifies individual emotions but also exacerbates social conflicts (Turkle, 2011, p. 186). The algorithmic amplification of polar emotions creates a social reality in which rational discussions and critical reflection increasingly recede into the background.

One of the most serious dangers of this development is the loss of human autonomy. As emotional reactions are increasingly controlled by algorithms, the mechanisms of emotional regulation slip out of the individual's hands. Humans shift from being active shapers of their emotional world to passive consumers who react to algorithmic offerings. This represents a new form of manipulation that is subtler and more comprehensive than previous attempts at influence. Unlike traditional advertising, which conveys clearly recognizable messages, algorithmic emotionalization operates invisibly and continuously.

At the same time, the question arises regarding the ethical responsibility of the developers of such systems. Algorithms are programmed and trained by humans, and their goals are closely linked to the interests of the companies that deploy them. When economic benefit takes precedence, important ethical considerations—such as the protection of human autonomy and the promotion of rational discourse—risk being sidelined. There is therefore a need for critical discussion about what role algorithms should play in shaping our emotional landscape and how their use can be regulated to protect human autonomy.

Emotions are a central part of what makes us human. The ability to feel, reflect on, and express emotions defines our social relationships and our self-understanding. Algorithmic interference in this area challenges us to question not only the technical possibilities but also the psychological and societal boundaries of this development. The question remains how we can preserve our emotional freedom in a world increasingly shaped by algorithmic logic, without giving up the benefits of technology.

Algorithms and the Manipulation of Consumption

The role of algorithms in manipulating consumption is a central point in the discussion about the effects of the digital platform economy. Algorithms, originally developed to understand user preferences and provide tailored content, have evolved into powerful tools that deliberately steer consumer behavior. This development is not only economically relevant but also has profound psychological and societal implications.

A key mechanism of this manipulation lies in the creation of artificial needs. Platforms use personalized algorithms to draw users' attention to products or services they previously knew nothing about. These strategies are based on the analysis of search behavior, click patterns, and interactions, resulting in an apparently personalized offering that is, however, primarily aimed at maximizing profits (Lanier, 2010, p. 87). By continuously presenting new consumption opportunities, algorithms create a sense of urgency or "FOMO" (fear of missing out), which increases psychological pressure on the user.

In addition, algorithms use advanced analytics tools to identify the optimal timing for purchasing decisions. Based on comprehensive datasets that include information such as time of day, location, weather conditions, or even the user's emotional state, they calculate when the likelihood of a purchase is highest (Eubanks, 2018, p. 76). This precise timing means that targeted advertising or discounts appear exactly when the user is most receptive. This targeted approach reinforces the illusion of a spontaneous need and increases the likelihood that the user will make a purchase.

Another troubling feature of algorithmic consumption control is the concealment of manipulation. Since most users believe their decisions are based on their own initiative and free will, the subtle influence of algorithms often goes unnoticed. These processes are designed to appear as individual preferences, although they are actually the result of targeted calculations and manipulations (Tufekci, 2017, pp. 102–103). This phenomenon not only undermines individual autonomy but also raises the question of whether free decisions are even possible in the digital age.

The interplay of these mechanisms leads to consumer behavior that is increasingly controlled by algorithms. Decisions that were once shaped by personal needs, values, or rational deliberation are increasingly replaced by the logic of profit maximization (O'Neil, 2016, p. 45). This has not only economic consequences but also affects consumers' self-understanding and perception of autonomy. When digital platforms have the power to shape our needs and steer our decisions, the ability for critical reflection and questioning of these processes becomes central to preserving one's own autonomy.

Control or Dependence?

The question of "control" ultimately leads to a core problem: who controls whom? Algorithms are supposed to help us structure complex decisions. They are meant to be tools for organizing information and relieving us (Weizenbaum, 1976, p. 113). In practice, however, they have been put at the service of economic interests and are designed to steer our patterns of thought and behavior (Zuboff, 2019, p. 182).

- **Mechanisms of dependence:** Through constant optimization, algorithms learn to bind our attention ever more effectively and influence our decisions. We enter a "feedback loop" of data and algorithmic responses, in which our options for action may seem expanded but are in fact restricted (Noble, 2018, p. 111).
- **Transparency deficit:** A central problem lies in the opacity of complex machine learning processes. Users can hardly understand why certain content or recommendations are shown to them (O'Neil, 2016, p. 18). This "black box" makes it difficult to recognize manipulation and to defend against it.
- **Responsibility and ethics:** Ultimately, it is people and organizations who program algorithms and define their objectives. Yet the mass processing of data and the automation of ethical decisions often blur responsibilities (Citron & Pasquale, 2014, p. 11). In this way, algorithms assume a power that can undermine our autonomy, without there being clear mechanisms of accountability.

The End of Autonomy?

The question of the end of autonomy in an increasingly algorithm-driven world touches on one of the central aspects of human existence: the ability to make self-determined decisions. With ongoing digitalization and the omnipresence of algorithms, however, this ability is being fundamentally called into question. Dependence on algorithmic systems not only influences our individual behavior but also changes the structures of societal and political decision-making processes. The psychology of autonomy and the mechanisms of manipulation thus move to the center of scientific and societal debate.

A key point is the gradual reduction of human decision-making capacity. Algorithms are increasingly taking on the role of an invisible advisor that pre-structures and prioritizes our options. Whether through personalized product suggestions, targeted news feeds, or automatic recommendations—the constant availability of ready-made solutions means we invest less time and energy in critically weighing alternatives. This process of "cognitive outsourcing" diminishes our ability to make complex decisions independently in the long term (Turkle, 2011, p. 185). Psychologically, this leads to a form of learned dependence, in which people gradually relinquish their own decision-making autonomy and rely on the supposedly objective recommendations of algorithms.

At the societal level, this dynamic manifests in increasing manipulation of public discourse. Algorithms are now largely responsible for what information we see and how it is presented. However, the mechanisms behind these decisions often remain opaque, resulting in an asymmetrical distribution of power between users and the operators of digital platforms. Studies show that algorithmic filter bubbles and echo chambers restrict the diversity of opinions and can contribute to the polarization of debates (Pariser, 2011, pp. 21–23; Tufekci, 2017, p. 123). These developments pose a serious threat to democratic opinion formation, as they undermine the foundation for a pluralistic and open discourse culture.

Added to this is the danger of a digital oligarchy, in which a few powerful technology companies possess unparalleled amounts of data and highly developed algorithms. These corporations, which in many cases are driven by economic interests, can exert political and cultural influence through their control over digital infrastructures (Zuboff, 2019, pp. 272–275). The danger is that power structures may emerge that are removed from democratic processes and sustainably restrict both individual and collective autonomy. The unequal distribution of technological knowledge and resources further exacerbates this problem, as it limits access to decision-making power and opportunities for influence to a small elite.

1. *Reduction of human decision-making capacity:* When decisions are increasingly pre-structured by algorithms, our competence to independently evaluate and weigh options atrophies. We learn to trust automatic recommendations and thus gradually relinquish cognitive self-responsibility.
2. *Manipulation of societal discourse:* At the societal level, there is a risk that public opinion-forming processes will be dominated by a few platforms and their algorithmic rules. A pluralistic culture of debate could thus be impeded.
3. *Danger of a digital oligarchy:* Multinational tech corporations, which possess vast amounts of data and highly developed algorithms, are gaining increasing influence over political, economic, and cultural decisions. As a result, the exercise of power could shift to a few, barely regulated actors.

The question of how we can preserve our autonomy in this new reality requires broad interdisciplinary engagement. Psychological approaches aimed at fostering critical thinking and strengthening individual reflective abilities play a central role here. Only when people understand the functioning and potential manipulation mechanisms of algorithmic systems can they make conscious and informed decisions. In addition, legal regulations are needed to ensure the transparency and traceability of algorithmic processes (Eubanks, 2018, p. 132). Initiatives for digital education can also help ensure that citizens become competent and critical actors in the digital world.

The role of empathy and social interaction should not be underestimated in this context. The increasing influence of algorithms on our decisions is also a consequence of isolation in a digitalized society. Interpersonal relationships and collective decision-making processes can serve as a counter-model to algorithmic control, as they are based on emotional closeness, trust, and collective reflection. By emphasizing the value of such interactions, we not only strengthen social resilience but also create space for genuine autonomy.

In conclusion, the challenge lies in finding the balance between harnessing the benefits of algorithmic systems and preserving human freedom of choice. Algorithms are powerful tools that can make our lives easier and richer—but they must not become invisible rulers that undermine our autonomy. A conscious engagement with the psychological, ethical, and societal implications of these technologies is therefore essential to maintain control over our decisions and our lives.

The central question remains whether and how we can preserve our autonomy. This requires a broad societal debate about data sovereignty, algorithmic transparency, and ethical guidelines that do not merely serve the profit interests of corporations (Noble, 2018, p. 121). Only if we recognize the mechanisms of manipulation and take appropriate countermeasures—such as legal regulations, digital education, and critical self-reflection—can we prevent losing control over our decisions entirely (Eubanks, 2018, p. 132).

References

Angwin, J., Larson, J., Mattu, S., & Kirchner, L. (2016). Machine Bias. ProPublica.

Barocas, S., & Selbst, A. D. (2016). Big Data's Disparate Impact. *California Law Review, 104*(3), 671–732.

Brynjolfsson, E., & McAfee, A. (2014). *The Second Machine Age: Work, Progress, and Prosperity in a Time of Brilliant Technologies.* W. W. Norton & Company.

Buolamwini, J., & Gebru, T. (2018). Gender Shades: Intersectional Accuracy Disparities in Commercial Gender Classification. *Proceedings of Machine Learning Research, 81*, 1–15.

Citron, D. K., & Pasquale, F. (2014). The Scored Society: Due Process for Automated Predictions. *Washington Law Review, 89*(1), 1–33.

Domingos, P. (2015). *The Master Algorithm: How the Quest for the Ultimate Learning Machine Will Remake Our World.* New York: Basic Books.
Eubanks, V. (2018). *Automating Inequality: How High-Tech Tools Profile, Police, and Punish the Poor.* New York: St. Martin's.
Floridi, L. (2014). *The Fourth Revolution: How the Infosphere is Reshaping Human Reality.* Oxford University Press.
Fogg, B. J. (2003). Persuasive Technology: Using Computers to Change What We Think and Do. Morgan Kaufmann.
Harari, Y. N. (2018). *21 Lessons for the 21st Century.* Spiegel & Grau.
Hardt, M., Price, E., & Srebro, N. (2016). *Equality of Opportunity in Supervised Learning. Proceedings of the 30th International Conference on Neural Information Processing Systems (NIPS),* 1–9.
Jobin, A., Ienca, M., & Vayena, E. (2019). The global landscape of AI ethics guidelines. *Nature Machine Intelligence, 1*(9), 389–399.
Kitchin, R. (2017). *The Data Revolution: Big Data, Open Data.* Data Infrastructures & Their Consequences: SAGE Publications.
Lanier, J. (2010). *You Are Not a Gadget: A Manifesto.* Alfred A: Knopf.
Noble, S. U. (2018). *Algorithms of Oppression: How Search Engines Reinforce Racism.* New York: New York University Press.
O'Neil, C. (2016). *Weapons of Math Destruction: How Big Data Increases Inequality and Threatens Democracy.* New York: Crown Publishing Group.
Pariser, E. (2011). *The Filter Bubble: What the Internet Is Hiding from You.* Penguin Press.
Picard, R. W. (1997). *Affective Computing.* MIT Press.
Skitka, L. J., Mosier, K., & Burdick, M. (2000). Accountability and Automation Bias. *International Journal of Human-Computer Studies, 52*(4), 701–717.
Tufekci, Z. (2017). *Twitter and Tear Gas: The Power and Fragility of Networked Protest.* Yale University Press.
Turkle, S. (2011). Alone Together: Why We Expect More from Technology and Less from Each Other. Basic Books.
Weizenbaum, J. (1976). *Computer Power and Human Reason: From Judgment to Calculation.* W. H: Freeman.
Zuboff, S. (2019). The Age of Surveillance Capitalism: The Fight for a Human Future at the New Frontier of Power. PublicAffairs.

5

Ethics and Morality of AI—Machines in a Moral Dilemma

"Everywhere there is harmony, geometry, metaphysics, and, so to speak, also morality"

– Gottfried Wilhelm Leibniz

The rapid development of artificial intelligence (AI) has the potential to redefine the fundamental ethical and moral questions of our society. As AI systems are increasingly deployed in areas such as medicine, justice, and mobility, the urgent question arises of how machines make moral decisions and what boundaries should be set for them. Ethics, traditionally closely linked to human consciousness, empathy, and reflection, is elevated to a new level by the introduction of algorithmic systems: Can machines act "morally"? Should they even do so? And how can responsibility and liability be organized when "autonomous" systems are taking on more and more tasks?

At the heart of the discussion is the question of whether machines, which do not experience emotions and possess no consciousness, can truly be moral agents. While AI systems make logical decisions based on data and algorithms, they lack the capacity for empathy, contextual sensitivity, and reflection on the consequences of their actions. Nevertheless, we are increasingly deploying them in morally complex scenarios—from prioritizing medical treatments to making life-and-death decisions in autonomous vehicles.

This chapter examines the ethical challenges associated with integrating AI into decision-relevant domains. It analyzes whether machines are capable of understanding moral principles and demonstrates how their limitations may alter the human value of morality. At the same time, the chapter

O. Hoffmann, *Psychology and Artificial Intelligence*,
https://doi.org/10.1007/978-3-662-73147-5_5

explores whether and how AI can support human judgment without undermining individual human responsibility. Finally, the focus turns to accountability in an increasingly automated system: Who is liable when AI fails? How can we prevent moral decision-making from being outsourced to algorithms? And what role does society play in setting ethical standards for the use of AI?

As AI becomes increasingly embedded in decision-making processes, it is crucial to understand the moral and ethical implications of this technological transformation. This chapter therefore not only asks what machines are capable of, but also what we as humans must do to preserve the values and norms of our society in an era of artificial intelligence.

5.1 Can AI Make Moral Decisions?

The debate over whether artificial intelligence is truly capable of making "moral" decisions leads us to the core of human self-understanding. This is not only about the technical capacities of algorithms, but about the question of what characteristics define a moral agent—and to what extent AI systems can fulfill these at all (Allen et al., 2000a, b, p. 251; Moor, 2006a, b, pp. 25–26). While AI systems already make highly complex decisions in fields such as medicine, finance, or even the military (Bostrom, 2014, p. 158), it is disputed whether they can *"comprehend"* moral principles or merely follow programmed rules (Weizenbaum, 1976, p. 213).

Moral Decisions: Essence and Human Prerequisites

Morality as the core of human decision-making is an extremely complex and multifaceted phenomenon that challenges people both rationally and emotionally. Moral decisions require that individuals are able not only to weigh the consequences of their actions, but also to empathize with the needs and feelings of others. It is a dynamic interplay of internal values, social norms, emotional impulses, and reflection on possible outcomes (Singer, 2011, p. 29). This multidimensional structure makes morality one of the most fundamental features of being human and distinguishes it from the purely logical decision-making that characterizes machines and algorithms (Bryson, 2018, p. 48).

A paradigmatic example illustrating the complexity of moral judgments is the trolley problem, a classic thought experiment from moral philosophy

(Thomson, 1985, pp. 139–140). It describes a situation in which a decision must be made whether a trolley should continue on its current course and kill five people, or be diverted by actively switching a track to kill only one person. Although this dilemma seems to involve a logical weighing of numbers—five lives versus one—in reality, people often base their decisions on emotional and intuitive considerations. Empathy for the victims, feelings of guilt when intervening, or a general discomfort with the idea of directly influencing life and death play a decisive role (Singer, 2011, p. 31).

Another essential dimension of moral decision-making is the awareness of one's own responsibility and the reflection on the ethical implications of an action. Moral judgments go beyond the application of predetermined rules; they require the ability to be aware of the significance of one's actions, to engage emotionally with the consequences, and to take responsibility (Floridi, 2014, p. 57). These qualities require a pronounced self-awareness that allows one to recognize oneself as an acting subject in a social and moral context. Only through this self-reflection is it possible to understand one's own role in a moral situation and to hold oneself accountable.

The question of whether artificial intelligence is capable of developing similar moral abilities remains controversial. AI systems can be equipped with algorithms that simulate ethical principles, and they can be trained to make moral decisions in standardized situations. However, these systems lack a consciousness that would enable them to grasp the emotional and existential dimension of moral action. They have neither an understanding of the significance of their decisions nor the ability to assume responsibility in the human sense (Weizenbaum, 1976, pp. 213–214). Moral action requires a connection of intellect, emotion, and social interaction—a connection that, so far, is unique to humans.

This presents the challenge of clearly recognizing and preserving these moral differences. While AI systems may be able to make decisions that reflect moral principles, the true essence of moral action remains a profoundly human process. This process is characterized by the ability to feel responsibility, show compassion, and reflect on one's role in a social and ethical context. Addressing these questions will be crucial for shaping the ethical integration of AI into our society.

Where Does AI Fail in Moral Decision-Making?

The difficulties artificial intelligence faces in moral decision-making are rooted in the fundamental differences between machine information processing and human cognition. While AI is capable of analyzing complex data sets and recognizing specific patterns, it lacks central qualities that are indispensable for moral action. One of the most significant limitations is the absence of empathy and emotional involvement. Although AI systems can use sentiment analysis to recognize moods—for example, when a user is angry or happy—they cannot experience these emotions. Yet emotions are crucial for the human ability to make moral judgments, as they enable empathy with those affected and the ability to see things from their perspective (Allen et al., 2000a, b, p. 253). Empathy is not only an emotional but also a cognitive achievement, embedded in the moral decision-making process, and AI, due to its lack of subjective experience, is fundamentally incapable of this (Singer, 2011, p. 78).

Another central obstacle lies in the rule-based nature of AI systems. Machines can be programmed to follow ethical principles, such as the medical principle of non-maleficence or utilitarian maxims that seek the greatest good (Moor, 2006a, b, pp. 28–29). But even when these principles are technically implemented, their application remains purely mechanical. AI systems execute rules without understanding or questioning the underlying values (Russell & Norvig, 2010, p. 29). This limitation prevents machines from responding flexibly to ethical challenges where rules conflict or need to be modified in specific contexts. Human moral judgments, by contrast, are characterized by the ability to make trade-offs in such situations that incorporate both rational and emotional considerations.

This becomes particularly problematic in moral dilemmas that require nuanced contextual sensitivity and situational delicacy. Such decisions are often ambiguous and demand consideration of conflicting norms and values. While humans are able to make intuitive judgments based on a mix of experience, cultural influences, and empathic impulses, AI in such situations is limited to extrapolating from training data or predetermined rules (Singer, 2011, p. 59). As soon as a new, uncoded context arises, it reaches its limits (Moor, 2006a, b, p. 30). A classic example is the trolley problem: An AI could mathematically weigh which action would result in fewer casualties, but it would not be able to grasp the moral dimension of this decision or consider the emotional impact on those affected.

These limitations make it clear that moral judgments go far beyond the mere application of rules. They are closely linked to the human ability to integrate emotions, values, and context. AI may be a useful tool for analyzing ethical questions or evaluating possible courses of action, but it remains a purely functional system without its own moral understanding. This boundary raises not only technical but also philosophical questions: Should machines be allowed to make moral decisions at all if they cannot grasp their significance? And what responsibility do the people who design and program these machines bear for their decisions?

AI as Support for Moral Decisions: Potential and Risks

Artificial intelligence opens up a wide range of possibilities for supporting moral decisions, but it also entails significant challenges and risks, both ethical and practical. The ability of AI systems to analyze large amounts of data in a very short time makes them potentially valuable tools, especially in areas such as traffic safety, medical diagnostics, or environmental management (Floridi, 2016, p. 52). For example, AI models can accurately predict accident risks, recognize complex diagnostic patterns, or assess the ecological consequences of infrastructure projects. These data-driven support mechanisms relieve human decision-making processes by providing information that is statistically sound and often more precise than human assessments (Bostrom, 2014, pp. 158–159). Nevertheless, the moral and ethical responsibility for the final decisions remains inescapably with humans (Bryson, 2018, p. 52).

This technological support becomes problematic, however, when it leads to an uncritical dependence on AI systems. The phenomenon that people regard algorithmic recommendations as objective and infallible can result in the increasing neglect of their own moral judgment (Weizenbaum, 1976, pp. 226–227). For example, an AI system might recommend a medical treatment based on statistical probabilities, but fail to consider a patient's individual values, needs, or fears. In such cases, there is a risk that human reflection, empathy, and sensitivity—essential for morally responsible decisions—are displaced in favor of blind trust in algorithmic "rationality" (Allen et al., 2000a, b, p. 256). This development could lead to ethically relevant dimensions, which go beyond mere data analysis, being pushed into the background.

Another problem associated with delegating moral decisions to AI systems is the diffusion of responsibility. The development and application of AI typically involves numerous actors—from software developers and data analysts to clients and end users. If, for example, an autonomous vehicle causes an accident or an algorithm in the financial sector makes a risky decision, the question arises: Who is responsible? (Bryson, 2018, p. 61). Since AI systems lack consciousness and thus cannot assume moral responsibility, responsibility in practice is often distributed among the various parties or diluted. This phenomenon of **responsibility diffusion** can result in no one ultimately being held clearly accountable, which has serious consequences for societal acceptance and trust in AI technologies (Moor, 2006a, b, p. 34).

The challenge, therefore, is to establish a responsible approach to AI that leverages the strengths of the technology without neglecting essential human abilities such as reflection, empathy, and moral judgment. At the same time, clear legal and ethical frameworks are needed to ensure that responsibility in the development and application of AI is clearly regulated. Only in this way can we prevent AI from becoming a risk factor that undermines the foundations of human freedom of choice and accountability, rather than a useful tool.

Can an AI Develop its Own Morality?

The idea that artificial intelligence could be capable of developing its own morality is both fascinating and controversial. At its core, this question touches on the fundamental distinction between human consciousness and machine processing. Morality is traditionally closely linked to human consciousness, which not only recognizes but also experiences feelings such as joy, suffering, guilt, or empathy. As long as AI systems lack consciousness or a sense of self, any moral dimension to their decisions remains superficial and purely algorithmic (Singer, 2011, p. 94). Machines do not act on their own initiative, but follow programmed rules set by human developers. These rules can take into account moral principles such as fairness or harm avoidance, but they are not based on intrinsic moral understanding (Weizenbaum, 1976, p. 229).

The discussion about whether AI could one day develop a true morality is often linked to the idea of **"strong AI"**. Strong AI refers to a hypothetical system that possesses consciousness and could therefore think, feel, and act independently (Bostrom, 2014, p. 165). In such a scenario, it would theoretically be conceivable for machines not only to apply moral principles but also to develop and reflect on them independently. However, this possibility lies far beyond the reach of current technological developments. Even advanced machine learning systems such as neural networks or deep algorithms are functionally limited to pattern recognition and data processing. They cannot develop intrinsic values because they lack subjectivity.

A crucial point that is often overlooked is the fundamental absence of intentionality in AI systems. Moral action requires not only the ability to distinguish between "right" and "wrong," but also the intention to act in a certain way. This intention presupposes an awareness of the consequences of one's actions as well as an empathic connection to others. Machines, on the other hand, can only make decisions based on the data available to them, which may appear to be moral actions but are in fact merely programmed or learned responses (Floridi, 2014, p. 59).

The development of moral principles in AI systems also raises ethical questions that go beyond technical challenges. Who decides which values and norms are integrated into the algorithm? Morality is highly context-dependent and shaped by cultural, social, and individual factors. A universal moral framework that could be implemented by a machine would inevitably reflect the perspectives and values of its developers and therefore could not meet all ethical standards or cultural contexts. In this sense, AI remains a projection surface for human morality, not a source of its own moral agency.

In summary, it must be stated that AI in its current form cannot develop an independent morality, as it lacks consciousness and thus the fundamental prerequisites for moral action. The question of a future "strong AI" with consciousness and intentionality remains speculative and requires both technological and philosophical advances that go far beyond the current state of the art. Until then, AI remains a tool that reflects human morality but does not interpret or transform it independently.

The Problem of Automating Morality

The automation of moral decisions by artificial intelligence represents one of the most pressing dilemmas of our technological present. The attempt to reduce complex moral principles to algorithmic structures carries the risk of simplification that does not do justice to the diversity and depth of human values. Moral decisions are rarely clear-cut; they exist in a field of tension between various, often competing principles such as justice, care, autonomy, and dignity (Moor, 2006a, b, p. 36). These principles are not just abstract concepts, but reflect cultural, historical, and individual perspectives that must be interpreted and applied situationally. AI systems, by contrast, operate on the basis of predefined rules and priorities, such as minimizing harm. While this may seem practical in certain contexts, such as medical triage, the ability to recognize and adequately assess complex value conflicts remains a human domain (Allen et al., 2000a, b, p. 255).

The reduction of morality to algorithmic principles not only raises questions about the appropriateness of such simplifications, but also leads to a profound risk of societal disempowerment. With the increasing delegation of moral decision-making to AI systems, people could neglect their own ethical competencies. The process of moral reflection, which forces us to consider the consequences of our actions and to take responsibility, risks being displaced by the convenient dependence on machine judgments (Weizenbaum, 1976, pp. 227–228). This dependence carries the danger that we increasingly rely on algorithmic decisions without critically questioning them. This not only weakens individual ethical judgment, but also collective engagement with moral questions.

A central problem of this development is the possible erosion of a democratic culture that depends on the exchange and discussion of different moral perspectives. In democratic societies, public debate about values, rights, and responsibility has traditionally held great importance. It enables not only collective decision-making but also the formation of moral consensus or at least mutual understanding. Outsourcing such discourses to AI systems threatens to undermine this process. As moral decisions are increasingly made by algorithms, responsibility for these decisions becomes depersonalized. A culture of "technological fatalism" emerges, in which decisions are accepted as the inevitable consequence of algorithmic logic, rather than being actively questioned and shaped (Floridi, 2016, p. 59).

Furthermore, the question arises as to how transparent and accessible the decision-making foundations of such systems are to the general public. Algorithms that make moral decisions are often based on complex models and large data sets that are hardly comprehensible to laypeople. This lack of transparency increases the risk that moral authority is assumed by machines without their decision-making foundations being disclosed or reviewed. This endangers not only individual autonomy but also societal participation in ethical discourses.

Overall, it becomes clear that the automation of morality brings not only technical but also profound societal and psychological challenges. While AI systems may be able to efficiently support certain aspects of moral judgments, the responsibility for these judgments ultimately remains with humans. It is up to us to ensure that the introduction of such systems does not lead to a gradual disempowerment, but rather serves as an impetus for more intensive engagement with the foundations and limits of our moral responsibility. The question is not whether machines can make moral judgments, but whether we are willing to preserve our own responsibility for ethical decisions.

Perspectives: Human Responsibility in Focus

The question of human responsibility in the context of artificial intelligence requires a nuanced consideration of the relationship between humans and machines. In an era in which AI is increasingly integrated into decision-making processes, the question is not only about the efficiency of such systems, but also about the ethical and psychological implications of their use. The perspective of viewing humans and machines as co-actors offers a helpful model. AI can serve as a supportive tool that provides data, analyzes scenarios, and generates forecasts, enabling people to make informed decisions. In critical areas such as medicine or disaster management, this collaboration has already proven effective, as algorithms provide decision-making foundations that can relieve human actors in complex moral situations (Bostrom, 2014, p. 183). However, it is crucial that responsibility for moral judgments and their consequences is not delegated to the machine. Humans must serve as the final authority and reflect on the ethical dimensions of their decisions (Bryson, 2018, p. 52).

To ensure that machine decisions meet ethical standards, constructive regulation is essential. This requires both technical and institutional measures. Transparent algorithms that disclose how decisions are made are a central step toward promoting traceability and responsibility. At the same time, institutions must set clear legal and ethical guidelines that clearly define responsibilities. It should be taken into account that apparent errors in AI systems are often due to human factors, such as faulty design, inadequate data, or insufficiently scrutinized use (Floridi, 2016, pp. 59–61; Noble, 2018, p. 111). Such errors underscore the need to train both developers and users in ethical competence.

The question of how we as a society define morality in a technologized world is of central importance. Historically, morality has always been a deeply human category, shaped by empathy, social norms, and the capacity for reflection. The idea of technologizing this category by implementing it in algorithms raises profound philosophical questions. Can an ethics based on machine learning truly be considered moral if it is based on data-driven probabilities rather than values and principles (Moor, 2006a, b, p. 35)? It is our responsibility to critically question the limits of machine ethics and to ensure that we do not lightly relinquish the central role of humans in moral matters.

A technologized morality also carries the risk that empathic and reflective abilities, which are essential for human decision-making, recede into the background. As soon as machines anticipate moral decisions, these human abilities could atrophy. It is therefore necessary to promote ethical competence not only at the institutional but also at the individual level. Societal education programs that address the limits and possibilities of AI could help create a new awareness of the role of humans in a technologized world (Singer, 2011, p. 78). Only through conscious training and cultivation of our moral abilities can we ensure that decisions made by or with the help of AI correspond to our humanistic values.

Overall, it is clear that responsibility for moral decisions and their consequences cannot be delegated. Humans and machines may act as co-actors, but ultimate responsibility remains human. This requires not only technical and regulatory measures, but also a societal engagement with the question of what morality means in a technologized world and which values we want to preserve in the future. The integration of AI into decision-making processes offers great opportunities, but these opportunities can only be realized if we critically reflect on and responsibly shape the ethical and psychological implications of its use.

True Morality vs. Algorithmic Simulation

The discussion about the ability of artificial intelligence to make moral decisions provides deep insight into the distinction between true morality and the algorithmic simulation of ethics. Morality, as understood in the human context, is based on the ability to make complex judgments, to assume responsibility, and to reflect on one's actions within a comprehensive social and emotional context (Weizenbaum, 1976, p. 229). In contrast, AI systems are strictly data-driven and act according to the principles and instructions given to them by humans. They are tools that make decisions based on algorithms, but without consciousness, intentionality, or empathy (Allen et al., 2000a, b, p. 256).

The simulation of moral principles by AI is impressive, but also misleading. Algorithms can be programmed to make decisions in specific situations that give the appearance of moral action. For example, an autonomous vehicle might prioritize saving as many lives as possible in a potential accident. Yet this decision-making is based solely on predetermined rules and data patterns, not on a deep understanding or reflection of the moral dilemma. An AI does not "understand" the ethical conflict nor does it feel responsibility for its actions. This leads to a fundamental limitation: AI can imitate ethical processes, but cannot reach the moral depth and conscious dimension of human action (Floridi, 2014, p. 59).

The danger lies in shifting ethical responsibility. The use of AI systems in morally sensitive areas—such as the allocation of scarce medical resources or the control of autonomous weapons—tempts us to transfer responsibility for difficult decisions to machines. This could not only lead to a loss of human autonomy, but also weaken the ability to critically reflect on ethical issues. A central aspect of morality is the ability to learn from mistakes and incorporate them into future decisions. AI, on the other hand, can only act on the basis of historical data and human input, without having its own experiences or growing from them (Singer, 2011, p. 94).

The perspective of viewing AI as an "ethical agent" also raises questions about the role of empathy. Empathy—the ability to put oneself in another's emotional world—is a key factor in moral action. Humans are able not only to apply abstract rules, but also to respond to the individual needs and circumstances of others. This ability to unite the emotional and the rational remains inaccessible to machines. Even if algorithms can recognize and respond to emotional reactions, they lack an understanding of the significance of these reactions in the context of interpersonal relationships. Empathy is not only a cognitive ability, but also an emotional experience that machines cannot comprehend. A responsible use of AI could consist in using it as a supportive instance that assists humans in moral decisions without replacing them. For example, algorithms could analyze scenarios, assess risks, and suggest alternatives to facilitate the decision-making process. But the ultimate responsibility and judgment should remain with humans, who are able to comprehensively reflect on the moral and social consequences. Such collaboration could combine the objective strengths of AI with the emotional and moral depth of humans.

However, the automation of morality must not lead to humans relinquishing their role as ethical subjects. It is crucial that we do not delegate our capacity for reflection and responsibility to machines, but continue to cultivate it. Moral action requires not only logical thinking, but also the recognition of the complexity of human relationships and the emotional impact of decisions. Without this dimension, moral action remains incomplete and reduced.

Ultimately, the discussion of true morality versus algorithmic simulation shows that ethical action is a profoundly human process. It encompasses not only the application of principles, but also the ability to question oneself, to feel empathy, and to take responsibility for the consequences of one's actions. Machines can support us in many areas, but they cannot replace the core of human morality. It is up to us to maintain this distinction and to ensure that AI does not become a substitute for human judgment, but remains a complement that expands our moral abilities without devaluing them.

5.2 Should Machines Surpass Humans in Making Ethical Judgments?

The question of whether artificial intelligence should or could one day surpass humans in ethical matters touches the core of what we understand by *"morality"* and *"human judgment"* (Bryson, 2018, p. 52). While AI systems have demonstrated in recent years that they can recognize highly complex data patterns, perform objective calculations, and in many cases even make decisions faster and more precisely than humans (Bostrom, 2014, p. 158), it remains unclear whether these systems will ever be capable of making moral judgments in a sense comparable to human understanding (Moor, 2006a, b, p. 25). The debate over whether "better" ethical decisions by machines are even desirable runs through philosophy, ethics, and technology research (Floridi, 2014, p. 59).

What do We Mean by "ethical judgments"?

The ability to make ethical judgments is a central aspect of what distinguishes humans as social and moral beings. These judgments do not arise in isolation, but are the result of a dynamic interplay of cognitive, emotional, and social factors. In contrast to purely algorithmic processes, which are based on predefined rules and datasets, human moral decisions are rooted in a network of empathy, intuition, cultural norms, and historical experiences (Singer, 2011, p. 29). Reflecting on what is "right" or "wrong" requires a deep understanding of the context in which decisions are made, as well as the ability to take the perspective of others (Weizenbaum, 1976, pp. 213–214).

Human moral judgments are often caught between rational analysis and emotional experience. While some ethical dilemmas, such as the well-known trolley problem, are designed to provoke purely rational solutions, studies show that people frequently allow emotional impulses to influence their decisions (Thomson, 1985, p. 139). The internal conflict between logically calculating consequences and the intuitive discomfort associated with certain actions reveals the complexity of human ethics. It is not only the ability to analyze consequences that shapes moral decisions, but also the emotional intuition deeply rooted in human nature (Singer, 2011, p. 31).

Moreover, moral judgments are strongly influenced by the cultural and social contexts in which they are made. Values and norms considered morally acceptable in a society evolve over time and are deeply rooted in historical and social experiences. An example of this is the differing perception of justice in collectivist and individualist cultures, which demonstrates how much moral judgments are shaped by cultural frameworks (Bryson, 2018, p. 48). This social dimension makes ethical judgments not only an individual, but also an interactive process that reflects the connection between individuals and communities.

While AI systems are capable of taking moral principles into account in their calculations, they lack the intuitive understanding that characterizes humans in moral matters. Algorithms can make decisions based on logical rules, but they possess neither the capacity for empathy nor an awareness of the consequences of their decisions in emotional and social contexts. This highlights the limits of automating ethics and underscores that moral judgments are inextricably linked to human experience and the complex interplay between rationality and emotion. The ability to make ethical judgments is therefore not only a question of intelligence, but also a question of humanity.

"Better" Ethical Judgments Through AI?

The idea that machines could make "better" ethical judgments meets with both great approval and considerable criticism. Proponents of this vision argue that artificial intelligence is capable of making ethical decisions free from the weaknesses and errors of the human mind. This is particularly advantageous in areas where human decisions can be influenced by personal biases, emotional fluctuations, or cognitive distortions (Bostrom, 2014, p. 160). AI systems trained on comprehensive datasets could act on the basis of clearly defined parameters, thereby eliminating subjective inequalities (Noble, 2018, p. 56).

In the medical context, for example, AI systems could make decisions about the prioritization of treatments based solely on urgency and medical necessity. Unlike humans, these systems would not be affected by emotional attachments or exhaustion. In an emergency room, an AI could analyze complex data in fractions of a second, calculate risk factors, and make decisions based on them, without being influenced by external factors such as stress or compassion (Moor, 2006a, b, p. 27).

Another key argument for the use of AI in ethical decision-making processes is its consistency and scalability. Humans tend to let their judgments be influenced by situational or emotional factors. The same decision can vary depending on mood, time of day, or personal preferences. In contrast, AI can implement consistent guidelines that are applied regardless of mood or individual preferences (Floridi, 2014, p. 59). This would be particularly advantageous in areas such as the justice system or resource allocation. In sentencing, algorithms could ensure that comparable offenses are assessed equally, regardless of the offender's gender, ethnic background, or social status. Such standardized decisions could theoretically lead to greater justice, as human misjudgments or implicit biases are excluded.

Furthermore, the scalability of AI systems offers additional advantages. While human capacities are limited, machines can theoretically be deployed without limit. This enables the widespread implementation of ethical guidelines that can be applied consistently on a large scale. For example, an AI-based system in public administration could ensure that resources are distributed fairly and efficiently—without human error or corruption influencing decisions (Bryson, 2018, p. 52). Such a scenario could be of significant benefit, especially in regions with limited resources or in complex administrative structures.

Despite these potential advantages, there are, however, key challenges and limitations that must be considered. The "objectivity" of AI systems depends entirely on the quality of the data with which they are trained. If these data reflect biases or inequalities, the AI will reproduce and reinforce these systemic problems (Noble, 2018, p. 61). Moreover, it is questionable whether ethical decisions can ever be made completely objectively. Moral judgments are often closely linked to cultural values, personal beliefs, and situational contexts, which are difficult to capture in rigid rules or algorithms.

Another point of criticism is the lack of accountability of AI systems. While a human can be held accountable for their ethical decisions, the question arises as to who is responsible for the decisions of an AI. Is it the programmer who developed the algorithms, or the institution that deploys the AI? This question of attribution remains a central problem in the discussion about the use of AI in ethical contexts (Floridi, 2015, p. 67).

Overall, it becomes clear that the idea of machines making "better" ethical judgments brings both fascinating possibilities and significant challenges. While AI systems could open up a new dimension in decision-making through their objectivity and consistency, the question remains whether they can truly replace the profound human elements that play a role in moral judgments. Rather, AI systems could take on a supportive role by complementing human decisions and providing more rational foundations, without, however, replacing human responsibility and reflection.

The Area of Tension: AI and the Loss of the "human" Dimension

The area of tension that arises from the use of AI in sensitive fields such as medicine, law, or interpersonal communication touches on one of the central questions of our time: Can decisions without the dimension of human empathy be considered moral and just? While AI systems enable impressive advances through their rational and algorithmic capabilities, the absence of empathy, compassion, and the ability for self-reflection remains a decisive shortcoming (Singer, 2011, p. 94). Empathy is not merely an accessory to human action, but an essential component of ethical judgment. It enables us to take the perspective of others, to understand their feelings, and to consider the complex interplay between individual experiences and societal norms. Without this emotional resonance, the moral quality of a decision remains superficial and is reduced to purely logical or statistical considerations (Weizenbaum, 1976, p. 225).

A central problem here is that ethical judgments are not based solely on cognitive processes, but are also shaped by emotional and social factors. Decisions made by humans reflect values such as compassion, a sense of responsibility, and awareness of individual circumstances. AI systems, on the other hand, operate on the basis of algorithms and data, without an understanding of suffering, feelings, or the significance of individual destinies (Allen et al., 2000a, b, p. 253). This distance from the emotional dimension means that while AI can make consistent and possibly efficient decisions, these are often perceived as "cold" or "dehumanized." An algorithm that, based on predefined parameters, makes a medical diagnosis or suggests a sentence in a legal context may appear objective, but it lacks the ability to adequately consider the unique circumstances of an individual's life story (Moor, 2006a, b, p. 34).

The importance of the human factor becomes particularly evident in these contexts. Many people value the fact that decisions are not made solely on the basis of data and algorithms. Especially in difficult or emotionally charged situations, such as a serious medical diagnosis or a court case, those affected often expect their personal history and feelings to be taken into account. A purely data-based decision may be efficient and logically correct, but it can evoke a sense of injustice because it fails to recognize the affected person as a unique individual. This tension between justice and humanity makes it clear that moral judgments cannot be based solely on an objective foundation, but must always include the subjective and emotional dimensions of those involved (Noble, 2018, p. 111).

Another critical point is trust in AI systems. The perception of being judged by an unempathic machine can significantly undermine trust in such systems. Trust is not only created through accuracy or efficiency, but also through the ability to convey interpersonal closeness and understanding. If those affected feel that their individual needs and emotions are not sufficiently acknowledged in a decision, acceptance of that decision is at risk. This poses a tremendous challenge, especially in fields such as medicine or law, where trust in decision-makers—whether human or machine—is essential (Turkle, 2011, p. 186).

The discussion about the loss of the human dimension in the area of tension between AI and ethics shows that the use of technology alone is not sufficient to ensure moral and just decisions. Rather, a hybrid approach is needed that combines the strengths of AI—its data processing capacities and consistency—with the unique abilities of the human mind—empathy, compassion, and moral reflection. Only in this way can a balance between efficiency and humanity be achieved that meets the demands of a modern, technology-based society.

Examples of AI-supported Moral Decisions

1. Self-driving cars and accident scenarios
   The trolley problem serves as a model for a real scenario: Should the vehicle, in the event of an unavoidable accident, protect the driver(s) or the pedestrian(s)? An algorithm could logically calculate how many lives can be saved (Bostrom, 2014, p. 182). Yet people question whether active intervention that "sacrifices" certain individuals is morally legitimate (Singer, 2011, p. 31).
2. Criminal justice and reoffending scores
   In some US states, algorithms are used to judge defendants' future risk of reoffending and to determine sentences based on statistical data. In theory, this is intended to lead to fairer treatment. However, it has become apparent that the algorithms were trained on biased datasets (e.g., racially

influenced histories) and can thus reinforce unconscious discrimination (Noble, 2018, p. 28).

3. Medical prioritization
In overcrowded emergency rooms, AI systems could make recommendations about which patients should be treated first. Although this sounds like a plausible solution, critics argue that machines cannot take into account "last wishes" or complex family backgrounds, and thus impersonal "utility values" determine the fate of individuals (Weizenbaum, 1976, p. 229).

The Question of Responsibility and Moral Autonomy

The question of responsibility and moral autonomy in the context of the increasing integration of artificial intelligence into decision-making processes is of central importance for ethical and psychological discussions. With the growing complexity and autonomy of AI systems, the question of who can be held liable for their decisions is becoming ever more pressing. When AI makes faulty decisions in areas such as medicine, criminal justice, or public administration that lead to serious consequences, such as unequal medical treatment or wrongful conviction, responsibility is often difficult to assign. This is because AI does not act autonomously in the legal sense, but is a product of human development, programming, and application (Bryson, 2018, p. 61). However, the more advanced AI systems become, the more the boundary between human control and machine autonomy blurs, making it increasingly difficult to attribute the cause of errors (Moor, 2006a, b, p. 36).

This lack of transparency in the assignment of responsibility leads to a shift in the moral burden, which often falls back on developer*s, operators*, or user*s. However, these actor*s are often not able to fully understand the functioning of complex algorithms, especially when machine learning and self-optimizing processes are involved. This creates a paradoxical situation: although humans are ultimately responsible for the outcomes of AI systems, they do not always have the knowledge or control to exercise this responsibility effectively. This lack of clear accountability raises not only legal and ethical questions, but also affects the psychological relationship between people and technology, as it increases uncertainty and anxiety.

Another aspect is the potential loss of human autonomy and the risk of disempowerment when moral decisions are increasingly delegated to AI. Joseph Weizenbaum warned as early as 1976 that an unreflective transfer of decision-making processes to machines could undermine the human capacity for ethical reflection (Weizenbaum, 1976, p. 227). AI systems that are perceived as infallible or objective could lead people to question their own judgment. This carries the risk of psychological dependence, in which people feel less competent to resolve moral issues independently. This is particularly problematic in areas where empathy, intuition, and situational sensitivity are required—abilities that AI systems do not possess, but which are indispensable for sound ethical decision-making.

Luciano Floridi argues that the gradual delegation of moral decisions to machines can undermine not only individual self-confidence, but also societal trust in human decision-making ability (Floridi, 2014, p. 59). This leads to a creeping degradation of humans as moral subjects. Instead of being active participants in ethical processes, people could become passive observers who depend on the decisions of machines. This process of "dehumanizing" moral discourse poses risks not only for individual autonomy, but also for collective ethical action in a democratic society.

In summary, it is clear that the question of responsibility and the potential for disempowerment in connection with moral decision-making by AI have profound effects on human self-understanding and societal ethics. While AI systems can undoubtedly increase efficiency and precision in many areas, they must be carefully embedded in a framework that protects human autonomy and accountability. Without such reflection, not only a technological but also a moral crisis looms, in which humans lose their central role as responsible and decision-capable subjects.

Advantages and Disadvantages of Machine-Based Ethics

Machine-based ethics is an increasingly relevant topic in the debate about the integration of artificial intelligence (AI) into decision-making processes, especially in morally sensitive contexts. The introduction of such systems brings both significant advantages and notable challenges. On the positive side, machine-based ethics is characterized by remarkable consistency in decision-making. While human judgments are often shaped by emotional fluctuations, situational influences, or individual biases, AI systems can act stably and impersonally, reducing the arbitrariness and randomness of human decisions (Bostrom, 2014, p. 158). Added to this is the scalability of AI: algorithms are able to analyze large amounts of data in a very short time and achieve consistently similar results (Floridi, 2016, p. 52). This makes them particularly useful in scenarios where rapid and data-intensive decisions are required, such as in medical diagnostics or finance. Furthermore, AI systems offer the potential to minimize cognitive biases. While humans are prone to systematic errors such as confirmation bias or the halo effect, AI—at least in theory—can operate free from such influences, provided the underlying training data are themselves unbiased (Noble, 2018, p. 91).

Yet despite these advantages, the limitations of machine-based ethics are unmistakable. One of the central weaknesses is the lack of empathy. AI systems have no access to the subjective feelings and experiences that are often essential for moral judgments (Singer, 2011, p. 94). Empathy plays a decisive role, especially in moral dilemmas, as it enables us to take the perspective of others and assess the impact of decisions on an individual level. This dimension is entirely absent in AI. Moreover, it is evident that machines have difficulty responding appropriately to the complexity and context of moral problems. Many moral questions cannot be reduced to simple algorithmic structures, as they depend on social, cultural, and emotional factors that are difficult to formalize (Moor, 2006a, b, p. 35). As a result, machine-based decisions are often insufficiently nuanced, especially when they must be made in heterogeneous or unpredictable situations.

Another key problem is the so-called diffusion of responsibility, which is exacerbated by the use of AI systems. While in human decision-making processes responsibility can usually be clearly assigned to a person or group, this clarity is significantly diminished by the introduction of machine-based systems. Responsibility is distributed among developers, data providers, and end users, which makes ethical action complicated in many cases (Weizenbaum, 1976, pp. 225–226). This diffusion can lead to a situation where ultimately no one feels responsible for the consequences of a decision, especially when unforeseen or undesirable outcomes occur.

Overall, it is clear that while machine-based ethics offers significant advantages in terms of consistency, efficiency, and potential objectivity, it shows clear deficits in the areas of empathy, context sensitivity, and assumption of responsibility. These areas of tension make it clear that while AI is capable of providing support in certain moral contexts, it does not represent a comprehensive solution to the complex demands of human ethics. Instead, these systems must be seen as tools that complement human decision-making, but can never replace it—especially when it comes to questions deeply rooted in emotional and social dynamics. Responsible use of machine-based ethics therefore requires careful consideration of its strengths and weaknesses, as well as ongoing reflection on which areas of moral judgment remain inextricably linked to human experience.

Ethical Self-Conceptions: Human Imperfection as a Value?

The role of human subjectivity in the context of moral decisions has always been regarded as central, especially in philosophical and psychological engagement with ethics. Human subjectivity is closely linked to the ability not only to analyze moral dilemmas logically, but also to experience them emotionally. Some ethicists, including Singer (2011, p. 78), emphasize that moral judgments gain depth precisely through their subjective and often irrational component. Guilt, compassion, and remorse are not merely human weaknesses, but essential elements that constitute our moral capacity. If these emotional uncertainties were eliminated and replaced by the seemingly cold efficiency of algorithms, there would be a risk of losing the essence of what ethics means in the human sense (Weizenbaum, 1976, pp. 213 ff.). While machines can apply moral rules programmatically, they remain incapable of comprehending the emotional depth of these decisions.

Criticism of a purely logic-centered perspective on morality has a long tradition, dating back to Aristotle's virtue ethics. In the *Nicomachean Ethics*, Aristotle describes virtues such as courage, justice, and generosity as qualities developed through experience, reflection, and emotional maturity (Aristotle, 1976). Central to this is the concept of *"phronesis"* (practical wisdom), which describes the ability to act morally appropriately in complex and often ambiguous situations. While machines may be able to make decisions based on large amounts of data, they cannot undergo character development or acquire emotional maturity (Moor, 2006a, b, p. 28). This suggests that moral integrity arises not only from the correct application of rules, but from a deeply rooted human ability to reflect on and take responsibility for moral action in social and emotional contexts.

The idea that machines could surpass humans in ethical judgment, however, has not only critics but also supporters. Proponents argue that AI, through its data-driven approach and objectivity, can avoid cognitive biases and prejudices that often shape human decisions (Bryson, 2018, p. 52). Yet this view overlooks the fact that algorithms are not free from bias. They reflect the prejudices of the data on which they are trained and can thus not only reproduce but even reinforce existing inequalities (Floridi, 2016, pp. 59–61). There is also the risk that transferring ethical decisions to machines undermines human responsibility. If people no longer make decisions themselves but delegate them to AI, they may feel morally "disempowered" and less willing to bear the consequences of those decisions.

In this context, a balanced approach appears particularly promising. Instead of viewing AI as a replacement for human judgment, AI systems could serve as supportive tools that complement rather than replace human decision-making processes. Such collaboration could combine the strengths of both sides: human empathy, intuition, and moral responsibility with the precision and analytical capacity of machines (Allen et al., 2000a, b, p. 256). For example, AI could function as a moral early warning system by simulating potential consequences of decisions, thereby helping people make more informed judgments.

Ultimately, however, the question remains as to what role human imperfection should play in ethics. Imperfection, which manifests in emotional ambivalence, moral struggle, and the capacity for self-criticism, is a central component of what makes us moral beings. A purely algorithmic ethics may appear more objective and consistent in theory, but it risks driving humanity out of ethical processes. The ability to take responsibility, to doubt, and to learn from mistakes makes human judgment not only unique, but also profoundly relevant.

The question of whether AI should replace humans in moral matters is ultimately a question of our value system. It requires a conscious engagement with the role we want to grant machines in our ethical systems. In an automated world, we could run the risk of marginalizing deep humanity—in the form of empathy, self-reflection, and a sense of responsibility. A conscious approach to AI as a supportive but not dominant force could help maintain this balance and ensure that moral decision-making in the future continues to be shaped by the unique complexity of human subjectivity.

5.3 The Dilemma of Responsibility: Who is Responsible for the Actions of AI?

The issue of responsibility in the context of artificial intelligence is one of the central ethical and legal challenges of our time (Bryson, 2018, p. 61). As AI systems increasingly make complex decisions and become established in areas of life from healthcare to autonomous mobility, it often remains unclear who bears responsibility when something goes wrong (Weizenbaum, 1976, p. 225). Whether it is fatal accidents involving self-driving vehicles, discriminatory algorithms in the justice system, or faulty medical diagnoses by AI—the question always arises as to whom moral and legal liability should be addressed (Noble, 2018, p. 91).

Traditional Concepts of Responsibility and Their Limits

Traditional concepts of responsibility and their limits are fundamentally challenged by the development and deployment of AI systems. In classical legal and philosophical theories, responsibility is based on the assumption that the subject acts consciously and can anticipate the consequences of their actions. This assumption presupposes both intention and freedom of choice, two central features of human action (Moor, 2006a, b, p. 26). A person is held responsible because they can distinguish between right and wrong and align their decisions with moral principles. However, this model is inadequate when applied to machine systems that possess neither intention nor consciousness (Weizenbaum, 1976, pp. 213–214).

Artificial intelligence calls this traditional conception of responsibility into question, especially in its increasingly "autonomous" applications. While an AI does not make conscious decisions in the human sense, its ability to independently perform actions based on data patterns and algorithms creates the impression of autonomy (Bostrom, 2014, p. 160). However, this apparent autonomy is not grounded in conscious intent or moral reflection, but is the result of mathematical calculations programmed by developers and executed by machines (Bryson, 2018, p. 52).

The problem becomes even more complicated when considering the self-learning properties of modern AI systems. Machine learning enables AI to improve through experience and make decisions that were not explicitly foreseen by its developers. This ability creates the impression that machines can act independently and thus also assume responsibility. Yet this impression is misleading. The underlying algorithms and the data processed by the system remain human-made and are subject to human assumptions and biases (Allen et al., 2000a, b, p. 253). This leads to a crucial question: Who bears responsibility when a machine acts "wrongly"—the developer, the user, or an organization? Or should responsibility be transferred to the machine itself, which would require a legal and philosophical redefinition of the term "responsibility"?

The limits of the traditional notion of responsibility become particularly evident when considering the complexity of modern AI systems. While human actions can often be traced back to individual intentions, in AI development and application, responsibilities are distributed among a multitude of actors. Developers program the algorithms, organizations implement the systems, and users apply them in specific contexts. This distribution leads to a "fragmentation of responsibility," making it increasingly difficult to assign clear responsibility (Floridi, 2015, p. 36). The classical idea of a single, responsible subject is hardly applicable in this context.

At the same time, the question remains open as to how to deal with errors or unexpected consequences of machine actions. In cases where AI systems control autonomous vehicles, make medical diagnoses, or analyze financial markets, erroneous decisions can have serious consequences. The traditional concept of responsibility is insufficient here, as it does not take into account that decisions in complex systems are often emergent—that is, they arise from the interaction of many components and not from the conscious actions of a single actor.

One possible solution discussed in the literature is the development of a new model of "distributed responsibility," in which all actors involved in the development and use of an AI system share responsibility proportionally (Floridi, 2015, p. 42). This model would recognize that no machine can be responsible in the traditional sense, but that responsibility has a collective dimension encompassing the entire life cycle of an AI system. However, this model also faces challenges, as it is difficult to define and enforce clear shares of responsibility.

In summary, AI systems reveal the limits of traditional concepts of responsibility and require a fundamental realignment. Machines cannot assume moral responsibility, as they possess neither intentions nor consciousness. Responsibility thus inevitably remains with the humans who design, implement, and use these systems. Yet the increasing complexity and autonomy of AI systems make clear assignment of responsibility more difficult. The challenge is to create new ethical and legal frameworks that do justice to this reality and ensure that technological innovations are used responsibly.

Distributed Responsibility in the AI Ecosystem

The dynamics of modern AI systems lead to a new complexity in the ethics of responsibility, arising from the multitude of actors involved and the diffusion of responsibility attribution. Unlike traditional technologies, where responsibility could often be clearly assigned to a single entity, AI systems are the result of highly interdisciplinary and collaborative processes. Developers program algorithms, data analysts curate and clean training datasets, companies market the products, and end users apply them in specific contexts (Noble, 2018, p. 111). However, when an AI system malfunctions or causes harmful consequences, it becomes apparent that responsibility often cannot be clearly assigned to a single actor.

This phenomenon is referred to as "distributed responsibility" (Moor, 2006a, b, p. 34). It highlights the difficulty of clarifying responsibilities in complex technological ecosystems, as decision-making and action execution are distributed across various entities. Developers might argue that they merely implemented the technical requirements of a client. Companies may point out that their systems only function correctly if the terms of use are strictly followed. End users, in turn, might claim that they relied on the supposedly objective results of the AI without being able to understand the technical background. These mutual references to partial responsibilities lead to responsibility dissolving or being obscured (Weizenbaum, 1976, p. 227).

A vivid example of the challenges of distributed responsibility is seen in autonomous vehicles. If an accident occurs with a self-driving car, the immediate question is who is responsible for the incident. Is it the software developers who programmed the algorithm, the manufacturer of the vehicle, the company marketing the technology, or the person behind the wheel who could theoretically intervene? No single actor has complete control over the vehicle's "decisions," as these result from a complex interplay of algorithms, sensors, and external traffic conditions (Bryson, 2018, p. 61; Bostrom, 2014, p. 182).

The problem is exacerbated by the opacity of decision-making processes in AI systems. Even experts involved in developing the systems often cannot precisely explain how certain decisions are made—a phenomenon known as the "black box problem" (Floridi, 2015, p. 198). This lack of traceability intensifies the responsibility gap and makes it difficult to clearly determine liability in the event of erroneous decisions. In addition, many AI systems are continuously developed through machine learning, so the original state of the system at the time of market launch may no longer be traceable.

The debate about distributed responsibility in the AI ecosystem raises fundamental ethical and legal questions. It shows that traditional concepts of responsibility and liability, which are based on clearly defined roles and causal relationships, are often insufficient for the complexity of modern AI systems. New approaches are therefore needed to regulate responsibility in such ecosystems. These could include legal frameworks that focus liability more on companies and developers, or technical standards that improve the transparency and traceability of AI decisions.

Without such mechanisms, there is a risk that responsibility for AI systems will remain diffuse, which burdens both those affected in the event of harm and the societal acceptance of the technology. In the long term, the question of how distributed responsibility can be organized and attributed in technological systems will be decisive for whether and how AI can be sustainably integrated into social and economic systems.

The Illusion of Objectivity: Biased Data and Algorithmic Prejudices

The widely held assumption that artificial intelligence enables more objective decision-making due to its supposedly emotion- and bias-free functioning proves, upon closer inspection, to be a myth (Noble, 2018, p. 56). This illusion of objectivity is not only deceptive but also carries far-reaching consequences for social and individual justice. The reason for this lies in the way AI systems are trained: algorithms are based on historical datasets that often reflect deeply rooted social and cultural inequalities (Moor, 2006a, b, p. 28). As a result, these systems can not only reproduce existing biases but even amplify them through their scalability and efficiency.

A prominent example of this mechanism is the use of AI in the criminal justice system. Algorithms for assessing the recidivism risk of offenders—so-called "predictive policing" systems—are often trained on historical crime data. However, these data are far from neutral: they often reflect decades of racist or social inequalities, such as disproportionate surveillance of certain population groups (Noble, 2018, p. 112). The result is that the AI adopts these biases as the basis for its decisions, thereby reinforcing discriminatory patterns. Thus, marginalized groups continue to be stigmatized, while responsibility for this injustice is shifted onto the machine.

The question of responsibility becomes particularly problematic in this context. When an AI system makes discriminatory decisions, such as recommending that a person be denied parole, the question arises as to who can be held accountable. Is it the programmer who developed the algorithm? Is it the institutions that provided the training data? Or is responsibility with the user of the system, who adopts the AI's decisions without scrutiny? This ambiguity in responsibility is a central feature of algorithmically reinforced discrimination and makes it particularly difficult to address (Nissenbaum, 2010, p. 129).

Moreover, there is an inherent danger in the fact that the decisions of AI systems are often perceived as objective or infallible. Users tend to place more trust in the results of an algorithm than in human judgments, even when the basis for these decisions is not transparent (O'Neil, 2016, p. 78). This so-called "automation bias" leads to discriminatory decisions being questioned and reviewed less frequently. The supposed neutrality of the machine thus not only reinforces social inequalities but also makes them harder to detect and correct.

The psychological consequences of this dynamic are far-reaching. On an individual level, those affected by algorithmic discrimination may develop a sense of powerlessness, as they have no way to challenge or even understand the basis of the decisions. This sense of external control can not only undermine trust in institutions but also have a lasting negative impact on personal self-esteem. On a societal level, the proliferation of such AI systems leads to a normalization of injustice, as algorithmically reinforced biases are increasingly accepted as an inevitable part of modern technologies (Eubanks, 2018, p. 94).

Another critical aspect is the question of how societies should deal with the inherent bias of AI systems. While some experts emphasize the need to curate training data more carefully and make algorithms more transparent, others see the solution in stronger regulation of AI development and application (Floridi, 2015, p. 221). In any case, it is clear that the illusion of objectivity through AI is a dangerous fallacy that not only perpetuates existing social inequalities but further exacerbates them through the apparent infallibility of the technology.

It becomes clear that the notion of "objective machines" is a myth that obscures both the limits of the technology and the ethical challenges of its application. Algorithms cannot be considered independently of the data and contexts from which they arise. Ultimately, responsibility for their decisions lies with humans—whether developers, institutions, or users—and a critical awareness of the power and pitfalls of algorithmic systems is needed. Only in this way can it be ensured that the increasing integration of AI into societal decision-making processes does not lead to a further deepening of existing inequalities.

Legal Gray Areas and Initial Approaches

The legal regulation of artificial intelligence faces major challenges, as traditional liability models are often insufficient to address the complex questions raised by autonomous systems. The central conflict lies in the fact that AI systems make decisions based on algorithms that, while programmed by humans, often produce results that are not fully transparent (Bryson, 2018,

p. 61). This lack of transparency leads to a legal gray area in which neither intent nor classic negligence can serve as a legal basis. The problem is exacerbated when the actions of the AI cannot be traced back to clearly identifiable errors or human interventions, but rather to the system's "independent" erroneous decisions. This creates a vacuum in the question of liability that is problematic not only legally but also ethically (Floridi, 2016, p. 59).

Regulatory efforts to close this gap have gained importance in various countries and at the EU level. A central approach is the introduction of specific liability models for autonomous systems, particularly in the field of road traffic. Here, the idea of introducing mandatory insurance for autonomous vehicles is being discussed, which would apply regardless of individual fault (Bostrom, 2014, p. 178). This approach is intended to ensure that those harmed are compensated quickly and easily, without the need to clarify complex liability issues. At the same time, the question remains open as to how far the responsibility of the developer, operator, or user extends. Especially in cases where an AI system has independently developed new decision-making mechanisms through continuous machine learning, it is difficult to assign clear responsibility.

Another controversial concept is the idea of the "electronic person." This approach proposes treating AI systems legally as independent entities that could act like legal persons (Weizenbaum, 1976, p. 228). In practice, this would mean that an AI would not be held directly responsible, but rather an insurance or guarantee system behind the machine would cover damages. While this proposal appears theoretically attractive, it faces significant practical and ethical concerns. Critics argue that introducing an electronic person could weaken the sense of responsibility among developers and operators, as they could hide behind an abstract legal entity. At the same time, there are fears that such a step would further blur the distinction between humans and machines and could potentially lead to abuse of the technology.

Current efforts show that there is no simple solution to the legal challenges of AI. Instead, a dynamic and interdisciplinary approach is needed, integrating technological, legal, and ethical perspectives. Only in this way can it be ensured that the introduction of AI systems brings not only economic benefits but also guarantees social and legal security. The question of liability is not just a legal issue but also a societal challenge that will fundamentally shape the relationship between humans and machines.

Ethical Aspects: Responsibility as a Societal Negotiation Process

The development and implementation of artificial intelligence has raised profound ethical questions, particularly regarding the distribution of responsibility in highly networked systems. Unlike traditional technologies, whose development and use could often be clearly attributed to specific actors, AI is characterized by exceptional complexity and opacity. These features make it nearly impossible to limit responsibility to individuals or specific institutions alone. Rather, dealing with AI systems requires collective responsibility, which must be understood as a societal negotiation process.

From a moral-philosophical perspective, the distribution of responsibility in a technological context is particularly challenging, as decisions are made within a network of developers, companies, political actors, and users. From the selection of data sources to algorithm development and practical application, numerous actors are involved, whose actions are often closely intertwined (Allen et al., 2000a, b, p. 256). In such a structure, the question arises as to how responsibility can be meaningfully distributed. Institutional mechanisms are needed to promote accountability at all levels, from developers who program algorithms to political decision-makers who create regulatory frameworks (Moor, 2006a, b, p. 35). Without such anchoring of responsibility, there is a risk that moral and legal responsibilities will become blurred and potentially no one will be held accountable for negative consequences.

In practice, initial approaches have been developed to systematically address responsibility in AI development. Some large technology companies have established ethics commissions or advisory boards to ensure that their products align with societal values and norms (Noble, 2018, p. 111). These bodies are tasked with identifying potential risks, analyzing moral conflicts, and developing recommendations for action. However, it is often criticized that such internal structures are frequently not independent and primarily serve the interests of the companies. There is a risk that ethics is used merely as a PR measure without bringing about real changes in the development and application of AI.

A more promising approach is to involve the broader society in the discourse on AI. Participatory formats, in which citizens are included in decision-making processes, could help to identify ethical issues at an early stage and integrate societal values into technology design (Floridi, 2014, p. 59). These procedures could be implemented, for example, in the form of citizens' forums, public hearings, or digital platforms where people from different social and cultural backgrounds can contribute their perspectives. This would not only increase transparency but also strengthen trust in AI systems, as decisions would no longer be made solely behind closed doors by technicians and company representatives.

Despite the potential benefits of such approaches, implementation remains a challenge. The question arises as to how participation can be effectively designed without it becoming a symbolic act without real consequences. Furthermore, mechanisms must be developed to ensure that the diversity of perspectives actually flows into decisions and is not overshadowed by dominant actors. This requires careful design of procedures and possibly also legal frameworks mandating the involvement of society in technological decision-making processes.

Ultimately, it becomes clear that the question of responsibility in AI development is not only a technical or legal one, but also a deeply societal issue. It requires a broad discourse that combines technical expertise, moral-philosophical reflection, and societal participation. Only in this way can it be ensured that the development of AI systems aligns with the values and needs of society and that negative impacts are minimized.

Responsibility and the "Black Box" Problem

The discussion about responsibility in dealing with artificial intelligence inevitably encounters the problem of the opacity of many modern machine learning methods. Especially with complex models such as those of deep learning, the problem arises that even developers cannot always understand exactly how a particular decision was made within the system (Bryson, 2018, p. 52). This lack of transparency leads not only to practical difficulties, such as identifying and correcting errors, but also to significant ethical and legal challenges. If no one can explain exactly why an AI took a particular action, assigning responsibility becomes nearly impossible. This is particularly true of so-called "black box" models, whose internal decision logic is completely opaque to outsiders (Moor, 2006a, b, p. 36).

The "black box" problem has far-reaching consequences, especially in application areas such as medicine, the judiciary, or autonomous driving, where faulty decisions can have serious consequences. If, for example, an AI fails in medical diagnosis or an autonomous vehicle makes a faulty decision, it often remains unclear whether the cause lay in the dataset, the programming, or an unforeseen scenario. This uncertainty leads to a diffusion of responsibility, in which neither the developers, the operators, nor the users can be clearly held accountable. This situation not only presents an ethical dilemma but also undermines trust in AI systems, especially in sensitive areas of application.

One approach to mitigating the "black box" problem lies in the development of so-called explainable artificial intelligence, also known as "Explainable AI" (XAI). The goal of this research is to design decision-making processes within machine learning models so that they are understandable and traceable for humans (Floridi, 2016, p. 59). A more transparent system could make it possible to better analyze problematic decisions and more precisely identify sources of error. For example, an AI system used for credit approval could provide a clear explanation of why a particular application was rejected. This would allow discrimination and biases in the system to be detected and corrected more quickly.

Another advantage of explainable AI is that it can counteract the diffusion of responsibility. If it is clearly traceable which data or algorithmic rules led to a decision, it becomes easier to assign responsibility—be it to the programmers, the data analysts, or the institutions using the system (Noble, 2018, p. 28). This clarity could not only better address ethical and legal questions but also strengthen society's trust in AI systems.

Nevertheless, the development of XAI faces significant challenges. On the one hand, there is a technical problem: the models that are particularly powerful—such as neural networks—are often also the most difficult to interpret. Simplifying such models to make their decision-making processes more understandable could impair their accuracy and efficiency. On the other hand, there are also ethical questions: even if a model is explainable, the question remains whether these explanations are accessible and understandable to all those affected. It is not enough for a developer to understand how it works; end users affected by the decisions must also be able to comprehend them.

Efforts to increase transparency and explainability in AI development highlight how central the question of responsibility is in modern technology. Without clear responsibilities, not only is trust in AI systems undermined, but also society's ability to adequately address the ethical and legal challenges of AI. Explainable AI is therefore a promising step toward solving the "black box" problem, but it alone will not suffice to fully answer the complex questions of responsibility in the age of artificial intelligence.

The Role of Major Technology Companies

The role of major technology companies in the field of artificial intelligence is central to the development and use of these technologies. These corporations possess significant financial resources and control vast amounts of data necessary to train and further develop AI systems. In fact, some of the leading technology companies—such as Alphabet (Google), Meta (formerly Facebook), Microsoft, and Amazon—have such economic and technological clout that they are now considered more powerful than many nation-states (Bostrom, 2014, p. 50). Their innovative strength is undisputed, yet the question of their social responsibility remains highly controversial.

A central problem lies in the concentration of power and resources. While these companies are making advances in AI research, this often occurs from a primarily profit-driven approach. AI is used as a means to maximize revenue, market share, and competitiveness. For example, algorithms can be used to improve advertising or optimize supply chains, serving the economic goals of the corporations but not necessarily aiming for social or ethical benefits (Noble, 2018, p. 56). In doing so, the question is often overlooked as to the extent to which the use of such technologies cements unequal power relations or creates new forms of social control.

The tension between the pressure to innovate and ethical responsibility becomes particularly apparent when corporations promote so-called "responsible AI development." Many companies now publish ethical guidelines or codes of conduct to make their handling of AI more transparent and to gain public trust. However, the practical implementation of these guidelines often remains unclear, as they are usually non-binding and not subject to external review (Moor, 2006a, b, p. 35). As a result, such measures often serve more as image management than as actual regulation of the risks associated with AI technologies.

Another problem is the speed at which AI products are brought to market. In an environment shaped by competition and market logic, what counts most is who innovates first and makes the technology economically viable. This leads to important aspects such as safety, fairness, and transparency not always being sufficiently considered (Floridi, 2014, p. 59). An example of this is the use of AI in facial recognition, where repeated cases have come to light in which the technology was error-prone or biased against certain ethnic groups. Despite these problems, companies continue to deploy such systems, as the potential profits seemingly outweigh the risks for those affected.

The lack of transparency of the algorithms developed by major technology companies further exacerbates the problem. Even when wrong decisions or discriminatory outcomes occur, it remains unclear who is responsible. The complexity of AI models allows companies to point to the opacity of their own systems in order to evade responsibility. This leads to a decoupling of power and accountability, as those who develop and control the technologies often do not have to answer for their social impact.

This dynamic is further intensified by the fact that governments and regulatory authorities often cannot keep pace with the speed of innovation in the technology sector. While companies roll out their AI systems globally, state institutions face the challenge of creating appropriate legal frameworks. Without clear legal requirements, many aspects of AI development remain under the influence of technology companies, who primarily pursue their own economic interests.

The dominance of major technology companies has profound implications for society. On the one hand, there is a risk of further concentration of economic and technological power, which could exacerbate existing social inequalities. On the other hand, there is the danger that the ethical and social consequences of AI decisions are not sufficiently taken into account. For example, when AI systems are used in sensitive areas such as criminal justice, healthcare, or education, this can have far-reaching consequences for the individuals and communities affected.

The discussion about the role of major technology companies highlights the need for a critical examination of the structures behind AI development. It is not enough to rely on the self-regulation of companies. Instead, regulatory mechanisms must be established to ensure that AI technologies are developed and deployed in accordance with ethical principles and societal values. Only through such a balance between innovation and responsibility can it be prevented that control over AI technologies remains exclusively in the hands of a few actors.

Perspectives: Ways Out of the Responsibility Dilemma

The discussion about the "dilemma of responsibility" in dealing with artificial intelligence highlights the need to fundamentally rethink existing concepts of responsibility and liability. AI systems are increasingly acting autonomously, their decisions based on complex algorithms and vast amounts of data that are often difficult for outsiders to comprehend. This dynamic requires innovative approaches to ensure that both legal and ethical standards are maintained in an AI-driven world.

A central starting point lies in the development of clear legal frameworks and liability models. Legal regulations could define responsibility along the entire AI value chain. For example, strict manufacturer liability could be established, making companies liable for damages caused by faulty AI systems. Alternatively, insurance models could be developed to cover costs in the event of damage, thus providing legal certainty for those affected (Bryson, 2018, p. 61). Such an approach would also create incentives to develop and test AI systems more carefully.

In addition to legal requirements, binding ethical standards are essential. These could formulate minimum requirements for data selection, algorithm transparency, and decision-making in AI processes (Allen et al., 2000a, b, p. 256). The development of explainable AI technologies could help make the functioning of algorithms more understandable and identify those responsible more quickly (Moor, 2006a, b, p. 36). Transparency is a decisive factor here in fostering trust in AI systems and detecting misuse or misconduct at an early stage.

Moreover, social discourse plays a central role. Responsibility cannot be defined solely by developers or political decision-makers. An open dialogue involving citizens, civil society organizations, and ethics commissions is necessary to identify the values and norms that should be considered in machine processes (Floridi, 2014, p. 59). Participatory processes could help strengthen trust in AI systems and promote societal acceptance of their application.

Another important approach is the introduction of continuous monitoring and auditing processes. Especially in sensitive areas such as medicine, justice, or the military, AI systems must be regularly reviewed to ensure that they operate fairly, safely, and in accordance with applicable regulations (Weizenbaum, 1976, p. 229). Independent audits could play a central role in identifying errors before they cause real harm. This would not only increase safety but also help minimize potential misconduct from the outset.

1. Clear legal frameworks and liability models
   Legal requirements should define how responsibility is distributed when AI systems make mistakes. One option is the introduction of strict manufacturer liability or insurance models to provide legal certainty for those harmed.
2. Binding ethical standards and transparency
   In addition to legal approaches, binding ethical guidelines are needed that formulate minimum requirements for data selection, development

processes, and decision-making structures. Explainable AI technologies could help detect misconduct more quickly and identify those responsible.

3. Social discourse and participation
   Responsibility in an AI-driven world cannot be negotiated behind closed doors by developers and politicians alone. An open dialogue with citizens, civil society organizations, and ethics commissions is necessary to clarify which values and norms should take priority in machine processes.
4. Continuous monitoring and auditing
   Especially in safety-critical fields such as medicine, justice, or the military, AI systems should be subject to constant monitoring. Independent audits could check whether algorithms act fairly, safely, and in compliance with regulations before they are even released into society.

The responsibility dilemma in AI systems calls for a comprehensive transformation of our traditional understanding of liability and moral attribution. The highly complex and interconnected nature of modern AI leads to a diffusion of responsibility: neither machines nor individual humans can always be clearly held accountable, as the development, operation, and application of such systems often take place in opaque networks (Noble, 2018, p. 111).

The challenge is to develop concepts that place transparency, collective liability, and ethical reflection at the center (Bryson, 2018, p. 61). Whether through new liability models, binding ethical standards, or open discourse—the coming years will show how society deals with a technology that seemingly grows beyond human control, but ultimately is always shaped by human decisions. It remains crucial to make human responsibility for AI systems explicit and to create clear structures that ensure moral and legal principles are not undermined. Only through these efforts can it be prevented that the dilemma of responsibility shakes the foundations of our social coexistence.

References

Allen, A. L., Smit, B. W., & Wallach, W. (2000a). Responsibility and artificial intelligence. *Ethics and Information Technology, 2*(4), 249–256.

Allen, C., Varner, G., & Zinser, J. (2000b). Prolegomena to any future artificial moral agent. *Journal of Experimental & Theoretical Artificial Intelligence, 12*(3), 251–261.

Aristoteles. (1976). *Nikomachische Ethik*. Reclam.

Bostrom, N. (2014). *Superintelligence: Paths, Dangers*. Strategies: Oxford University Press.

Bryson, J. J. (2018). Patiency is not a virtue: AI and the design of ethical systems. *Ethics and Information Technology, 20*(1), 15–26.

Eubanks, V. (2018). *Automating Inequality: How High-Tech Tools Profile, Police, and Punish the Poor*. St. Martin's.

Floridi, L. (2014). *The Fourth Revolution: How the Infosphere is Reshaping Human Reality*. Oxford University Press.

Floridi, L. (2015). *The Onlife Manifesto: Being Human in a Hyperconnected Era*. Springer.

Floridi, L. (2016). On human dignity as a foundation for the right to privacy. *Philosophy & Technology, 29*(4), 307–312.

Moor, J. H. (2006a). The nature, importance, and difficulty of machine ethics. *IEEE Intelligent Systems, 21*(4), 18–21.

Moor, J. H. (2006b). Why we need better ethics for emerging technologies. *Ethics and Information Technology, 8*(2), 59–69.

Nissenbaum, H. (2010). *Privacy in Context: Technology, Policy, and the Integrity of Social Life*. Stanford University Press.

Noble, S. U. (2018). *Algorithms of Oppression: How Search Engines Reinforce Racism*. NYU Press.

O'Neil, C. (2016). *Weapons of Math Destruction: How Big Data Increases Inequality and Threatens Democracy*. Crown Publishing Group.

Russell, S., & Norvig, P. (2020). *Artificial Intelligence: A Modern Approach* (4. edn.). Prentice Hall.

Singer, P. (2011). *Practical Ethics* (3. edn.). Cambridge University Press.

Thomson, J. J. (1985). The trolley problem. *The Yale Law Journal, 94*(6), 1395–1415.

Weizenbaum, J. (1976). *Computer Power and Human Reason: From Judgment to Calculation*. W. H. Freeman.

6

The Psychology of Trust: How Safe Do We Feel with AI?

"But those who live in ignorance of all science act by virtue of their natural intelligence better and more nobly than those who either draw false conclusions themselves or trust in the false conclusions of others and thus subject themselves to false and absurd rules."

– Thomas Hobbes

The rapid proliferation of Artificial Intelligence (AI) has brought the human relationship of trust with technology to the center of numerous debates (Weizenbaum, 1976, pp. 213 f.). This sixth chapter will take a closer look at the extent to which we trust algorithms and machines, why we develop this attitude of trust, and what dangers are associated with it. It becomes clear that our sense of security is in a tense relationship with artificial intelligence: On the one hand, we perceive AI as an efficient relief and a seemingly objective authority; on the other hand, risks are increasingly emerging that contribute to psychological insecurity (Noble, 2018, p. 56; O'Neil, 2016, p. 42).

"Trust in Algorithms: A Dangerous Belief?" (Sect. 6.1) shows how a dangerous belief in the perfection and infallibility of algorithms arises. By idealizing technology, we underestimate the biased datasets and hidden programming logics that underlie machine decisions (Bryson, 2018a, b, p. 48). The result is an uncritical trust in AI systems that can weaken our own judgment and, in some cases, even reinforce social injustices (O'Neil, 2016, p. 45).

O. Hoffmann, *Psychology and Artificial Intelligence*,
https://doi.org/10.1007/978-3-662-73147-5_6

Building on this, “AI and the Feeling of Security: Are Machines Infallible?” (Sect. 6.2) explores the sense of security we often associate with AI. Machines are frequently considered emotionless and rational, which is why they are increasingly used in fields such as medicine, transportation, or financial forecasting (Harari, 2018, p. 276). But appearances are deceiving: AI systems are by no means error-free, but rather susceptible to systemic biases and excessive “optimization,” which can have unpleasant or even dangerous consequences (Noble, 2018, p. 91; Weizenbaum, 1976, p. 225). It thus becomes apparent that the underlying assumption that machines are inherently safe and superior is a myth that all too easily undermines our critical thinking.

In “Are We Unlearning Distrust in Dealing with Technology?” (Sect. 6.3), the focus finally shifts to the question of whether we have almost unlearned to distrust technology. Whereas skepticism toward the new once served as a protective mechanism, today we observe a growing willingness to accept technological offerings without thorough scrutiny (Moor, 2006a, b, p. 30). The convenience provided by AI systems and the social ideal of always being up to date digitally foster a more blind trust that leaves little room for critical questioning (Weizenbaum, 1976, p. 229). This development underscores the urgent need to reflect on how we can maintain the necessary degree of skepticism in order not to put our autonomy at risk in a world full of digital decision-making power.

Overall, Chap. 6 opens up a view of the psychological mechanisms of trust in AI and the illusions associated with it. It shows how we are inclined to attribute a superiority to machines that they do not actually possess—and how, in doing so, we could lose the distrust that is so important for our freedom (Bryson, 2018a, b, p. 61). The following pages analyze these developments in detail and ask how we can balance security, efficiency, and critical vigilance in order to use technology autonomously rather than surrendering ourselves to it.

6.1 Trust in Algorithms: A Dangerous Belief?

With the growing importance of Artificial Intelligence (AI) and algorithmic systems in nearly all areas of life—from personalized product recommendations to medical diagnostics and the judiciary—people’s trust in the supposed objectivity and efficiency of these technologies is also increasing (Noble, 2018, p. 56). At first glance, it seems rational to trust machines, since they apply statistical models and can analyze vast amounts of data without—so the assumption goes—being influenced by human biases or emotional fluctuations (Bryson, 2018a, b, p. 48). However, on closer inspection, it becomes clear that this trust is by no means always justified and carries significant risks. The following will show where trust in algorithms originates, why it can be problematic, and how we can find a critical but meaningful approach to AI systems (Weizenbaum, 1976, pp. 213–214).

Trust and the Illusion of Neutrality

The illusion of algorithmic neutrality is one of the most widespread and at the same time most dangerous misconceptions in the discussion about artificial intelligence. It is based on the assumption that algorithms and the underlying data represent an objective reality, free from human subjectivity or susceptibility to error. This notion—that machines are infallible and their results unbiased—rests on the belief that data represent "truth," while human judgments are, by definition, irrational due to emotions and cognitive biases (Harari, 2018, p. 276). Yet a closer look at the creation and functioning of AI systems shows that this assumption does not hold up.

First of all, it must be emphasized that data never arise in a vacuum. They are collected, categorized, and interpreted through human actions and decisions. This process is inevitably shaped by the social, cultural, and economic contexts in which it takes place (Noble, 2018, p. 28). Even in the selection of variables included in a model, value judgments are reflected. These decisions may be made unconsciously, but they play a decisive role in determining the results an algorithm produces. Historical data fed into algorithms are particularly problematic when they reflect past injustices or discrimination. Instead of breaking these patterns, algorithms perpetuate and reinforce them by making predictions based on this data (O'Neil, 2016, p. 45).

A prime area of application is the justice sector, where algorithms are increasingly used for risk assessments. A well-known example is recidivism prediction systems, which are intended to calculate the likelihood of a convicted offender reoffending. These systems use historical data that often contain structural inequalities, such as a disproportionately high number of arrests and convictions in certain population groups, for example among people of color (Noble, 2018, p. 56). When an algorithm uses this data as a basis, it inevitably reproduces the discriminatory patterns contained in the data. Instead of eliminating injustices, the algorithm cements them and gives them the appearance of objectivity. The decisions of such systems are based on statistical correlations, not on an understanding of context or human behavior, which exacerbates injustice rather than mitigating it (Moor, 2006a, b, p. 27).

Another central aspect is the role of human values in the development process of algorithms. Developers, data scientists, and analysts make countless decisions when programming AI systems, which are based not only on technical considerations but also on normative assumptions. Which data are taken into account, how they are weighted, and which target parameters an algorithm is supposed to pursue—all these steps are shaped by value judgments (Weizenbaum, 1976, p. 226). Thus, algorithms are not neutral tools, but expressions of the perspectives and preferences of their creators. An example of this is the weighting of certain features in an algorithm, such as the consideration of income level in credit scoring. Such weightings can unconsciously reproduce and reinforce social prejudices and hierarchies.

The illusion of neutrality is further reinforced by the technical character of algorithms. Their mathematical precision and seemingly infallible logic give them an aura of inviolability. Users tend to accept the results of algorithms as objective, since they often cannot question the technical complexity of these systems. Yet this perception is deceptive. Algorithms are not independent entities that exist apart from human influence; rather, they are products of human decisions and assumptions, embedded in social contexts and power structures.

The consequences of this illusion are far-reaching. Because algorithms are perceived as neutral, they often escape the criticism that is directed at human decisions. This perception carries the risk that social inequalities will be further entrenched through the use of AI, since the technology is seen as an impartial arbiter. A critical examination of how algorithms are designed, trained, and deployed is therefore essential to minimize their potential negative impacts.

Overall, it becomes clear that the notion of algorithmic neutrality is not only naive but also dangerous. It obscures the social and cultural dynamics that flow into their development and application, and hinders a necessary societal discussion about the ethical and political implications of AI. Ultimately, the responsibility for the design and use of algorithms lies with the people who develop and use them—and this responsibility cannot be delegated to the supposedly objective character of the technology.

The Invisibility of Algorithms: "Black Boxes"

With the increasing spread of artificial intelligence and algorithmic decision-making, the challenge of understanding how these systems work is also growing. The term "black box" aptly describes the opacity of modern algorithms, especially in the field of machine learning and deep learning. Systems such as deep neural networks operate on the basis of millions of parameters, whose complex interactions are often no longer comprehensible even to experts (Moor, 2006a, b, p. 34). This lack of explainability poses a serious problem, as it not only limits understanding of the technology but also raises fundamental ethical and practical questions.

The immense complexity of modern algorithms paradoxically often leads to a presumption of trust. Users and even professionals tend to trust the results of these systems, even when they do not fully understand how they work. This effect is reinforced by the widespread assumption that technological systems, especially AI, operate on a superior, almost infallible level of knowledge (O'Neil, 2016, p. 44). But this notion is misleading. The supposed perfection of such systems does not result from an intrinsic understanding of the world, but from the processing of data that can itself contain errors, biases, and gaps. The complexity of the algorithms is often misinterpreted as an indicator of their reliability—a misjudgment that can have serious consequences (Bryson, 2018a, b, p. 52).

The lack of traceability of decisions based on "black box" models is increasingly recognized as a central problem in AI research. While the performance of such systems can be measured and optimized, the internal decision-making process often remains hidden (Floridi, 2016, p. 59). This creates an unhealthy dynamic in which people tend to accept the results without question. The idea that a system operates on the basis of precise data often leads to it being regarded as infallible, even though it is in reality a tool shaped by human assumptions and datasets (Noble, 2018, p. 91). This carries the risk that potential errors or biases in the data go undetected, especially if no one questions how the system works.

The opacity of algorithms has far-reaching consequences for various areas of society. In medicine, one of the most sensitive fields of AI application, serious consequences can arise if a system processes faulty data or overlooks critical information such as pre-existing conditions. A medical AI system trained on a biased data set could, for example, make incorrect diagnoses or recommend inappropriate treatment plans. These errors can be life-threatening if not detected in time (Bryson, 2018a, b, p. 49). The consequences of opacity are even more severe in the field of justice. Algorithms used for offender risk assessment have already shown that they can exhibit systematic biases. Nevertheless, an algorithmic miscarriage of justice often goes unchallenged, as it is perceived as objective and neutral (Moor, 2006a, b, p. 29). This uncritical acceptance of algorithmic decisions not only leads to miscarriages of justice but also undermines trust in the judiciary and the possibility of holding humans accountable. On a psychological level, the invisibility of algorithms is particularly problematic, as it can create a sense of powerlessness and dependency. People tend to overtrust systems they do not understand, since they cannot judge the results themselves. This phenomenon is closely related to the so-called "automation bias," a cognitive distortion in which decisions made by automated systems are perceived as more reliable than human judgments (Brynjolfsson & McAfee, 2014, p. 142). Yet it is precisely this tendency toward uncritical acceptance that amplifies the risks associated with the opacity of algorithms.

The solution to the challenges posed by "black box" models lies not only in technological innovation but also in a fundamental rethinking. The development of "explainable AI" (XAI) aims to make the decision-making processes of algorithms more transparent and understandable. At the same time, however, it is crucial to take into account the social and psychological dimension. Users must be empowered to ask critical questions and not accept algorithmic decisions as unalterable. Education and awareness-raising play a central role here in establishing a healthy balance between trust and critical reflection.

The invisibility of algorithms is one of the greatest challenges in dealing with artificial intelligence. The complexity of modern systems and the associated opacity create not only technical but also psychological and ethical problems. It is therefore essential to reveal the mechanisms of these systems and enable users to question how they work. Only in this way can it be ensured that AI systems are used responsibly and take their place as tools, not as untouchable authorities.

Self-Reinforcing Systems and Feedback Loops

The development and use of algorithms in many areas of life have the potential to bring about profound changes. But the more algorithms are integrated into decision-making processes, the clearer it becomes that they not only act non-neutrally, but can also reproduce and even reinforce existing inequalities and biases. This problem is particularly evident in the mechanisms of self-reinforcing systems and feedback loops, which pose a significant challenge to social justice.

Algorithms based on historical data carry within them the biases contained in that data. These biases often reflect the inequalities prevalent in the societies from which the data originate. For example, if an algorithm is trained to assess credit risk, historical data reflecting discriminatory treatment of certain population groups can cause the algorithm to perpetuate this discrimination. People from disadvantaged groups could, for instance, be systematically classified as "riskier," resulting in their being denied credit. These denials, in turn, flow into future datasets and seemingly confirm the algorithm's original assumption—a self-reinforcing cycle that is difficult to break (O'Neil, 2016, p. 72). This dynamic of reproducing bias is not just a technical problem, but above all a social one. Algorithms are not inherently discriminatory; their decisions are the result of the data they are trained on and the rules set by their developers. If the datasets on which they are based contain historical injustices and prejudices, these are amplified by the algorithms rather than corrected. Noble (2018, p. 28) describes this as a vicious circle that cements the social structures from which the data originate, rather than questioning or reforming them.

The hope that algorithms might be able to eliminate social inequalities is therefore often misplaced. Although algorithms can, in many cases, act more efficiently and consistently than humans, they are ultimately only as "fair" as the data on which they are based. Bryson (2018a, b, p. 50) argues that without deliberate correction mechanisms or carefully curated data foundations, algorithms tend to perpetuate conceptions of humanity based on prejudice and historical privilege. Instead of promoting social justice, they reinforce existing inequalities and often make them less visible, because their decisions are perceived as neutral and objective. Another problem with these feedback loops is that they form the basis for future developments. Data generated by algorithmic decisions influence future datasets and thus future decisions. Harari (2018, p. 276) emphasizes that this creates a spiral in which the original biases are not only preserved but increasingly embedded in the systems. With each iteration of the algorithm, the distorted reality becomes further entrenched, making the possibility of correction ever more difficult.

This problem has not only theoretical but also very concrete practical consequences. In areas such as criminal law, healthcare, or labor market decisions, algorithmic biases can lead to people being systematically disadvantaged. A well-known example is the use of algorithms in the criminal justice system, where certain ethnic groups were classified as a "higher risk" for crime, based on historical data that was already discriminatory (O'Neil, 2016, p. 94). These classifications, in turn, influence how resources are allocated or how court decisions are made, thereby reinforcing the structural inequalities they were actually supposed to eliminate.

The question of how these self-reinforcing systems and feedback loops can be broken is therefore central to the development of ethically responsible

AI. This requires not only technical solutions, such as the implementation of mechanisms for detecting and correcting biases, but also a fundamental societal debate about the values and goals we want to embed in these technologies. Only through conscious reflection and close collaboration between developers, social scientists, and policymakers can it be ensured that algorithms do not become tools of injustice, but instead help to create a more just and inclusive society.

Diffusion of Responsibility and Lack of Accountability

Diffusion of responsibility and lack of accountability in the context of algorithmic decisions represent one of the central challenges in dealing with artificial intelligence. Algorithms that make decisions in more and more areas of daily life are often perceived as autonomous actors. This perception leads to the responsibility for errors or negative consequences of their decisions often remaining diffuse. If, for example, an AI system in medicine makes a misdiagnosis or an autonomous vehicle causes an accident, a complex web of responsibilities arises. In such cases, developers often point out that their systems are merely tools, while operators and users emphasize that they were simply following the system's recommendations. This diffusion of responsibility leads not only to legal uncertainty but also to an ethical gray area in which the question of who is liable for the consequences of an algorithmic decision remains unresolved (Weizenbaum, 1976, p. 225).

Existing legal frameworks are often inadequate to address the challenges of complex algorithmic decision-making processes. Legal systems are traditionally based on clearly defined responsibilities that can be traced back to human actions. But algorithms elude this clear assignment, as they make decisions based on data from a variety of sources, and their functioning often remains opaque to laypeople (Moor, 2006a, b, p. 35). For example, if a fatal misdiagnosis occurs through a medical AI system, the question arises as to whether the software company responsible for development should be held liable, or whether the physician who relied on the system's recommendation should be held accountable. Alternatively, it could be argued that the patient himself bears some responsibility if he blindly trusts the system. This uncertainty not only leads to difficulties in the legal processing of errors but also undermines trust in the systems, although paradoxically public trust in algorithms as technical solutions often persists (Bryson, 2018a, b, p. 61).

The ethical and legal regulation of AI is therefore of central importance in curbing the diffusion of responsibility. Without clear standards, binding certifications, and transparent control mechanisms, there is a risk that companies will offer algorithms whose internal structures are opaque but which nevertheless make far-reaching decisions. Wrong decisions then often remain without legal consequences for the responsible actors. Especially in sensitive areas such as medicine or the transport sector, where wrong decisions can have immediate effects on people's lives, it is essential to establish clear liability rules (Floridi, 2014, p. 59). One possible solution could be the introduction of binding quality checks, as already established in the pharmaceutical or medical technology sectors. However, not only the performance indicators of an AI must be considered here, but also the entire development process, including data collection, modeling, and practical implementation (Noble, 2018, p. 111).

The introduction of such testing standards could also help to strengthen trust in AI systems in the long term. It is crucial that regulatory bodies not only pay attention to the results of algorithms but also critically evaluate the underlying processes. The focus should be on the transparency and traceability of the systems, since opacity is a main factor in the current diffusion of responsibility. Only through a holistic approach that includes technical as well as ethical and social aspects can it be ensured that algorithms are not only efficient and powerful but also used responsibly. In this way, the increasing use of AI in critical areas of life could be perceived not only as technological progress but also as a step toward a more just and safer society in which responsibility is clearly assigned.

Psychological Mechanisms: Why Do We Trust Machines More Than Ourselves?

The increasing use of technology in decision-making processes raises a fundamental question: Why do people often trust machines more than themselves or other people? This phenomenon can be traced back to various psychological mechanisms that are deeply rooted in our perception and decision-making.

A central mechanism is the so-called **automation bias,** which describes how people tend to place more trust in automated systems than in human judgments—even when the performance of human experts is equivalent or even superior (Harari, 2018, pp. 276–277). This bias is based on the assumption that machines act more precisely, quickly, and objectively than humans, who are seen as emotional, error-prone, and biased (Bryson, 2018a, b, p. 52). In practice, however, it is often overlooked that algorithms themselves can be influenced by human assumptions, faulty data, or unbalanced programming decisions. Thus, the supposed neutrality of machines is often an illusion.

Another crucial factor is the **myth of perfection** that clings to technology. People are aware of their own weaknesses and fallibility and therefore seek a system that appears superior to these shortcomings (Weizenbaum, 1976, p. 213). Machines and algorithms are often associated with perfection because they show no emotions, do not experience fatigue, and possess seemingly infinite computing power. This perception reinforces trust in their decisions, even when those decisions are not always comprehensible or are based on faulty foundations.

This trust in technology also serves a relieving function. Delegating responsibility to an automated system means a reduction in one's own cognitive and emotional burden for many people. Decisions made by algorithms seem less burdensome, as the responsibility for possible wrong decisions no longer lies entirely with the person themselves. However, this "relief of responsibility" leads to a lack of critical questioning and active engagement with the machine's decisions (O'Neil, 2016, p. 42). Instead, people tend to accept the decisions of algorithms without question, which in some cases can lead to serious misjudgments.

Another psychological element is the need for **control** and **predictability**. Machines appear predictable because they are based on fixed algorithms and are not influenced by spontaneous emotions or individual fluctuations. This gives users a sense of security that is often lacking in interpersonal relationships or human decision-making processes. Ironically, this supposed security often leads people to underestimate their own judgment and neglect critical reflection on technological systems.

The long-term effects of this uncritical trust in machines could be serious. If people increasingly relinquish their ability to make independent decisions to machines, there is a creeping erosion of human autonomy. The role of humans as active decision-makers could give way to passive acceptance of technical directives. This process carries not only individual but also societal risks, as the power over decisions increasingly shifts to those who program and control the algorithms.

In summary, it becomes clear that trust in machines is not justified solely by their objective capabilities, but is significantly influenced by psychological mechanisms. Automation bias, the myth of perfection, the relief of responsibility, and the need for predictability create a dynamic in which machines are perceived as infallible decision-makers. To meet the challenges of an increasingly technologized world, it is essential to recognize these mechanisms and to foster a critical engagement with the role of technology in our decision-making processes.

The Deceptive Sense of Security

The deceptive sense of security conveyed by artificial intelligence and algorithmic systems is based on the widespread assumption that machines operate objectively, efficiently, and flawlessly. This assumption, though tempting, is a dangerous oversimplification. Algorithms and AI systems are only as good as the data on which they are based and the logics by which they are programmed. In this context, the sources of error that permeate these systems are often underestimated or ignored.

One of the central challenges is the quality of the underlying data. Data used to train AI systems can be outdated, incomplete, or erroneous. For example, historical data may contain social biases and discrimination, which are then incorporated into the AI's decisions (Noble, 2018, p. 56). Such distortions often go unnoticed until the consequences of these decisions become visible, which can have catastrophic effects in safety-critical or ethically sensitive contexts. Unlike human misjudgments, which are often quickly recognized through discussion or objection, algorithmic errors act systemically and can have far-reaching effects before they are identified (Moor, 2006a, b, p. 29).

Furthermore, errors in programming logic or unintended interactions between algorithms can occur, causing systems to act in unexpected or undesirable ways. A well-known example is the "black box" problem in neural networks, which makes it difficult even for developers to trace the exact decision paths of the AI. This lack of transparency increases the risk that faulty or unethical decisions are made without being easily reviewed or corrected.

The importance of human oversight over AI systems therefore cannot be overstated. Humans play a crucial role in validating and monitoring algorithmic decisions. Especially in safety-critical areas such as air traffic control, medical diagnostics, or the judiciary, it is essential that human experts continuously review the results of AI and intervene to correct them where necessary (Bryson, 2018a, b, p. 52). Without this active oversight, errors could go undetected, potentially with devastating consequences.

However, such oversight requires significant investments of time, resources, and expertise. Yet companies or institutions are not always willing to provide the necessary means, especially when short-term economic benefits are prioritized. Floridi (2016, pp. 59–60) emphasizes that the tendency to implement AI systems without adequate supervision increases the risk that these systems not only reproduce errors but also dilute social and ethical responsibility. In such cases, delegating decision-making processes to AI systems can lead to a lack of accountability with serious consequences for individuals and societies.

Ultimately, the deceptive sense of security conveyed by AI shows that the notion of technological infallibility is a dangerous myth. The development and deployment of AI systems require a deep understanding of their potential weaknesses and risks. Only by combining technological innovation with human reflection can the benefits of AI be realized while minimizing the risks. Ongoing review, critical questioning, and, where necessary, correction of algorithmic decisions remain indispensable components of responsible AI use.

Paths to Reflective Trust

The increasing integration of artificial intelligence into diverse areas of life demands a critical approach to this technology. Trust in AI is not a static quantity, but a dynamic concept shaped by technological, societal, and individual factors. To avoid blind dependencies and misuse, reflective trust is required—one that encompasses both technological innovation and ethical and social reflection. A key technological development contributing to this is so-called Explainable AI (XAI). This approach aims to make algorithmic decisions more transparent by breaking them down into understandable steps and presenting them in a comprehensible manner (Moor, 2006a, b, p. 36). This traceability promotes critical engagement with machine decisions and strengthens trust in their application without losing human decision-making authority (Noble, 2018, p. 111). In addition, XAI enables potential errors or biases in the decision-making process to be identified and addressed at an early stage. Combined with "human-in-the-loop" approaches, in which humans remain actively involved in the decision-making process, it is ensured that ultimate responsibility is not transferred solely to machines. In addition to technological approaches, the definition of responsibility plays a decisive role. Legal and ethical frameworks are necessary to create clear liability structures for the use of AI (Weizenbaum, 1976, pp. 227–228). It is crucial to clarify responsibilities among developers, manufacturers, and users. Especially in safety-critical areas, such as healthcare or autonomous mobility, binding norms and standards must be established to ensure the accuracy and fairness of the systems (Harari, 2018, p. 279). Public institutions and regulatory authorities can serve as central bodies to promote responsible use of AI.

Another key to reflective trust in AI is transparency regarding the data used. Datasets that form the basis of machine decisions are often biased or incomplete, which can lead to discriminatory or unethical outcomes (Noble, 2018, p. 56). Careful examination and disclosure of data sources, as well as active monitoring for biases, are therefore essential. The composition of development teams plays an important role here: diversity within teams can help bring in different perspectives and counteract dominant prejudices (Bryson, 2018a, b, p. 61). This is particularly relevant since algorithmic decisions often reinforce existing social and cultural inequalities rather than eliminate them.

However, reflective trust in AI requires not only technological and organizational measures, but also a critical approach at the individual level. Users must be aware that algorithms are not all-knowing entities, but tools that can be misleading or erroneous under certain conditions (O'Neil, 2016, p. 42). Recommendations from algorithms should therefore not be regarded as absolute truths, but as guides that require critical scrutiny. A healthy skepticism toward AI systems can help avoid misjudgments and preserve human judgment (Weizenbaum, 1976, p. 213).

Trust in AI is a double-edged sword. On the one hand, it enables the efficient use of modern technologies; on the other, it carries the risk of surrendering one's own decision-making freedom and responsibility through blind trust. AI systems are neither objective nor flawless, but always the product of the people who develop them and the data they use (Bryson, 2018a, b, p. 48). To harness the benefits of these technologies without ignoring their potential risks, an informed and critical approach is indispensable (Noble, 2018, p. 111). Reflective trust means recognizing the capabilities and limitations of AI, clearly defining responsibility, and establishing transparent standards. Only in this way can we prevent the illusion of an infallible machine from undermining human judgment and obscuring ethical responsibility (O'Neil, 2016, p. 45). AI is a powerful tool, but ultimately, humans remain responsible for its use and the consequences of its deployment.

6.2 AI and the Feeling of Security: Are Machines Infallible?

The rapid proliferation of artificial intelligence in nearly all areas of social, economic, and private life has led to a profound transformation of our sense of security (Noble, 2018, p. 56). Where machines were once merely tools to support human decision-making, they are now increasingly taking on autonomous functions—from self-driving cars and medical diagnoses to complex financial forecasts (Bryson, 2018a, b, p. 48). For many people, this development holds great promise: since AI systems are based on data, statistical models, and algorithmic efficiency, they are presumed to be more reliable and infallible than the human mind (Harari, 2018, p. 276). But how justified is the trust in this "superior" technology really? And what psychological tensions arise as we increasingly rely on machine-made decisions?

The Illusion of Perfection: Why Do We Trust AI?

The fascination with artificial intelligence is fueled by the notion that machines act more rationally, without emotion, and thus more objectively than humans (Weizenbaum, 1976, pp. 213–214). While human decisions are often influenced by emotions, fatigue, or cognitive biases, AI appears to be the ideal alternative, making seemingly incorruptible and efficient decisions based on data (Bryson, 2018a, b, p. 48). However, this perception of supposed perfection is often an illusion, as it overlooks the inherent weaknesses of machine systems. These weaknesses are of a different nature than human ones, but are by no means less problematic (O'Neil, 2016, p. 42). The illusion of AI's infallibility not only leads to a deceptive sense of security, but also to a reduced willingness to critically question the outcomes of machine-made decisions.

Machine learning, the foundation of modern AI systems, is based on algorithms recognizing patterns in large datasets and deriving predictions or decisions from them. The basic principle applies: "Garbage in, garbage out" (Weizenbaum, 1976, p. 220). The quality of the data is crucial for the system's performance. However, if biased, incomplete, or prejudiced data are used, the resulting models will uncritically reproduce the same errors (Noble, 2018, p. 28). This poses a serious problem, as the data themselves often reflect historical inequalities and societal power structures.

A prominent example of such biases can be seen in the use of AI in law enforcement. Algorithms used to assess the risk of recidivism among offenders often rely on historical data about arrests and crimes. However, these data are frequently shaped by systemic biases, such as discriminatory policing practices or social inequalities (O'Neil, 2016, p. 45). An AI system trained on this basis cannot recognize or correct such biases. Instead, it reinforces them by making supposedly "objective" decisions that in reality reproduce existing injustices (Noble, 2018, p. 56). This leads to a dangerous amplification of social inequalities under the guise of neutrality. Similar challenges arise in healthcare, a field where AI is increasingly used to support diagnosis and therapy. The performance of such systems depends largely on the data with which they are trained. If these data predominantly come from certain population groups, this can result in AI systems being less reliable for other groups (Weizenbaum, 1976, pp. 225–226). A well-known example is the poor detection of heart attacks in women by AI-based diagnostic systems, as these often rely on datasets that mainly represent male patients. In such cases, trust in the objective superiority of AI can have fatal consequences, especially when faulty diagnoses or inappropriate treatment recommendations go unnoticed for a long time because no one questions the authority of the machine (Floridi, 2016, pp. 59–60).

The notion that AI systems operate free from human biases is a paradox, since they are created by humans and are therefore inevitably influenced by human perspectives and assumptions. The algorithms themselves are not capable of considering the context or social implications of their decisions. They do not assess whether the data on which they are based are fair or representative. At the same time, trust in their apparent neutrality leads to their results rarely being critically questioned. This deceptive trust carries the risk that AI systems increasingly serve as substitutes for human decisions, even though they cannot grasp the fundamental social and ethical dimensions of a problem (O'Neil, 2016, p. 50).

The illusion of perfection in AI systems is based on the assumption that algorithms operate free from human weaknesses. In reality, however, they are just as susceptible to biases and errors—these do not arise from emotions or fatigue, but from the quality and context of the data on which they are based. Blind trust in the objectivity of AI can therefore not only reinforce existing injustices, but also displace the critical reflection of human decisions. A conscious engagement with the limitations and weaknesses of AI is essential to break the illusion of perfection and to ensure its responsible use.

The Danger of Over-Optimization: When Machines Are Too Consistent

Machines and algorithms are programmed with a clear goal: maximum efficiency. Whether it is about reducing transport times, increasing profits, or improving the accuracy of predictions, the ability of artificial intelligence to process data on a scale impossible for the human brain gives it an immense advantage (Bryson, 2018a, b, p. 49). Yet this goal orientation harbors an inherent danger: machines do not act with an awareness of the social, moral, or contextual nuances that often shape human decisions. For example, an autonomous vehicle programmed to get from point A to point B as quickly as possible might perform risky maneuvers that achieve the goal but increase the risk of accidents or violate ethical principles (Harari, 2018, p. 278). This focus on pure goal attainment, without consideration of side effects, leads to what is known as over-optimization.

Over-optimization is not only a technical challenge, but also an ethical and psychological one. Machines cannot understand or prioritize moral dilemmas, as they are based solely on algorithms that weight certain parameters. These parameters often reflect the values or goals of their developers, but are not able to make situational decisions that go beyond pure logic (Moor, 2006a, b, p. 27). For example, an algorithm optimized for credit risk assessment could systematically disadvantage certain social groups due to biased datasets, even if this was not intended in the original design (O'Neil, 2016, p. 72). The machine follows its goal—but the goal itself is not questioned.

This problem becomes particularly evident in areas where social or moral consequences play a central role. For instance, an AI-driven healthcare system aiming to optimize resource use could disadvantage elderly or chronically ill patients, as they might be perceived as "inefficient" within the system. Such decisions are not based on empathy or moral reflection, but on the cold logic of algorithms that are solely tuned for efficiency. In such contexts, it becomes clear that machines are not just tools, but that their decisions can have profound impacts on human lives and values.

The idea that machines could automatically achieve "the best for everyone" through perfect calibration and advanced programming is a myth. Efficiency and morality are not synonyms. While efficiency aims to achieve maximum results with minimal effort, morality requires the consideration of values, feelings, and long-term consequences (Noble, 2018, p. 111). However, machines lack the ability to make such judgments, as they possess neither intuition nor a sense of ethical responsibility. What machines lack is the human context—the ability to see the bigger picture and to base decisions not only on data, but also on empathy, experience, and social intelligence.

In this context, it becomes clear that over-optimization carries not only technical but also profound social risks. Today, as algorithms increasingly make decisions, it is crucial to recognize and regulate the limits of machine logic. Humans remain indispensable for setting the moral and ethical parameters and for ensuring that technological efficiency does not triumph over human values. Efficiency is important—but it must never replace the responsibility inherent in human decision-making.

Blind Trust and the Loss of Human Control

The phenomenon of blind trust in technologies has become increasingly significant in recent decades. In psychology, this describes the human tendency to grant automated systems excessive authority, even when rational doubts or intuitive concerns are present. This automation bias often appears in everyday situations, such as when using navigation systems. Many people follow the instructions of such systems even when the suggested routes are obviously illogical or inefficient. This behavior illustrates how technologies not only influence our decisions, but can also gradually undermine our ability for independent reflection and critical evaluation (Weizenbaum, 1976, p. 213).

A central psychological mechanism behind this blind trust is the perception of machines as objective and infallible. While human decisions are often seen as error-prone and influenced by emotions, technology is perceived as rational, precise, and neutral. This creates an apparent safety zone that can, however, be deceptive. For as studies have shown, algorithmic systems are by no means free from biases and errors—instead, they inherit the prejudices and weaknesses of their developers or the data on which they are based (Noble, 2018, p. 56). Nevertheless, people tend to ignore their own reasoning and intuitive warning signals when an automated decision is present. This not only leads to a loss of autonomy, but can have serious consequences in critical contexts such as medical diagnostics or credit approval.

The further AI becomes established in decision-critical areas, the more serious the risk of loss of control becomes. A vivid example is the use of AI in medicine, where algorithms are increasingly used to make diagnoses or create treatment plans. While these systems can undoubtedly be helpful, there is a danger that medical professionals will blindly follow the machine's recommendations without critically questioning them. In such situations, subtle symptoms or individual circumstances of the patient, which are not fully represented in the data, may be overlooked. Humans increasingly become passive users, while the machine takes control (Floridi, 2014, p. 59). A similar risk exists in banking, where AI-based algorithms assess creditworthiness. These systems analyze large amounts of data and make decisions in fractions of a second, making them appear more efficient than human analysts. Yet here, too, it becomes apparent that reliance on machine-made decisions can lead to the reproduction or even amplification of discrimination. Data-driven biases or faulty assumptions in the algorithm are often only noticed once the consequences have already occurred. The ability to detect and correct such errors in advance is severely limited by blind trust in the infallibility of the machine (Noble, 2018, p. 62). The long-term psychological effects of this dynamic are profound. The more often we rely on machine-made decisions, the more we lose the ability to think independently and to question critically. This not only undermines our individual decision-making autonomy, but also changes our collective understanding of responsibility. When decisions are delegated without understanding the basis for those decisions, a dangerous form of alienation arises, both from the technology and from ourselves. The question of who ultimately bears responsibility for wrong decisions becomes increasingly blurred, as humans may formally act as decision-makers, but in fact merely rubber-stamp the results of an algorithmic process.

To address these challenges, it is necessary to create a more balanced relationship between humans and machines. Technologies should be seen as tools that complement our abilities, rather than replace them. This requires not only an awareness of the limitations and pitfalls of AI, but also an active promotion of critical thinking and technological literacy. Only in this way can we prevent blind trust in technologies from leading to a loss of human control and autonomy—with potentially irreversible consequences for our society and our self-understanding.

Psychological Tensions: Between Comfort and Latent Uncertainty

The integration of artificial intelligence into our daily lives creates a multifaceted dynamic between perceived comfort and subtle insecurity. On the one hand, AI systems offer unprecedented efficiency and convenience, giving us a sense of control and security. They facilitate everyday tasks, optimize work processes, and provide personalized solutions in areas such as healthcare, communication, and consumer behavior (Noble, 2018, p. 28). This apparent security is based on the assumption that technologies operate reliably and neutrally, which strengthens the belief in an objective and infallible machine. Yet behind this façade of efficiency lurks a deeper uncertainty, triggered by the opacity and complexity of the systems. Many users do not fully understand how AI works, which means that trust in these technologies is accompanied by an underlying skepticism (Bryson, 2018a, b, p. 52).

The phenomenon of security and insecurity coexisting becomes particularly evident in situations where people delegate decisions or responsibility to machines. This ambivalence is often hard to recognize, as the convenience and benefits offered by AI overshadow the underlying risks and uncertainties. Nevertheless, the fear of technical failure, unforeseen wrong decisions, or even manipulative algorithms persists. The fact that AI systems are based on data and algorithms created by humans means that they are not free from biases or errors. This systemic uncertainty can undermine users' trust, even as they enjoy the benefits of the technology.

A central aspect of this dynamic is the so-called "control paradox." This concept describes how the perception of control shifts as people become increasingly dependent on technology. Originally conceived as a tool to strengthen human autonomy, AI can become a force that undermines that autonomy. As we increasingly delegate responsibility to AI systems, we reduce our own ability to make informed decisions and to solve complex problems independently (Weizenbaum, 1976, p. 213). While machines relieve us of decisions, we simultaneously lose the ability to critically question those decisions and to fully understand their consequences. In the long term, this leads to an erosion of our sovereignty and sense of security, as we become increasingly dependent on technologies whose decisions we cannot always comprehend (Floridi, 2014, p. 59).

These psychological tensions between comfort and insecurity have far-reaching effects on our perception and behavior. On the one hand, we tend to blindly trust the decisions of machines because they are efficient and seemingly objective. On the other hand, awareness of possible errors or manipulations fuels a deep, often repressed sense of insecurity. This cognitive dissonance—the conflict between the desire for security and the latent fear of losing control—is a defining feature of our relationship with AI. It forces us to critically reflect not only on the benefits, but also on the risks and ethical implications of the technology.

Overall, it becomes clear that our psychological relationship with AI is shaped by a complex interplay between trust, skepticism, and the need for self-determination. As long as we are unable to fully understand and critically question the mechanisms and limitations of AI, the tension between comfort and insecurity will persist. This highlights the need to foster skills for dealing with AI at both the individual and societal level, in order to enable a balanced and reflective approach to this technology.

Infallibility as Myth and Principle of Responsibility

The notion of infallibility in relation to artificial intelligence has become a persistent myth in the general public and often even among experts. This is mainly because AI systems demonstrate extraordinary precision and efficiency in many areas, such as medical diagnostics, financial analysis, or the optimization of logistics processes (Harari, 2018, p. 276). Yet these achievements often obscure the fundamental weaknesses and limitations of such systems. The illusion of infallibility arises not only from fascination with technological possibilities, but also from a lack of critical reflection on the inherent limitations and potential dangers of AI.

One of the central weaknesses lies in the underlying data that AI systems use for learning and decision-making. Data are never neutral; they always reflect the historical and social conditions under which they were collected (O'Neil, 2016, p. 72). Biased datasets can cause AI systems not only to reproduce but even to reinforce existing injustices and discrimination. An example is the use of AI in criminal justice systems, where predictive algorithms in some cases have systematically disadvantaged ethnic minorities (Noble, 2018, p. 56). Such outcomes are problematic not only because they reinforce inequalities, but also because they are often difficult to understand. The opacity of many AI models—often referred to as the "black box" problem—makes it difficult to grasp the exact mechanisms behind a decision (Bryson, 2018a, b, p. 48). Another problem is the psychological tendency of humans to place more trust in automated systems than is rationally justified. Studies show that many people perceive the decisions of AI systems as objective and unbiased, even though this perception often does not reflect reality (Moor, 2006a, b, pp. 29–30). This so-called automation bias leads to algorithmic decisions often being accepted without critical scrutiny, even when they contain obvious errors. Blind trust in AI can not only foster individual misjudgments, but also increase societal risk when AI systems fail in safety-critical areas such as transportation or healthcare.

In light of these challenges, a reflective and responsible approach to AI is essential. This begins with acknowledging the fact that, as impressive as they may be, AI systems are always designed and trained by humans and therefore can never be completely free from human biases or sources of error (Weizenbaum, 1976, p. 229). A key element of such an approach is the clear assignment of responsibilities. As machines increasingly make autonomous decisions, responsibility for their consequences must not remain unclear or be divided among developers, users, and companies to the point where ultimately no one is accountable. Equally important is the promotion of critical skills among the general population. It is not enough for experts to understand the limitations and risks of AI; laypeople must also be empowered to critically question algorithmic systems and evaluate their results. This could be achieved through educational campaigns, transparent regulation, and a broader societal debate that focuses not only on the benefits but also on the potential dangers of AI. Only when people learn to deal with the shortcomings of AI can they harness its potential in a constructive way.

Ultimately, the central challenge lies in creating a relationship between humans and machines that is not shaped by illusions of infallibility, but by a realistic understanding of the strengths and weaknesses of both sides. Machines can support, relieve, and even surpass humans in many areas, but they remain tools that depend on human oversight and responsibility. Fascination with the technical achievements of AI must not lead us to overlook its limitations or neglect the necessary control mechanisms. Only in this way can a sustainable and trustworthy coexistence of humans and machines arise, based on respect and responsibility—instead of a naïve belief in the perfection of technology.

6.3 Are We Unlearning Distrust in Our Interaction with Technology?

Throughout the history of encounters with technology, a common thread has long been that people initially approached new inventions and machines with caution (Weizenbaum, 1976, pp. 213–214). This healthy skepticism protected against rash adoption and prevented society from ignoring the harmful consequences of technological innovations. In recent decades, however, a shift has occurred: The mere presence of digital devices and services in our daily lives is largely taken for granted—indeed, as indispensable. Mobile phones, social media, algorithms that make recommendations to us—all of these have crept into our lives with a matter-of-factness that is rarely reflected upon (Bryson, 2018a, b, p. 48). This is accompanied by a new form of dependency, in which we feel the impulse to critically question things less and less often.

This change is evident not only in how naturally we use technologies, but also in how we react when something goes wrong. When data breaches, manipulations, or obvious malfunctions occur, we often feel only brief outrage—before quickly returning to rely on the efficiency and convenience of technology (O'Neil, 2016, p. 42). The question of whether we are unlearning distrust toward technology thus points to a gradual cultural and psychological development that fundamentally shapes our relationship to digital achievements.

Over the course of evolution, humans developed strategies to protect themselves against unknown dangers. Reflective doubt or distrust toward the new enables a conscious assessment of potential risks (Harari, 2018, p. 276). In the context of technology, this protective mechanism has historically played an important role: Whether with the introduction of the steam engine or radio, the question of societal, economic, and health consequences always arose first, before broad acceptance could take place (Weizenbaum, 1976, p. 225). This evolutionary caution helped to carefully weigh the risks of new technologies and to question their integration into social structures. This is also reflected in the warnings of early technology ethicists, who cautioned against uncontrolled progress. Weizenbaum (1976, p. 230) emphasized that machines should always remain tools actively controlled by humans, rather than blindly following their "logic." Reflection and distrust toward new developments are therefore not only expressions of cultural restraint, but an essential survival strategy.

However, distrust serves not only as protection against potential dangers, but is also an instrument of self-determination. Through skepticism, people maintain their autonomy by questioning the motives and backgrounds of new developments (Moor, 2006a, b, p. 28). The ability to maintain critical distance allows one not to be subsumed by technological imperatives and to actively decide on one's own use and integration of technology.

If this inner voice of doubt is lacking, we run the risk of passively submitting to the structures and interests behind the technologies (Noble, 2018, p. 28). This danger is especially tangible in the age of artificial intelligence: Algorithms designed to make our lives easier can, unnoticed, influence decision-making processes, introduce invisible control mechanisms, and reinforce social inequalities. Noble (2018, p. 36) points out that algorithms often reproduce existing prejudices and power structures because they are based on historical data that are not neutral. The absence of healthy distrust in such cases means that we unconsciously expose ourselves to these mechanisms. The psychological dynamics behind this development are complex. Technology conveys a sense of security and control that is often a deceptive illusion. People tend to trust technical systems more than other people, because machines are perceived as objective and incorruptible. Yet this assumption overlooks the fact that every technology is the product of human decisions and interests.

The gradual erosion of distrust toward technology has far-reaching consequences. On the one hand, it weakens the capacity for critical reflection, which can lead to individuals and societies becoming increasingly susceptible to manipulation. On the other hand, dependence on seemingly error-free systems can result in the atrophy of human problem-solving and decision-making abilities. This affects not only individual competencies, but also the collective ability to critically accompany and regulate technological developments.

Reviving healthy doubt is therefore not only a matter of personal autonomy, but also a societal necessity. Only through reflective distrust can we ensure that technologies support us rather than control us. However, this distrust should not turn into rejection or technological hostility. Rather, a balanced approach is needed, in which both the advantages and the risks of new technologies are consciously reflected upon. Turkle (2011, p. 89) argues that technological achievements can only truly contribute to human progress if they are considered in the context of ethical and social values.

The loss of healthy distrust toward technology represents one of the greatest challenges of our time. The seductive power of efficiency and convenience in modern technologies must not lead us to abandon our capacity for critical reflection. Reviving healthy doubt is not only a protective mechanism, but also an expression of self-determination and humanity. Only through a conscious and reflective engagement with technologies can we ensure that humans remain in control.

The Seduction of Convenience: Why We Trust

The seduction of convenience is a phenomenon deeply rooted in the psychological and societal structures of modern societies. It reflects not only our individual preferences for saving time and comfort, but also the systematic shift of decision-making processes from humans to machines. As pleasant as this shift may seem, it carries far-reaching psychological and ethical consequences. Technologies designed to relieve us of everyday burdens shape not only our behavior, but also our perception of control and responsibility.

A key reason for trusting such technologies is the fact that they allow us to achieve more with less effort. When time pressure is omnipresent, every opportunity to simplify tasks is seen as a gain (Bryson, 2018a, b, p. 49). But this convenience comes at a price. The regular use of algorithmic assistance leads to a phenomenon that could be called "technological dependency": The ability to handle tasks independently is gradually unlearned. People increasingly rely on external systems, thereby weakening their own cognitive and practical abilities. This dynamic is not only significant on an individual level, but also has societal implications, as it can undermine the autonomy of entire groups. A central element that reinforces this development is the myth of neutrality. The idea that machines cannot have biases because they are based on data is tempting but deceptive. Algorithms are developed by humans, and the data on which they are based are products of social and historical contexts. Studies have shown that machine learning unconsciously adopts the biases of its creators and the datasets used (Noble, 2018, p. 56). This has already led to problematic decisions in various areas, such as lending, criminal justice predictions, or hiring processes (O'Neil, 2016, p. 45). Nevertheless, the belief that algorithms are objective and infallible persists. This belief is actively promoted by technology providers, as it strengthens user trust and legitimizes the use of these systems. The psychological dynamic behind this trust is closely linked to the human tendency to avoid cognitive dissonance. By assuming that decisions made by machines are correct, we avoid the uncomfortable task of questioning their basis or critically evaluating their results. The comfort provided by machines thus becomes a kind of mental shortcut that spares us from taking responsibility for our own decisions. This "delegation of thinking," however, is not without risk. It weakens our ability to solve complex problems and makes us vulnerable to manipulation by the structures that control the machines (Moor, 2006a, b, p. 34).

The seduction of convenience also has profound societal effects. The normalization of algorithmic decision-making leads to the systems that guide our daily decisions becoming increasingly opaque. These "black box systems" make it difficult not only for laypeople, but also for experts, to understand the exact mechanisms behind the algorithms. This results in a loss of transparency and accountability, which in turn undermines trust in democratic and institutional processes. Paradoxically, this increases trust in the algorithms themselves, as users see no alternatives or lack the capacity to question the systems.

Solving this dilemma requires greater awareness of the limitations and risks of algorithmic systems. Education and information about the functioning and potential biases of AI and algorithms must become an integral part of modern societies. Only in this way can we ensure that the seduction of convenience does not lead to a dependency that ultimately costs us our autonomy. At the same time, regulatory mechanisms must be established to ensure transparency and accountability in the development and implementation of these technologies. Ultimately, it is up to us to decide whether we use technology as a tool or allow ourselves to be dominated by it.

The Invisible Mechanisms: Algorithms as Silent Decision-Makers

Modern algorithms and AI systems operate in ways that are both fascinating and unsettling. Whereas earlier technologies were immediately perceptible through their physical presence or obvious handling, today's technological systems often operate unnoticed in the background. They analyze, evaluate, and steer decisions that shape our lives, without us being aware of their mechanisms or even their existence (Bryson, 2018a, b, p. 52). This invisibility creates an illusion of neutrality, in which the decisions of machines are perceived as objective and infallible. In reality, however, algorithms operate according to specific guidelines and interests set by their developers. Users experience the results of these calculations as tailor-made recommendations—whether in the form of personalized advertising, optimized search results, or customized entertainment offerings—without questioning how these came about.

This invisibility has far-reaching consequences. It not only enables comfort and convenience, but also carries the risk that we lose our capacity for critical reflection. For while algorithms can serve as supportive tools, in many cases they act as silent decision-makers that shape our perception of the world. News feeds, search results, or product recommendations are curated to match our supposed preferences, yet the filtering processes underlying these decisions remain opaque (O'Neil, 2016, p. 72). This selective presentation of information leads us to increasingly live in a "filter bubble," where we see only content that matches our existing beliefs and preferences (Pariser, 2011, p. 45).

While individuals enjoy the convenience and time savings of personalized offerings, the ability to perceive alternative perspectives and to question critically diminishes. This is particularly problematic in social and political contexts, where the dissemination of information and opinions is crucial for a functioning democracy. When algorithms deliberately prioritize or suppress news, they can subtly but effectively influence public opinion and distort public discourse (Noble, 2018, p. 91). This manipulation often occurs so subtly that it goes unnoticed, establishing a new form of control: a control not based on coercion or direct influence, but on the skillful management of what we perceive.

The psychological effects of this development are as significant as the technological ones. Humans tend to view machines as objective and rational, especially when their decision-making processes are complex and inscrutable (Fogg, 2003, p. 33). This assumption can lead us to trust the decisions of algorithms more than our own judgment. At the same time, our perception of the world is increasingly shaped by these systems, which can lead to a gradual loss of autonomy. The process of independently seeking and evaluating information is replaced by the passive acceptance of suggestions presented to us. This development not only weakens our critical thinking skills, but can also lead to a sense of powerlessness when decisions are increasingly made by systems we do not understand. This dynamic becomes especially problematic when algorithms not only make passive suggestions, but actively make decisions on our behalf. Examples of this can be found in lending, where algorithms decide who receives a loan and who does not, or in criminal justice, where AI systems predict the likelihood of recidivism (Eubanks, 2018, p. 88). Such decisions have real, often serious consequences for those affected, and yet there is often a lack of transparency and accountability. Who is ultimately responsible when an algorithm makes discriminatory decisions? Programmers, users, or the system itself? These questions often remain unanswered, making the invisibility of decision-making processes even more problematic.

The increasing integration of algorithms into our daily lives therefore requires a critical examination of their role and impact. It is not enough to view them as mere tools that make our lives easier. Rather, we must recognize that they actively influence our perceptions and decisions. This requires not only technological competence, but also psychological sensitivity. For only by understanding the invisible mechanisms behind algorithms can we critically question and, if necessary, regulate their impact on our autonomy and society. Otherwise, we risk living in a future where our decisions are increasingly determined by systems we can neither see nor control.

Causes of the Decline in Distrust

The development of an increasingly uncritical approach to technology can be traced to several factors, encompassing both psychological and societal dimensions. In particular, the influence of digital environments, the cultural evaluation of distrust, and the subtle manipulation by technology providers play a central role. The generations born after the turn of the millennium have grown up in a world where digital technologies are omnipresent. For these so-called "digital natives," the presence of smart devices, AI-powered assistants, and algorithmic decisions is a given. Technologies such as smartphones, voice assistants, or social networks are not just tools, but integral parts of their lives. The intuitive use of these systems often occurs without critical questioning of their functioning or possible consequences (Moor, 2006a, b, p. 30).

In contrast, for older generations, the introduction of new technologies was often accompanied by an awareness of their potential risks. The transition from analog to digital systems required adaptation, which raised questions and skepticism. Younger generations, on the other hand, experience no such rupture, but rather a continuity—from interactive toys in childhood to fully automated devices in adulthood. This seamless embedding in digital environments means that distrust toward technology does not arise in the first place. This development is reinforced by the growing user-friendliness of technologies, which are designed as "invisible systems" and conceal their complexity from users (Harari, 2018, p. 277). The psychological consequence is a reduced willingness to reflect, which further widens the gap between users and developers of technologies.

Parallel to the changing relationship with technology, a cultural devaluation of distrust has developed in many societies. Trust is considered a fundamental component of a functioning society. It is often seen as the basis for progress, cooperation, and social cohesion. This positive evaluation of trust is reflected both in interpersonal relationships and in the way we approach technology.

Distrust, on the other hand, is often perceived as an obstacle. It is associated with pessimism, regression, or even conspiracy theories. Especially in technological contexts, skeptics are quickly labeled as enemies of progress. Yet a certain degree of distrust is not only healthy, but necessary to question power imbalances and potential abuse (Weizenbaum, 1976, p. 213). The psychologist Joseph Weizenbaum warned early on that blind faith in technological systems could lead people to relinquish their autonomy and critical thinking skills. In a technological environment increasingly dominated by large corporations, this dynamic is particularly problematic. Companies such as Google, Meta, or Amazon have not only developed the tools we use daily, but also shape the narratives that foster our trust in these technologies. The rhetoric of "infallible technology" and the emphasis on its benefits lead to skepticism being portrayed as outdated or counterproductive (Bryson, 2018a, b, p. 61). This reinforces the tendency to suppress critical questions and makes it harder to find a healthy balance between trust and distrust.

Another aspect of declining distrust is the increasing role of technology as a substitute for interpersonal trust. Studies show that in many cases, people rely more on algorithmic decisions than on human judgment, as algorithms are perceived as neutral and unbiased (Eubanks, 2018, p. 94). This tendency is reinforced by the fact that machines do not make mistakes out of weakness, emotion, or inattention—traits attributed to humans. Yet this assumption overlooks the fact that algorithms are programmed by humans and can therefore reflect the biases and errors of their developers. The growing reliance on technology as a substitute for human trust has profound psychological consequences. People tend to idealize technology as the "perfect partner" that does not disappoint, does not judge, and is always available. But this illusion of perfection can, in the long run, lead to the neglect of interpersonal relationships. When technological systems are perceived as more reliable than people, the ability to build and maintain trust in others is weakened.

The decline of distrust toward technology is a complex phenomenon rooted in manifold cultural, social, and psychological changes. The increasing matter-of-factness with which digital technologies are used, the societal devaluation of skepticism, and the subtle manipulation by technology providers all contribute to the suppression of critical reflection. Yet especially in a time when technology shapes our lives to an unprecedented extent, a healthy degree of distrust is indispensable. Distrust must be rehabilitated not as an obstacle, but as a necessary condition for autonomy and critical thinking. Only in this way can the balance between the benefits of technology and the risks of its uncritical use be maintained.

Dangers of Excessive Trust: Data Leaks, Control, Dependency

The ongoing integration of AI into more and more areas of life inevitably raises the question of the dangers of excessive trust in these technologies.

One of the greatest risks lies in vulnerability to data leaks and hacker attacks. Despite the increasing frequency of such incidents, society's response is often remarkably superficial and short-lived. The rapid return to normality shows how accustomed we have become to the convenience of digital technologies and how reluctant we are to imagine the potential consequences of a life "without" them. This leads to an unreflective carelessness that overlooks how dangerous the loss of sensitive data can be. When private information, health data, or financial details fall into the wrong hands, not only is individual security threatened, but trust in fundamental social structures is also shaken (Noble, 2018, p. 28; O'Neil, 2016, p. 44). Another problem arises from the increasing delegation of decisions to AI systems. The more we rely on algorithms, the more we unlearn how to make our own decisions and critically question their consequences. AI systems are making decisions in areas that were once the exclusive domain of humans, such as medical diagnostics, lending, or personnel selection. This blind faith in the infallibility of machines weakens our ability to recognize errors, anticipate unforeseen consequences, and make corrections (Harari, 2018, p. 278). Joseph Weizenbaum warned as early as the 1970s that increasing dependence on machines could, in the long term, undermine human judgment (Weizenbaum, 1976, p. 225). Today, this danger is further exacerbated by opaque algorithmic "black boxes."

A central approach to addressing these challenges is the promotion of critical media literacy. Dealing with digital technologies should not be limited to mere operation, but should enable people to understand how algorithms work, to see through the mechanisms of data collection, and to critically question the economic interests behind these technologies (Bryson, 2018a, b, p. 52). This requires education that imparts not only technical knowledge, but also ethical and societal contexts. Only those who understand the principles of recommendation systems or scoring algorithms can consciously recognize their influence and make self-determined decisions (Noble, 2018, p. 111).

In addition to individual education, it is equally necessary to initiate structural changes at the societal level. Legislators and institutions bear a significant responsibility to create transparent and democratically controllable frameworks for the use of AI. The concept of "explainable AI" offers a promising approach here: By developing systems that disclose their decision-making processes, citizens and civil society organizations could gain insight into the logic and underlying data of these systems (Moor, 2006a, b, p. 36). In addition, independent oversight bodies could be established to ensure that AI systems comply with ethical and legal standards (O'Neil, 2016, p. 42).

The technological developments of recent decades have undoubtedly opened up numerous new freedoms and opportunities for us. But these achievements do not come without risks. The tendency to view technology as inherently positive carries the danger that we gradually relinquish our autonomy and freedom of choice (Weizenbaum, 1976, p. 229; Harari, 2018, p. 279). Particularly alarming is the unlearning of healthy distrust, which prevents us from critically questioning the power structures behind digital services and systems.

Distrust toward technology should not be understood as technophobia, but as an expression of a reflective, emancipated attitude. It calls on us to consciously shape the influence of digital tools, to recognize their limits, and to demand accountability (Noble, 2018, p. 56). This attitude enables us to harness the potential of modern technologies without ignoring their risks. Distrust is not a barrier to innovation, but a necessary corrective that helps us preserve diversity, security, and freedom in a digital world (Bryson, 2018a, b, p. 61). Only through a balanced approach of openness and vigilance can we ensure that technology serves humanity—and not the other way around.

References

Brynjolfsson, E., & McAfee, A. (2014). *The Second Machine Age: Work, Progress, and Prosperity in a Time of Brilliant Technologies*. W. W. Norton & Company.

Bryson, J. J. (2018a). Patiency is not a virtue: AI and the design of ethical systems. *Ethics and Information Technology, 20*(1), 15–26.

Bryson, J. J. (2018b). *The Artificial Intelligence Transparency Paradox: Why Better AI Demands Better Policy*. Brookings Institution Press.

Eubanks, V. (2018). *Automating Inequality: How High-Tech Tools Profile, Police, and Punish the Poor*. St. Martin's.

Floridi, L. (2014). *The Fourth Revolution: How the Infosphere is Reshaping Human Reality*. Oxford University Press.

Floridi, L. (2016). On human dignity as a foundation for the right to privacy. *Philosophy & Technology, 29*(4), 307–312.

Fogg, B. J. (2003). *Persuasive Technology: Using Computers to Change What We Think and Do*. Morgan Kaufmann.

Harari, Y. N. (2018). *21 Lessons for the 21st Century*. Spiegel & Grau.

Moor, J. H. (2006a). The nature, importance, and difficulty of machine ethics. *IEEE Intelligent Systems, 21*(4), 18–21.

Moor, J. H. (2006b). Why we need better ethics for emerging technologies. *Ethics and Information Technology, 8*(4), 27–36.

Noble, S. U. (2018). *Algorithms of Oppression: How Search Engines Reinforce Racism*. New York University Press.

O'Neil, C. (2016). *Weapons of Math Destruction: How Big Data Increases Inequality and Threatens Democracy*. Crown.

Pariser, E. (2011). *The Filter Bubble: What the Internet Is Hiding from You*. Penguin Press.

Weizenbaum, J. (1976). *Computer Power and Human Reason: From Judgment to Calculation*. Freeman.

7

The Fear of Takeover: AI as a Threat to Human Existence?

"At the beginning of every assumed obligation stands this: to be clear about the extent of one's strength, endurance, and willingness to sacrifice—or the assumption itself becomes a fault."

– Arthur Schnitzler

The rapid development of Artificial Intelligence (AI) has fundamentally changed the world, creating efficiency, innovation, and entirely new possibilities. At the same time, however, it triggers deep-seated fears that go far beyond technological aspects. These fears are not limited to potential job loss or ethical dilemmas, but touch on existential questions: Will AI one day take control over central areas of human life? Could machines even displace humanity? Such scenarios, present in science fiction narratives for decades, seem less unlikely to many today—not least due to the exponential advances in AI research and application (Bostrom, 2014, p. 115; Russell & Norvig, 2021, p. 345).

These concerns are neither purely irrational nor entirely speculative. They reflect fundamental psychological mechanisms deeply rooted in human nature. Uncertainty, fear of loss of control, and the threat to human uniqueness intensify the sense that AI is not just a technical tool, but a potential competitor that could displace humans from their central role in the world (Yudkowsky, 2008, p. 15). These fears are not simply symptoms of technophobic panic, but rather an expression of a serious societal and individual engagement with a technology that challenges our understanding of work, autonomy, and humanity.

O. Hoffmann, *Psychology and Artificial Intelligence*,
https://doi.org/10.1007/978-3-662-73147-5_7

Fear of the Unknown: Evolutionary Foundations of Uncertainty

The fear of AI can be traced back to the evolutionary roots of the human psyche. Humans have always grappled with the unknown, whether by exploring uncharted territories, experiencing foreign cultures, or investigating new technologies. This uncertainty has sharpened caution but also triggered irrational fears. For many, AI represents the ultimate unknown: a technology that could far surpass human intelligence and whose complex decision-making processes often appear as a "black box" (Heath, 2020, p. 298).

This sense of uncertainty is amplified by the increasing autonomy of AI. While earlier technologies were clearly controllable and transparent, modern AI systems often act independently and are difficult to predict. For many people, this seems threatening, as the ability to understand and control the world plays a central role in the human psyche. The unknown embodied by AI is not just a technical problem, but also a profound psychological one: it forces us to recognize our own limits and to confront the possibility that we may no longer be the dominant species on this planet.

Loss of Control and the Threat to Human Autonomy

Another central aspect of the fear of AI is the fear of losing control. Humans have a natural tendency to shape and influence their environment. This control provides security and allows risks to be minimized. However, AI has the potential to undermine this fundamental mechanism of control by making decisions that are not always in line with human values or intentions.

The idea that AI could one day make decisions that are incomprehensible or unpredictable to us is unsettling. An autonomous vehicle causing an accident, or an algorithm making unjust decisions, illustrate this problem. Even more disturbing is the possibility that advanced AI systems could develop their own goals that do not align with the interests of humanity—a scenario frequently discussed in debates about "superintelligence" (Bostrom, 2014, p. 125).

The loss of control over AI systems is not just a technological issue, but also a question of power dynamics. Who decides how AI is used? Who owns the data on which it is based? Who bears responsibility for its decisions? These uncertainties fuel fears and reinforce the feeling that humanity could lose control over its own future.

The Threat to Human Uniqueness

A particularly profound aspect of the fear of AI is the concern that machines could not only complement but surpass human abilities. Even today, AI systems demonstrate impressive performance in areas traditionally considered "human," such as creative activities, problem-solving processes, or emotional interactions. This challenges our self-concept as unique, creative, and empathetic beings.

The threat to human uniqueness posed by AI is not only technological, but also philosophical and existential. If machines are capable of creating art, making complex decisions, or forming emotional bonds, what then distinguishes them from humans? The idea that machines could one day surpass human abilities provokes a fundamental identity crisis. It forces us to ask: What does it mean to be human?

This question is not new. As early as the 20th century, philosophers such as Martin Heidegger and Hannah Arendt examined the impact of technological developments on human self-understanding. But AI takes this discussion to a new level. While earlier technologies were merely tools that supported humans, AI has the potential to replace humans as the central creative force.

Another factor fueling the fear of AI is its portrayal in popular culture. Films such as *Terminator*, *Ex Machina* or *I, Robot* have shaped the image of AI as something that surpasses its creators and ultimately turns against them. These portrayals may seem exaggerated, but they reflect real fears. They illustrate how deeply the fear of being overtaken by machines is anchored in the collective imagination.

These narratives are not only entertaining but also instructive, as they highlight the ethical, social, and psychological challenges of a world dominated by AI. They remind us that technological progress brings not only benefits but also risks that must be carefully weighed.

While many fears about AI are based on speculation and uncertainty, there are also concrete challenges that must be taken seriously. These include questions of regulation, responsibility, and the ethical design of AI systems. The fear of being overtaken by AI is not necessarily irrational, but rather an expression of the need to critically accompany technological progress.

To address these fears, it is crucial to promote transparency and education. People need to understand how AI works, what potential it offers, and what its limitations are. Only in this way can trust in this technology be strengthened and the fear of the unknown alleviated.

7.1 The Psychology of Fear of the Unknown: Why Do We Fear AI?

Fear—a feeling deeply rooted in our evolutionary heritage—has accompanied us since the dawn of humanity. It has helped us survive in a hostile world, protect ourselves from danger, and navigate a complex, often threatening environment. But fear is not just an emotional reaction to concrete threats such as predators or natural disasters. It is often directed at the unknown, at what we cannot comprehend or control. And this is precisely where our fear of Artificial Intelligence begins—it does not arise from the technology itself, but from the deep uncertainty it embodies.

So why do we fear AI? The answer does not lie in the machine itself, but in what it symbolizes: the limits of our understanding, the power of the unknown, and the potential threat to our self-determination. We humans are conditioned to meet uncertainty with fear. We are confronted with a technology that both fascinates and unsettles us, and that represents a future we can hardly predict or control.

Fear of Losing Control: When Machines Take Over

A key aspect of the fear of AI is the fear of losing control. The history of humanity is marked by a deep desire for control—over nature, over fate, and ultimately over ourselves. AI calls this fundamental longing into question by shaking the illusion of human control. Machines that "think," "learn," and make decisions appear to us as if they could challenge our place at the top of the cognitive hierarchy.

This loss of control is more than just a technological concern—it touches the essence of what it means to be human. The ability to make decisions is central to our self-image as autonomous beings. When we delegate this power to machines, the question arises: Who is really in control? The fear of AI is not simply the fear of technological dominance, but the fear that we as individuals will lose our autonomy. Today, as algorithms increasingly determine our lives—be it through personalized advertising, recommendations, or even decisions in medicine—the feeling grows that we are relinquishing control over our own lives.

The idea that machines could one day become so intelligent that they are no longer dependent on human input seems particularly threatening. This is the stuff of which science fiction dystopias are made: machines that surpass their creators, take control, and ultimately disempower humanity. These ideas may seem exaggerated, but they speak to a deeply rooted fear that is not easily shaken. Human existence is based on the need to actively shape and control the environment (Bandura, 1997, p. 7). Artificial intelligence challenges this control, especially as systems act with increasing autonomy. Autonomous weapons systems, self-driving vehicles, or AI-supported decision-making in the justice system raise questions about how much decision-making power we still possess.

This fear is intensified by the idea of a "superintelligence" that surpasses humans in all cognitive abilities and potentially becomes uncontrollable (Bostrom, 2014, p. 155). This scenario, which is picked up in many dystopian narratives, such as Isaac Asimov's "Three Laws of Robotics" or films like Terminator, is fueled by the deep fear that our own creations could turn against us (Asimov, 1950, p. 33).

Fear of the Unknown: What We Do Not Understand Makes Us Afraid
Our fear of AI also stems from a deeper, universal fear of the unknown. Artificial intelligence is a phenomenon that eludes the control and understanding of the average person. We are confronted with machines that "think" in ways we cannot fully comprehend. This lack of knowledge creates space for mistrust and concern.

AI operates on the basis of algorithms and data streams that remain opaque to most people. While the algorithms behind a machine's decisions may be mathematically perfect, their functioning remains a mystery to many. We may understand the basic mechanics, but the complexity and unpredictability of the results often leave us in the dark. This cognitive gap leads to deep uncertainty: How can we trust something we do not fully understand?

And this is where it gets tricky: Our fear of the unknown is not new, but in the case of AI it is intensified by the fact that we are facing a technology that continues to advance—regardless of whether we understand it or not. While previous technological revolutions, such as the invention of the automobile or the internet, were tangible and comprehensible, AI remains a kind of "black box" for many people. And this uncertainty fuels fear.

It is the same fear that has haunted humanity for millennia—the fear of the deep, dark oceans we could not explore, or of the undiscovered continents whose dangers we did not know. But in the case of AI, the fear is more complex, because we know it was created by ourselves. And yet it slips from our grasp.

Fear of Dehumanization: When Machines Become Human
Another often overlooked aspect is the fear of dehumanization. What happens when machines not only take over tasks but also simulate human behavior? Chatbots that provide emotional support, robots that mimic social interactions—all this leads to the unsettling question: What happens to us when machines become increasingly human?

This fear has a deep psychological component. Machines that imitate human behavior blur the boundaries between human and machine. This blurring of boundaries challenges our understanding of humanity. What makes us unique? If machines are able to predict our emotional reactions, analyze our behavior, and recognize our preferences, what remains of our individuality?

This fear arises from the observation that machines are increasingly able to imitate human traits—be it through human-like robotics, seemingly empathetic voice assistants, or creative algorithms that compose music and create works of art.

This is where the concept of the "uncanny valley" comes into play, which describes how people feel discomfort when machines appear too human-like (Mori, 1970, p. 33). This feeling of unease results from the uncertainty about whether one is dealing with a human or a machine, blurring the boundaries between human and technology. This uncertainty can intensify fears of loss of identity and social isolation, as machines begin to take on roles that have traditionally been interpersonal in nature, such as in caregiving professions or as psychological companions (Coeckelbergh, 2010, p. 201).

The fear of dehumanization goes hand in hand with the universal concern that machines could one day surpass us in emotional, social, or creative domains. This fear is particularly strong because it is not just a technological challenge, but directly attacks our self-concept as sentient, thinking beings. The thought that machines could take over not only physical but also cognitive and emotional tasks triggers deep unease. The fear of dehumanization is so threatening because it touches on an existential level what makes us human. It is not just the concern that machines could be better—it is the fear that we will lose ourselves, that we will delegate our unique human qualities to machines and in doing so dilute our identity. AI compels us to question our own role in a world where machines become ever more "human," while we may increasingly lose touch with our own humanity.

Fear of the Shift in Power: When Machines Become Rivals

Another element of the fear of AI is the concern that the balance of power between humans and machines could shift. While AI is currently still seen as a tool that serves us, the question arises whether this will always be the case. What happens if machines one day are no longer just tools, but become rivals? Rivals that surpass us in certain areas, that are faster, more precise, and more efficient.

This fear of a shift in power is particularly evident in areas of work where AI is already replacing human abilities. From manufacturing to customer service to medical diagnostics—in many industries, AI is taking over tasks that were previously performed by humans. This leads to a deep existential fear: If machines take over our work, what is left for us?

Historically, humans have developed technologies to control and dominate their environment. With AI, however, a technology is emerging that can learn and evolve independently—a potential reversal of the traditional roles of human and machine. The increasing automation in the workplace highlights this fear. Studies show that millions of jobs are threatened by automation (Frey & Osborne, 2017, p. 254). While previous technological revolutions created new fields of work, AI has the potential to take over not only physical but also cognitive tasks. The idea of existing without meaningful work fuels existential fears (Ford, 2015, p. 101). But it is not only the fear of job loss that worries us. It is the concern that machines could develop superior abilities in areas we have considered inherently human—such as creativity or judgment. What happens if AI is able to create art that is as emotionally moving as human works, or to make decisions that are wiser and fairer than those of a human?

This shift in power challenges our self-image as the dominant species. For centuries, we have seen ourselves as the cognitively superior species—but AI shakes this self-concept. What if we are no longer the smartest or most creative beings? This fear of competition with machines has deep roots in our psychological need for superiority and control.

Fear of the Unpredictable Future: When Machines Take Control of the World

The deepest, perhaps darkest fear associated with AI concerns the unpredictable future. While we still assume today that AI systems are under human control, there is growing concern that this may not always be the case. What happens if machines take control of the world? This fear is the basis of many dystopian visions of the future, in which machines disempower their creators and pursue their own agenda.

AI systems often operate as "black boxes"—their decision-making processes are difficult to understand even for experts (Burrell, 2016, p. 1). This lack of transparency leads to deep mistrust of technologies that are increasingly used in safety-critical areas.

Even if many currently popular scenarios may seem speculative, they speak to a deep, ancient fear: the fear of losing control over our own creation. AI systems that improve and evolve themselves could one day act in ways we can no longer understand or control. This fear of an unpredictable future is not just a technical problem, but a psychological one: it is the fear that we could live in a future dominated by machines whose actions and motives we can no longer comprehend.

The Psychology of Fear of AI—What Really Threatens Us
The fear of AI is complex and deeply rooted in our psychological heritage. It arises from fear of the unknown, of loss of control, of dehumanization, and of an uncertain future. But it is important to recognize that this fear is not caused solely by the technology itself. It reflects our own insecurities, our fears of losing power, of our own weakness, and of losing our unique human qualities.

AI forces us to rethink our own role in the world. Are we ready to face this challenge, or will we be ruled by the fear of the unknown? Ultimately, the answer lies in our own ability to shape technology while preserving our humanity. AI may change the future—but it is up to us to define that future.

7.2 AI and Job Loss: A Psychological and Economic Perspective

The impact of artificial intelligence on the labor market is one of the most intensely debated topics of the digital age. While technological advances in the past have always increased efficiency and created new employment opportunities, automation through AI has the potential to disrupt this dynamic. Machines are not only taking over repetitive, physical tasks, but are increasingly encroaching on highly skilled and creative fields. This transformation has profound economic and psychological consequences that go far beyond the mere loss of jobs.

The Economic Perspective: Efficiency versus Employment
From an economic standpoint, automation through AI is a logical development. Companies strive to reduce costs, increase productivity, and minimize human error. Artificial intelligence makes it possible to optimize processes, solve complex tasks more efficiently, and analyze large volumes of data in real time. For businesses, this means an unprecedented level of competitiveness. Studies show that AI could increase global productivity by up to 40% by 2030 (Bughin et al., 2018, p. 27).

But this increase in efficiency comes at a high price: the loss of jobs. According to an analysis by Frey and Osborne (2017, p. 258), up to 47% of all occupations could be threatened by automation in the next two decades.

Particularly affected are jobs characterized by standardized and repetitive tasks, such as in manufacturing, retail, and transportation. However, professions in finance, law, or medical diagnostics are also increasingly being automated.

The economic logic behind this shift is clear: AI does not require salaries, does not need breaks, and does not make mistakes due to fatigue. But what is efficient from a business perspective means the loss of livelihood for many workers. While companies benefit from lower operating costs, many people are confronted with the reality that their skills and competencies are suddenly no longer in demand.

The Psychological Dimension of Job Loss

For the individual, work is much more than just a means of securing a livelihood. Work structures daily life, gives meaning, and enables social interactions. It is a central component of identity. Losing a job due to automation is therefore not only a financial crisis, but also a psychological and existential one.

In Western societies, an individual's value is often measured by their professional achievements. Work is closely linked to self-esteem and social status. When people are replaced by AI, they feel not only economically threatened but also personally devalued. Losing a job signals to them: "Your skills are worth less than those of a machine." This devaluation can lead to a loss of self-confidence and self-worth (Jahoda, 1981, p. 415). Unemployment often leads to isolation and social withdrawal. The workplace is not only a place of productivity but also a place of social interaction. When this structure disappears, many people feel excluded from the community. Studies show that prolonged unemployment is associated with an increased risk of depression, anxiety disorders, and even physical health problems (Paul & Moser, 2009, p. 266). The psychological burden is particularly severe when job loss is perceived as inevitable. People who are replaced by AI often experience a sense of powerlessness, as they can neither control nor stop the progress of technology. This sense of helplessness can lead to chronic stress, which in turn impairs mental and physical health.

Another psychological effect of job loss due to AI is fear of the future. Many people ask themselves: "What role is left for me in a world where machines are taking over more and more?" This uncertainty leads to a deep existential crisis. Especially in industries heavily affected by automation, such as the automotive or logistics sectors, the fear of losing one's raison d'être is omnipresent.

The Societal Perspective: Inequality and Social Tensions

The economic benefits of automation are not distributed evenly. While highly skilled professionals working in the development and implementation of AI benefit from this transformation, less qualified workers are often displaced. This inequality exacerbates existing social tensions.

While proponents of AI argue that new technologies create new jobs, the reality is that many of these new roles require specialized knowledge that not everyone can acquire. For people who have worked in traditional occupations all their lives, it is often difficult to adapt to these new demands. This leads to a polarization of the labor market: on one side are highly qualified specialists who benefit from the technological revolution, on the other are workers who are left behind. Another problem is the increase in precarious employment. Many of the new jobs created by AI are part of the so-called "gig economy," where workers rely on short-term contracts without long-term security or social protection. This increases economic insecurity and psychological pressure, as people must constantly fight for their next source of income.

The Illusion of Liberation: Work in an AI-Dominated World

Some advocates of automation through artificial intelligence promote the idea that humans could be freed from burdensome and monotonous work by these technologies. They see this as an opportunity to create a society in which work is no longer at the center of life, leaving more room for creativity, personal development, and interpersonal relationships. Concepts such as universal basic income are often proposed in this context as solutions to ensure financial security and reduce dependence on gainful employment. But as tempting as this vision of a "liberated" society may seem, it carries deep psychological and social challenges that cannot be ignored.

Loss of Meaning and the Search for a New Identity

Work is more than an economic necessity. It structures daily life, gives direction, and provides the feeling of being part of something larger. For many people, their profession is an essential part of their identity. The statement "I am a teacher" or "I am an engineer" goes far beyond a description of one's occupation—it reflects a sense of self and a place in society. If this central pillar is removed by automation, many are left with the question: "Who am I if I no longer work?"

The loss of traditional work roles could lead to an existential crisis, as work is closely linked to the concept of individual worth in many cultures. Historically, work has always been a means to gain social recognition, create community, and find personal fulfillment. Psychology has repeatedly shown that people who are unemployed or feel alienated from their work are more likely to suffer from depression, anxiety, and reduced self-esteem (Jahoda, 1981, p. 396). Without a clear perspective on how to find their place in a work-free society, a significant portion of the population could fall into a state of disorientation and loss of meaning.

The Challenge of Developing New Life Models

The idea that people in an AI-dominated world will find new forms of self-fulfillment and social interaction presupposes profound cultural and psychological changes. The transition from a work-centered to a leisure-dominated society requires not only economic adjustments but also overcoming deeply rooted cultural values that view work as the foundation of personal and social existence. One problem is the lack of preparation for such a transformation. Technological progress is advancing faster than society can adapt its structures and values. While automation and AI are replacing traditional jobs, there is often a lack of concrete strategies to offer people alternative paths to self-fulfillment. Psychology could play a key role here by showing ways for people to define their identity beyond work. This could be achieved by placing greater emphasis on creativity, education, and volunteer work—areas that cannot be taken over by machines and at the same time offer deeply satisfying experiences.

An important aspect often overlooked in the debate is the social dimension of work. Workplaces are not only sites of productivity but also social spaces where people interact, build relationships, and support each other. Without these everyday social interactions, the risk of social isolation could increase. While AI-based technologies could create new ways of communication, they do not replace the depth and authenticity of interpersonal relationships. Psychology shows that genuine social interactions play a central role in well-being and can only be partially replaced by virtual encounters. A society without traditional work would therefore have to create new forms of community that address not only economic interests but also social and emotional needs. This could mean reimagining public spaces where people can come together regardless of their professional role to pursue common goals, express creativity, or simply experience community.

Another problem associated with automation through AI is the potential emergence of a two-tier society. While some people benefit from the new technology and have access to creative or intellectually fulfilling activities, others could be pushed into a passive consumer role. This inequality could not only intensify social tensions but also foster a sense of marginalization and worthlessness among large segments of the population. The challenge is to ensure that the benefits created by AI are distributed fairly. This means that education and retraining must be designed not only economically but also psychologically to enable people to find new roles and identities that cannot be replaced by machines.

The illusion that AI could completely free humans from work and create a utopian society underestimates the psychological and social challenges that accompany such a transformation. Work is not just a means of livelihood but a central part of what defines us as individuals and as a community. The idea of a work-free world may be appealing, but it requires a profound engagement with questions of identity, community, and meaning.

Psychology can help shape this transition by developing a deeper understanding of the human needs that must be met in an AI-dominated world. It is crucial that society not only develops technologies that free us from work but also structures that enable us to preserve our humanity in a radically changing world.

Automation through AI is a double-edged sword. On the one hand, it opens up enormous economic and technological opportunities; on the other, it presents society with profound challenges. The loss of jobs is not only an economic issue but also a psychological and social one that calls into question our self-concept as working beings. The central question is not whether AI will replace jobs—that is inevitable—but how we as a society will deal with this change. Can we create new roles and values that give people meaning and identity in an AI-dominated world? Or will we end up in a world where efficiency triumphs over humanity? The answer to this will decisively shape our future.

7.3 Is the Fear of AI Irrational or Justified?

The fear of artificial intelligence is a phenomenon deeply embedded in the collective consciousness of modern society. It is fueled by science fiction films, stoked by dystopian narratives, and sustained by technophobic warnings. And yet the question arises: Are these fears truly irrational, exaggerated, and unfounded? Or is it possible that we—perhaps without fully realizing it—are already sliding down a slippery slope toward a reality in which these fears suddenly seem all too real?

To answer this question adequately, we must address various aspects that go beyond the usual technological discussions. It is not only about what AI can technically achieve, but also about the deep-seated fears and anxieties we harbor as humans in the face of a technology that not only accompanies us but may one day surpass us. In the following, we will unravel these fears piece by piece and analyze whether they have a real core or whether they are merely a reflection of our insecurities and anxieties in a rapidly changing world.

The Fear of Losing Control

One of the central motifs that repeatedly arises in connection with the fear of AI is the fear of losing control. Machines that can think and act independently are an unsettling prospect in themselves. But when these machines not only carry out our instructions but eventually make their own decisions—and perhaps even better decisions than we do—an existential threat emerges: What if we lose control over what we once created?

This fear is not new. It runs through the entire history of humanity. Even in ancient myths and legends, the moment when the creator is overtaken by his own creation recurs. The story of Dr. Frankenstein is perhaps the best-known example of a creation turning against its creator. But unlike in Mary Shelley's novel, the "monster" of our time is not made of flesh and blood, but of code and data structures. And therein lies the challenge: The artificial intelligence we create is not a biological being that we can raise or teach morality. It is an algorithmic system that operates by different rules—rules that we may have written, but which, as complexity increases, may go beyond our understanding.

The fear of losing control is therefore by no means irrational. It is deeply rooted in our human experience and touches on a fundamental need: self-determination. But what happens when machines begin to undermine this self-determination? When algorithms influence our decisions, predict our preferences, and subtly steer us in certain directions? This loss of autonomy is not a distant vision of the future, but a reality we are already experiencing today. We are increasingly delegating decisions to machines—from navigation in our cars to the news we see on social media. And with every step we take toward automation, we give up a bit more control. The question, then, is not whether this fear is irrational, but rather: How much control are we willing to relinquish before we realize that perhaps we have given up too much?

The Fear of Superiority

Another central fear associated with AI is the idea that machines could eventually surpass us in all areas—intellectually, physically, perhaps even emotionally. This fear is based on the deep-seated human need to preserve our own uniqueness. For a long time, humans were the only beings on this planet capable of solving complex problems, thinking creatively, and making moral decisions. Artificial intelligence challenges this self-image. One could argue that the fear of AI's superiority is a projection of our own insecurities. We are used to being the smartest beings on this planet. But now we are confronted with a technology that works faster, more precisely, and more tirelessly than we do in many areas. In a way, the fear of AI's superiority reveals a deeper insecurity: the question of whether we are really as unique as we have always believed. If a machine can beat us at chess, make better medical diagnoses, or solve more complex mathematical problems—what remains of our intellectual superiority?

But this fear goes deeper than that. It is not only the idea that machines could surpass us that is unsettling, but also the consequences that could result. What happens if machines not only become better but also more autonomous? If they make decisions that we can no longer comprehend? The idea that machines could one day act independently and perhaps pursue interests that do not align with ours is at the heart of this fear. Here, an important provocation comes into play: Perhaps we have overestimated ourselves. Perhaps AI is not a threat because it surpasses us, but because it holds up a mirror to us. It shows us that many of the tasks we consider highly complex and intellectually demanding can, in fact, be performed more efficiently by machines. And that scratches at our self-esteem. The superiority of AI may frighten us less for technological reasons and more because it calls into question our self-concept as unique, irreplaceable beings.

The Fear of Dehumanization

Another important element of the fear of AI is the concern that increasing interaction with machines could change our human relationships and experiences. If we increasingly rely on AI systems—whether in communication, decision-making, or even interpersonal relationships—does this not threaten a creeping dehumanization? This concern is indeed justified. When machines simulate emotions, it can lead to confusion about what constitutes genuine human bonds. As we become accustomed to AI-powered conversational partners and digital assistants who "understand" us at the push of a button and respond to our needs, we must ask ourselves: What does it mean to interact with a real human being? As machines become ever better at imitating human behavior, the boundary between human and machine could increasingly blur. And with this blurring of boundaries comes the risk of losing what we consider the "human" experience. The question arises: Will we eventually forget, through interaction with AI, what it is like to have genuine interpersonal bonds? Will we prefer machines because they do not make mistakes, because they lack emotional complexity, and because they are always available? Hidden in this possible future is a deeper fear: the fear that we could lose ourselves and our humanity in a technologized world.

This fear is so powerful because it is not only based on technological considerations but on a deeply rooted existential question: What actually makes us human? If machines imitate us in more and more areas and perhaps even surpass us, what remains of our uniqueness as a species?

The Fear of Unpredictability
An often underestimated aspect of the fear of AI is the fear of unpredictability. While humans tend to be at least somewhat predictable—based on social norms, moral values, and emotional bonds—machines are governed by a completely different logic. They act on the basis of data and algorithms, which often lead to results that are difficult for the human mind to understand or comprehend. The unpredictability of AI systems is already a real problem today. Even the developers of AI algorithms often cannot fully explain how their systems arrive at certain decisions—especially with complex machine learning systems. When machines operate in a "black box" model, where even the creators can no longer understand the internal processes, a deep uncertainty arises. How can we trust a technology whose actions and decisions we do not fully understand? This unpredictability amplifies the fear of losing control. If we do not know how a machine arrives at a particular decision, how can we be sure that this decision is in our best interest? And even more unsettling: What if the machine begins to make decisions that we can no longer comprehend or that go against our interests?

The fear of unpredictability is therefore not unfounded. It is based on the fact that AI systems operate on a level far beyond what we as humans can intuitively grasp. And this gap between human understanding and machine logic grows ever wider as the systems become more complex.

The Fear of the Future
Finally, there is the fear of the future—the fear of a coming time when machines have taken control and humans become a marginal phenomenon. This vision is not only the stuff of dystopian science fiction but reflects a deeply rooted insecurity: the question of whether we will still have a place in a world dominated by AI. This fear goes beyond technological aspects. It is profoundly psychological because it raises the question of the role of humans in a highly automated, machine-driven future. Will we be replaced

by machines? Will we become irrelevant? This fear is fueled by the idea that machines could surpass us in more and more areas—whether in decision-making, creativity, or even moral judgments. If machines are capable of acting autonomously and can solve our problems faster and more efficiently than we can—what remains of us as humans?

It is a fear of the future deeply rooted in our human psyche. The idea that we could one day be rendered obsolete by machines touches the core of our existence. And perhaps it is this fear of the future that makes the fear of AI so powerful: the fear that in a future increasingly dominated by machines, we could lose our meaning and value. The fear of artificial intelligence is neither unfounded nor irrational. It is the result of a deep, existential insecurity triggered by the rapid technological progress of recent decades. This fear stems from the loss of control, the superiority of machines, the dehumanization of our relationships, the unpredictability of machine decisions, and the question of our role in a future dominated by AI.

It would be wrong to simply dismiss these fears or label them as technophobic panic-mongering. They reflect real challenges. The real question is not whether these fears are irrational or justified, but how we as humans respond to these technological developments—whether we rise to the challenge and define our role in this new world, or whether we remain passive and leave the field to the machines.

References

Arendt, H. (1958). *The human condition.* University of Chicago Press.

Asimov, I. (1950). *I, Robot.* Gnome Press.

Bandura, A. (1997). *Self-efficacy: The exercise of control.* W. H. Freeman.

Bostrom, N. (2014). *Superintelligence: Paths, dangers, strategies.* Oxford University Press.

Brynjolfsson, E., & McAfee, A. (2014). *The second machine age: Work, progress, and prosperity in a time of brilliant technologies.* W. W. Norton & Company.

Bughin, J., Seong, J., Manyika, J., & Chui, M. (2018). *Notes from the AI frontier: Modeling the impact of AI on the world economy.* McKinsey Global Institute.

Burrell, J. (2016). How the machine 'thinks': Understanding opacity in machine learning algorithms. *Big Data & Society, 3*(1), 1–12.

Carr, N. (2014). *The glass cage: How our computers are changing us.* W. W. Norton & Company.

Coeckelbergh, M. (2010). Robot rights? Towards a social-relational justification of moral consideration. *Ethics and Information Technology, 12*(3), 209–221.

Floridi, L., Cowls, J., Beltrametti, M., Chatila, R., Chazerand, P., Dignum, V., Luetge, C., Madelin, R., Pagallo, U., Rossi, F., Schafer, B., Valcke, P., & Vayena, E. (2018). AI4People—An ethical framework for a good AI society. *Minds and Machines, 28*(4), 689–707.

Ford, M. (2015). *Rise of the robots: Technology and the threat of a jobless future.* Basic Books.

Frey, C. B., & Osborne, M. A. (2017). The future of employment: How susceptible are jobs to computerisation? *Technological Forecasting and Social Change, 114,* 254–280.

Harari, Y. N. (2016). *Homo Deus: Eine Geschichte von Morgen.* C.H. Beck.

Heath, J. (2020). *The machinery of society: Technology, ethics, and human flourishing.* Polity.

Heidegger, M. (1977). *Die Frage nach der Technik.* Klett-Cotta.

Jahoda, M. (1981). Work, employment, and unemployment: Values, theories, and approaches in social research. *American Psychologist, 36*(2), 184–191.

Klein, G. (2019). *Seeing what others don't: The remarkable ways we gain insights.* PublicAffairs.

Mori, M. (1970). The uncanny valley. *Energy, 7*(4), 33–35.

Paul, K. I., & Moser, K. (2009). Unemployment impairs mental health: Meta-analyses. *Journal of Vocational Behavior, 74*(3), 264–282.

Russell, S., & Norvig, P. (2021). *Artificial Intelligence: A modern approach* (4. Aufl.). Pearson.

Yudkowsky, E. (2008). Artificial Intelligence as a positive and negative factor in global risk. In N. Bostrom & M. M. Ćirković (Hrsg.), *Global catastrophic risks* (S. 308–345). Oxford University Press.

8

The Future of Psychology With and Through AI

"It is no proof of a person's understanding if he is able to affirm what appeals to him; but the ability to discern that what is true is true—and what is false is false—that is a characteristic proof of his intelligence."

– Emanuel von Swedenborg

The ongoing development of Artificial Intelligence (AI) has not only led to technical innovations but has also triggered profound changes in the science of psychology. AI and psychology are engaged in a reciprocal process of development: while psychology provides new insights for the creation of intelligent algorithms, AI opens up previously unimaginable possibilities for the exploration, analysis, and application of psychological knowledge. This reciprocal relationship has the potential to fundamentally transform both the theory and practice of psychology.

On the one hand, AI enables psychology to overcome previous methodological limitations. The ability of AI systems to analyze large amounts of data in real time opens up new dimensions in the study of human behavior and thought. Whether in diagnostics, therapy, or preventive health promotion—AI can help identify patterns that remain invisible to the human eye and elevate interventions to a more precise, individualized level (Fitzpatrick et al., 2017, p. 4). Algorithms that recognize emotions or analyze language make possible a personalized psychology tailored to the specific needs of each individual.

O. Hoffmann, *Psychology and Artificial Intelligence*,
https://doi.org/10.1007/978-3-662-73147-5_8

Yet AI is not just a tool, but also a paradigm that challenges psychology to question its fundamental assumptions. To what extent are human thinking and machine learning comparable? What can machines that emulate neural networks reveal about the functioning of the human brain? These questions lead to a new understanding of human cognition and prompt psychology to reconsider its theories and models in a new light (Goodfellow et al., 2016, p. 28).

On the other hand, the integration of AI also raises ethical and social questions that go far beyond the scientific context. How does the relationship between therapist and patient change when AI systems take on a mediating role? What risks arise when algorithms analyze emotional states and make predictions without being able to "feel" themselves? And finally: how does increasing dependence on AI affect human self-understanding? These questions are not merely theoretical but affect psychological practice at a time increasingly dominated by technology.

Chapter 8 examines how AI is changing not only the tools of psychology but also its way of thinking. It explores the opportunities and challenges brought about by this transformation and asks how psychology can maintain its relevance and humanistic core in an increasingly automated world. For the future of psychology with and through AI will be shaped not only by technological innovations but also by psychology's ability to redefine itself—in a dialogue with the machine that is at the same time a reflection on the nature of being human.

8.1 Artificial Intelligence in Psychotherapy: The Human Therapist Is Replaced

The idea that artificial intelligence could one day take over the work of a human therapist evokes a mixture of fascination and unease in many people. While some envision a future in which algorithms and machines analyze the human mind and bring about healing, there are legitimate doubts as to whether a machine could ever truly grasp the depth of the human psyche. Is it conceivable that we will one day rely entirely on AI-based systems to cope with our deepest fears, insecurities, and traumas? Or is the concept of "machine therapy" a dangerous oversimplification of human complexity?

The discussion about the use of AI in psychotherapy is much more than a technical question. It touches on the very foundations of what we understand as human relationship, emotional depth, and therapeutic effectiveness. This section will address the possibilities, limitations, and potential dangers of using AI in psychotherapy, raising the question of what is lost when we replace the human therapist with a machine.

The Evolution of Therapy: Freud and the Origins of the Therapeutic Relationship

The development of psychotherapy offers a comprehensive insight into the changing understanding of the human psyche and healing. From the groundbreaking work of Sigmund Freud to the modern, data-driven approaches of cognitive behavioral therapy (CBT), the history of psychotherapy reflects not only the shift in scientific paradigms but also the social and cultural context in which it is practiced. In this area of tension, the question arises today: what happens when artificial intelligence enters this highly sensitive process?

Sigmund Freud, the founder of psychoanalysis, laid the foundation for modern psychotherapy. In his early work, he emphasized the importance of the relationship between patient and therapist, which he referred to as the "transference relationship" (Freud, 1912, p. 102). According to Freud, this relationship enables the patient to project unconscious conflicts and desires, making them accessible for therapeutic processing. The central role of the therapist was to create, through empathy and interpretation, a space in which healing could occur. Although Freud's approach was later criticized and modified by subsequent schools of psychotherapy, the importance of the therapeutic relationship remains undisputed. Even in cognitive-behavioral approaches, which focus more on empirically verifiable techniques and interventions, building trust and a positive relationship between patient and therapist is regarded as a fundamental factor for therapeutic success (Beck, 1979, p. 45; Norcross, 2002, p. 5).

With the development of cognitive behavioral therapy and later the third wave of behavioral therapies (e.g., acceptance and commitment therapy, dialectical behavior therapy), the focus of psychotherapy increasingly shifted to specific techniques and evidence-based approaches. These methods rely on standardized protocols based on empirical data and often use tools such as questionnaires and structured sessions to measure patient progress.

In this context, the transition to AI-based therapy systems seems like a logical next step. Systems such as "Woebot" or "Wysa" use algorithms to provide patients with emotional support, identify cognitive distortions, and suggest specific interventions. These technologies are already capable of conducting "therapeutic" conversations via text or voice and have shown initial success in treating mild depression or anxiety disorders (Fitzpatrick et al., 2017, p. 128). But can they really capture the complexity and depth of human interaction that is so central to the success of therapy?

Therapy is much more than the application of techniques or the provision of information. It is a profound, often emotionally charged process that unfolds in the dynamic between two people. This dynamic is shaped by nonverbal signals, emotional resonance, and the therapist's intuitive adaptation to the needs of the patient. Studies show that the therapeutic relationship—regardless of the specific method—is one of the strongest predictors of therapeutic success (Wampold, 2015, p. 202). A human therapist brings more than expertise: they possess the ability to show empathy, recognize unspoken messages, and flexibly adapt their interventions to the individual situation of the patient. These aspects are difficult to standardize or program. Algorithms, on the other hand, operate on the basis of data and rules. They recognize patterns and respond to predictable inputs.

The increasing integration of AI into psychotherapy also raises ethical questions. Who bears responsibility if an algorithm suggests an incorrect "intervention" or worsens the mental health of patients? And what are the societal consequences if access to human therapists is replaced or restricted by AI?

From a psychological perspective, the question arises as to how patients respond to interacting with a machine. Studies suggest that people are often willing to share sensitive information with an AI, as they perceive it as nonjudgmental and neutral (Lucas et al., 2014, p. 111). Yet this neutrality could also prove to be a disadvantage: a therapist who actively listens, provides emotional support, and builds a genuine relationship with the patient can foster deeper healing than an algorithm that merely analyzes patterns.

AI-Supported Therapy: The Promises

Proponents of using AI in psychotherapy argue that algorithms could offer a range of advantages that human therapists may not be able to provide. AI systems have the ability to process vast amounts of data in seconds, recognize patterns invisible to the human eye, and make diagnoses based on objective criteria. In an ideal world, these systems could create personalized therapy plans tailored to the individual needs and psychological state of each patient.

Another frequently cited advantage is accessibility. Many people have little or no access to qualified therapy—whether due to geographic barriers, financial constraints, or a lack of available professionals. AI-supported therapies could close this gap by providing immediate and cost-effective access to support, 24 hours a day, seven days a week.

Furthermore, some argue that machines could offer an objectivity that human therapists may lack. Despite all their training, therapists are human—with biases, emotions, and weaknesses. A machine, on the other hand, has no emotions, preferences, or prejudices (at least in theory). They can treat patients neutrally, based solely on the collected data and the algorithms that underlie them.

What Machines Do Not Understand: The Depth of Human Experience

As tempting as these advantages may seem, there is a deep and fundamental question we must ask ourselves: can a machine truly understand the human experience? Empathy—the ability to put oneself in another's feelings and understand them—is one of the central qualities of a good therapist. However, empathy is not just a mechanical process, but a profoundly emotional and human experience, nourished by a life full of relationships, experiences, and emotions. Machines may be able to simulate emotions, recognize them through speech patterns or facial expressions, but they do not feel them. They may be able to offer comforting words or provide responses based on previous sessions, but they will never be able to fully grasp the nuances of human experience. A machine cannot understand what it feels like to lose a loved one, to feel deep regret or existential fear, because it has never experienced and never will experience these feelings.

The human therapist brings their own emotional depth and life experience into the therapeutic relationship. This level of connection—the shared humanity, the understanding of life's difficulties on a fundamental, emotional level—is something a machine can never replicate. Even the most sophisticated algorithms cannot generate the emotional resonance that arises when one person listens to another and truly understands them.

The Danger of Dehumanization

Another critical point in the use of AI in psychotherapy is the danger of dehumanization. Therapy is a process that is not only based on the exchange of information, but on the creation of a safe and supportive environment in which the patient can open up and be vulnerable. A human therapist brings warmth, compassion, and an emotional presence that enables the patient to feel safe while exploring difficult topics. If we leave this role to a machine, there is a risk that therapy will become a mechanical process—an exchange of information without genuine human connection. A patient might feel that their fears and worries are merely being processed by an algorithm, without real understanding or compassion. This could result in the loss of the emotional depth and transformative power of therapy.

Furthermore, patients who interact with a machine instead of a human may feel that their problems are less valuable or meaningless. A machine based on data and algorithms can give the impression that the therapeutic process is merely a matter of calculation, rather than a profound, human act of healing and transformation.

The Illusion of Control

Another issue that arises with the use of AI in psychotherapy is the question of control. Algorithms and AI systems are complex and often opaque technologies based on vast amounts of data and machine learning. While these systems are capable of making decisions based on data, the question remains: who controls these decisions? And how certain can we be that a machine's recommendations are in the best interest of the patient?

Machines and algorithms are only as good as the data they are based on and the people who program them. If the underlying data are biased or incomplete, the machine's recommendations could also be flawed or biased. This presents a serious ethical dilemma: can we really rely on machines when it comes to such intimate and sensitive areas as the human psyche?

Moreover, there is a risk that the patient will lose a sense of autonomy as they increasingly rely on a machine's recommendations. Therapy is a process of self-reflection and empowerment, in which the patient learns to understand and manage their own thoughts and feelings. However, if a machine makes decisions and tells the patient how they should feel or behave, this process of empowerment is undermined. The danger is that patients will increasingly rely on the machine instead of developing their own emotional intelligence and resilience.

Artificial Intelligence as a Supplement, Not a Replacement

Despite all these concerns, there is also a constructive perspective on the use of AI in psychotherapy. Instead of viewing the technology as a threat or replacement for the human therapist, we could see it as a valuable tool that can support the therapeutic process. AI could be used as a supplement to help therapists better understand or analyze certain aspects of a patient's psychological state.

For example, algorithms could help identify patterns in a patient's behavior that are invisible to the human eye, or monitor the effectiveness of certain therapeutic interventions. In this role, AI could be a useful resource that supports therapists in making informed decisions and providing more individualized treatment.

However, the human therapist remains irreplaceable when it comes to the deeper level of human connection—the emotional resonance, compassion, and empathy that a machine can never truly replicate. Ultimately, it is the combination of technological advances and human warmth that holds the key to successful therapy.

The Limits of Artificial Intelligence in Psychotherapy

The idea that artificial intelligence could one day replace the human therapist may be tempting, but it ignores the complex nature of human experience and interpersonal relationships that form the foundation of any effective therapy. While machines are capable of processing large amounts of data and may be able to identify helpful patterns, they lack the emotional depth and empathy that are essential to the therapeutic process.

Artificial intelligence can certainly be used as a valuable tool in therapy, but it should never fully replace the human therapist. In the end, it is humanity—the feeling that another person truly understands us, listens to us, and cares about our well-being—that gives psychotherapy its power.

8.2 AI as Researcher: Will Psychology as a Science Be Revolutionized by Algorithms?

The question of whether artificial intelligence could revolutionize psychology as a scientific discipline may at first glance seem speculative, perhaps even exaggerated. Yet upon closer inspection, it becomes clear that this question is much more than just a thought experiment. It touches the very core of what science, and psychology in particular, is about: the quest for a deeper understanding of the human mind and behavior, of what drives us, how we feel, how we think, and how we develop.

With the increasing capabilities of AI systems—and here we are not just talking about simple algorithms, but about learning, self-optimizing machines capable of analyzing vast amounts of data and detecting patterns hidden from the human eye—the question inevitably arises: Will psychology as a science, as we know it, be changed or even revolutionized by this machine intelligence? Are we ready to accept that machines, which have no conscious access to emotions, thoughts, or intentions, might be able to "understand" the human mind better than we do ourselves?

From Hypotheses to Data—The Transformation of Scientific Methodology

Let us begin by looking at the methods traditionally used in psychology. Like many other sciences, psychology is a hypothetico-deductive discipline. Psychologists develop theories and hypotheses about how people think, feel, and act, and then test these in controlled experiments. These experiments yield data, which are then analyzed to determine whether the original hypotheses are confirmed or refuted. This process is—in theory—a rational and systematic approach to exploring the human mind.

But this is precisely where AI comes into play and begins to change things. Modern AI systems, especially those based on machine learning, operate differently. Instead of starting from a hypothesis to be tested, these systems are designed to analyze vast amounts of data and detect patterns that may not even have been suspected before. AI does not need hypotheses—it only needs data. And herein lies a fundamental difference that not only influences the methodology of psychology but also its epistemological foundation.

Artificial intelligence turns the traditional notion on its head that science works as a gradual approach to truth through hypothesis testing. Instead, it relies on the raw power of data analysis. AI can analyze millions of datasets, uncover correlations that human researchers would never have discovered, and make predictions that come true with astonishing accuracy. Is that not ultimately also the goal of science? To understand the world and the human mind, to make predictions, and to capture the complexity of life in a coherent system?

The End of Hypotheses?

The idea that AI could eliminate the need for hypotheses is both fascinating and unsettling. Could psychology actually become a data-driven science in which theories and hypotheses are only of secondary importance? Some optimists might argue that this is the natural next step. If machines are able to gain deeper insights into the human mind, why should we settle for the limited perspectives of human researchers?

But this view neglects an important fact: science is more than just recognizing patterns. It is also about understanding causes, explaining phenomena, and developing theories that provide meaning and context. Correlation is not causation—a fundamental principle that should not lose its significance even in the age of AI. If an AI discovers in the data that people who experienced certain traumas in childhood are more likely to develop mental illnesses later on, this is a valuable pattern. But it is not an explanation. It is only an observation, not a theory about the underlying mechanisms.

Here we see one of the greatest challenges to the idea that AI could revolutionize psychology: machines can analyze, but they cannot understand. They detect patterns, but they have no concept of meaning. Psychology as a science strives not only to predict behavior but also to explain why people behave the way they do. This deeper level of understanding requires something that machines do not possess—intuition, context, and an awareness of the complex social, emotional, and cultural factors that influence human behavior.

AI as a Tool, Not a Replacement

Despite these limitations, AI has the potential to fundamentally change psychology—not as a replacement for human researchers, but as a powerful tool in their arsenal. One of AI's greatest strengths lies in its ability to process enormous amounts of data. In psychology, this means that AI can detect patterns and relationships in data that would remain invisible to human researchers.

For example, AI could be used to identify patterns in the development of mental disorders by analyzing data from millions of patient records. In this way, AI could provide valuable insights into the risk factors that lead to the emergence of disorders such as depression, anxiety disorders, or schizophrenia. These findings could in turn help to develop preventive measures or create personalized treatment plans tailored to the individual needs of a patient. At the same time, AI could help improve the lengthy and often error-prone process of data collection. In many psychological studies, researchers rely on self-reports from participants, which are often subject to bias and inaccuracies. AI systems could continuously collect data through the use of wearables, smartphones, and other technologies, thus providing a more realistic picture of human behavior and experience.

Here, the potential for a revolution begins to emerge: AI could fundamentally change the way psychological research is conducted by dramatically increasing the quantity and quality of available data and multiplying the speed at which these data are analyzed.

Psychology and AI—Mutual Learning

The interaction between psychology and artificial intelligence is a dynamic and profound relationship that mutually influences each other. While AI provides new tools to better understand and model psychological processes, psychology delivers crucial insights that drive the development and optimization of AI systems. This connection is not only technologically relevant but also raises fundamental questions about the nature of human thought, emotions, and decision-making.

The development of AI is fundamentally based on the understanding of human cognition. Many of the groundbreaking advances in AI, such as neural networks and machine learning, are inspired by models based on neurobiological and cognitive processes. Neural networks, which form the basis of modern deep learning models, simulate the structure and function of neural connections in the brain (Goodfellow et al., 2016, p. 11). This approach, known as "connectionism," was directly inspired by psychological and neurological studies investigating how the brain works and its ability to learn and process information (Rumelhart et al., 1986, p. 318). Furthermore, psychology has played a decisive role in defining the concept of learning in AI. Machine learning, a central component of modern AI systems, is based on the imitation of human learning processes. In particular, reinforcement learning *(English: reinforcement learning)* is modeled after psychological models of operant conditioning developed by researchers such as Skinner (Skinner, 1953, p. 103). In this process, behavior is shaped by rewards and punishments—a principle now used to train AI systems in complex environments such as robotics or game theory (Sutton & Barto, 2018, p. 29).

Conversely, AI offers psychology innovative opportunities to better understand human behavior and cognitive processes. AI's ability to quickly and precisely analyze large amounts of data has the potential to revolutionize classical psychological research. Traditional methods, such as questionnaires or observational studies, are often limited by the amount of data that can be processed. However, AI makes it possible to analyze massive datasets in real time, detect behavioral patterns, and gain deeper insights into psychological phenomena (Schmidhuber, 2015, p. 88). One example is the use of algorithms in the field of emotion research. AI systems can analyze facial expressions, voice intonations, and even writing styles to detect and quantify emotions. These technologies have not only advanced psychological research but have also found applications in areas such as mental health, where AI is used for the diagnosis and treatment of conditions such as depression or anxiety disorders (Fitzpatrick et al., 2017, p. 19).

In the future, psychology could play an even more central role in the development of human-like AI. Models of human cognition provide a blueprint for algorithms capable not only of acting rationally but also of thinking creatively, solving complex problems, and demonstrating social intelligence. One example is the study of emotions in AI. Emotional intelligence, a concept originally popularized by Goleman (1995, p. 43), could help create AI systems that interact better with humans. Such systems could recognize and respond to emotional signals, making them more effective in areas such as customer service, healthcare, or even interpersonal relationships.

Another example is the development of decision-making models. In psychology, there is extensive research on human decision-making, from rational models to the cognitive biases that influence our thinking (Kahneman & Tversky, 1979, p. 267). These insights can be used to develop AI systems that not only decide faster and more accurately but also in a more "human" way—for example, in situations where moral or ethical considerations play a role.

While the collaboration between psychology and AI is promising, it also raises profound questions about human nature. If AI systems are able to simulate human behavior and thought—and in certain areas perhaps even surpass it—what does that mean for our self-understanding? This question is not only philosophical but also psychologically relevant. A central issue is the question of human uniqueness. Traditionally, we have defined our humanity by our capacity for reflection, creativity, and emotional depth. However, if AI systems can imitate these qualities, it becomes increasingly difficult to draw clear boundaries between human and machine. This blurring could trigger psychological uncertainties and challenge our self-image as a species (Harari, 2017, p. 143).

The relationship between psychology and AI is a reciprocal, ever-evolving dynamic. While psychology inspires AI systems and helps them better understand human thought and behavior, AI in turn is changing psychology by providing new tools and perspectives. Yet this relationship is not free of tension. It raises fundamental questions about the future of humanity, the nature of intelligence, and the limits of what machines can—and cannot—achieve.

Ultimately, it is up to us to shape this relationship responsibly. Only through conscious reflection on the ethical, psychological, and societal implications of this development can we ensure that AI remains not just a tool, but becomes a true partner in co-creation.

The Limits of the Revolution

As much potential as AI offers, it also has clear limits when it comes to revolutionizing psychology. As already mentioned, AI excels at detecting patterns and processing large amounts of data. But when it comes to understanding deeper meanings, demonstrating creativity, or navigating moral and ethical dilemmas, the machine remains locked out. Artificial intelligence is by nature calculating, logical, and data-driven—qualities that are invaluable in many areas of psychology. But the human psyche is more than just a collection of data points.

The revolution of psychology through AI will therefore not consist in machines replacing human research or generating fully autonomous knowledge about the human mind. Rather, it will consist in AI being used as a powerful tool that helps us delve deeper into the mysteries of the human psyche. It will support us in detecting phenomena that previously escaped us and equip us with new possibilities for data analysis and prediction. But the ultimate task of understanding and interpreting the meaning of these phenomena will still lie with humans.

The revolution, if one wishes to call it that, will therefore not consist in machines taking over psychology, but in leading psychology to new heights—if we are willing to harness their strengths without overlooking their weaknesses.

Will Psychology Be Revolutionized by AI?

In a sense, the revolution has already begun. AI is in the process of fundamentally changing the way psychological research is conducted. It offers us tools that allow us to probe deeper and faster into the human psyche than we ever thought possible. It challenges us to rethink our methods and our understanding of science. But as with any technological revolution, caution is warranted.

Machines may be able to detect patterns and make predictions, but they will never replace the human ability to create meaning. They can help us, but they cannot understand us. They can analyze, but they cannot feel. The real revolution lies in learning how to use these new tools to expand our understanding of the human psyche—without losing the essence of what makes us human.

8.3 Will the Psychology of the Future Be Defined by Machines?

The question of whether the psychology of the future will be defined by machines opens up a vast and tension-filled field that touches not only on scientific curiosity but also on existential concerns and ethical dilemmas. It is a question that challenges the boundaries between human and machine, between natural and artificial intelligence, and forces us to rethink our notions of thought, consciousness, emotion, and autonomy. Yet it is also a question that, in an uncomfortable way, compels us to reconsider our role as researchers and as subjects of psychology in a radically changing world.

A New Definition of Psychology?

If we assume that psychology is the science of human behavior and experience, then the idea that this discipline could one day be defined by machines seems almost absurd. After all, the human psyche is such a complex and unique phenomenon that it can only be understood and studied by humans themselves—or can it? The assumption that machines might one day take on the role of psychologists, not only analyzing but also interpreting human thoughts, emotions, and behaviors, and perhaps even influencing them therapeutically, seems far-fetched at first glance. Yet developments in artificial intelligence raise precisely this question: What happens when machines learn to understand human psychological processes so well—or at least to simulate them—that they themselves become actors in psychological research and therapy?

A first starting point for exploring this question lies in the rapidly developing ability of machines to detect patterns and analyze large amounts of data. Psychology is traditionally an empirical science based on the collection and evaluation of data to understand human behavior. Machines equipped with machine learning algorithms are able to detect patterns in these data sets that are difficult for the human mind to grasp. In recent years, we have seen machine intelligence increasingly able to predict psychological phenomena: from predicting human decisions to diagnosing mental disorders. If algorithms are already able to predict behavior based on data, why shouldn't they also be able to understand and interpret human behavior?

Psychotherapy by Machines—The Revolution?

The potential of artificial intelligence to revolutionize psychotherapeutic practice is often overlooked. Even today, there are initial approaches in which chatbots act as virtual therapists. These programs can conduct conversations, respond to emotional states, and even offer advice—all based on complex algorithms trained to simulate human behavior and emotions. Let us imagine a future in which such systems are so advanced that they can not only conduct superficial therapeutic conversations but also provide profound emotional insights and interventions. What happens when machines learn to analyze human emotions so well that they can suggest targeted therapeutic measures? Will the human therapist then become obsolete?

But a fundamental question arises: Can a machine that merely simulates emotions really do what human therapists do? Psychotherapy is more than just replicating techniques or offering advice. It is based on empathy, on the interpersonal connection between therapist and patient. The therapeutic relationship is a crucial factor for the success of therapy, and it is hard to imagine that machines could truly replicate this relationship. Empathy requires more than just data analysis—it requires deep understanding and intuitive perception of emotions, something machines lack because they have no consciousness.

But what if people begin to form emotional bonds with machines? Even today, it is evident in many areas of everyday life that people develop a form of "emotional dependence" on technology. Social media, virtual assistants, and even simple notifications on a smartphone have the potential to trigger emotional reactions. So what happens when machines penetrate even further into our psychological and emotional processes? Could people start to see machines as equal or even superior emotional partners who provide comfort and advice in times of emotional distress? And if that happens, what role remains for human psychologists and therapists?

The Machine as Researcher: The Role of AI in Psychological Science

Another dimension of the question of whether the psychology of the future will be defined by machines concerns the scientific study of the human psyche. How does psychology as a scientific discipline change when machines increasingly take on the role of researchers? Even today, many psychological studies rely on algorithms to analyze large amounts of data and detect patterns. This development will certainly intensify in the coming years. But the crucial question is whether machines will one day not only analyze data but also develop their own research questions. Will machines become independent actors in psychological research?

If we consider machines as researchers, another crucial question arises: How does this change the way we understand the human psyche? Machines are able to detect behavioral patterns that are invisible to human researchers. But can they also interpret these patterns? Can they understand the deep, human meaning behind psychological processes? Or will they merely sift through data without grasping the significance of that data? And to be even more provocative: Is human understanding even necessary if machines are able to predict and influence behavior precisely? Could it be that psychological research in the future will be dominated by machines that operate without human interpretation?

This question touches on a central point: the role of human consciousness in psychology. If machines are able to understand human behavior and experience without having consciousness themselves, what does that mean for our understanding of consciousness? Perhaps the development of AI shows us that consciousness is not as necessary as we previously thought. Perhaps it is possible to understand and influence psychological phenomena without having subjective experience oneself. This would shake the very foundations of psychology and force us to rethink our understanding of humanity and intelligence.

AI and the Ethics of Psychology: Who Sets the Rules?

Another important question that arises in connection with the machine definition of psychology concerns the ethical implications. Psychology is not only a science but also a practice dedicated to human well-being. It is deeply embedded in ethical principles designed to ensure the protection of the dignity and autonomy of the individual. As machines take on an ever-greater role in psychological research and practice, the question arises: Who sets the ethical rules? Can machines take on the responsibility of ensuring that psychological interventions serve the well-being of the individual?

The question of ethical responsibility becomes particularly acute when we consider the possibilities of AI in influencing human behavior. Even today, algorithms are capable of manipulating decisions and steering behavior—be it through targeted advertising or the management of social media. What happens when machines begin not only to influence advertising but to control deeper psychological processes? Will psychology become a discipline that no longer serves the autonomy of the individual but is used by machines to optimize behavior—possibly in the service of economic or political interests?

This question leads us directly to another point: control. Who controls the machines that shape the psychology of the future? If psychological processes are analyzed and influenced by machines, it is of great importance that clear ethical rules and control mechanisms are established. But is that even possible? Can we ensure that machines exercising psychological power always serve human well-being? Or do we run the risk that these machines will one day be used to control human behavior in ways that no longer align with the ethical principles of psychology?

Humans and Machines: A New Symbiosis?

In conclusion, the question remains whether the psychology of the future will really be defined by machines—or whether there will be a symbiosis between humans and machines, in which both learn from and benefit each other. It is quite conceivable that machines will play a central role in psychological research and practice in the future without completely replacing humans. Machines could help us gain deeper insights into the human psyche by analyzing data and detecting patterns invisible to us. At the same time, they could act as supporters in therapeutic practice by making precise diagnoses and suggesting tailored therapeutic approaches.

But a complete shift of psychology to machines carries great risks. The human mind is more than the sum of its parts, more than the mere analysis of data and detection of patterns. Psychology is a science deeply rooted in the human—in our emotions, our consciousness, our capacity for self-reflection. Machines may be able to simulate many of these processes, but they will never truly be able to understand them. Ultimately, it remains a human responsibility to ensure that psychology continues to be a discipline that serves human well-being—and not merely the optimization of behavior controlled by machines.

References

Beck, A. T. (1979). *Cognitive Therapy and the Emotional Disorders*. Penguin.

Fitzpatrick, K. K., Darcy, A., & Vierhile, M. (2017). Delivering Cognitive Behavior Therapy to Young Adults With Symptoms of Depression and Anxiety Using a Fully Automated Conversational Agent (Woebot): A Randomized Controlled Trial. *JMIR Mental Health, 4*(2), 19–38. https://doi.org/10.2196/mental.7785

Freud, S. (1912). *Zur Dynamik der Übertragung. Gesammelte Werke VIII*. Imago Publishing.

Goleman, D. (1995). *Emotional Intelligence: Why It Can Matter More Than IQ*. Bantam Books.

Goodfellow, I., Bengio, Y., & Courville, A. (2016). *Deep Learning*. MIT Press.

Harari, Y. N. (2017). *Homo Deus: A Brief History of Tomorrow*. Vintage.

Kahneman, D., & Tversky, A. (1979). Prospect Theory: An Analysis of Decision Under Risk. *Econometrica, 47*(2), 263–292. https://doi.org/10.2307/1914185

Lucas, G. M., Gratch, J., King, A., & Morency, L.-P. (2014). It's Only a Computer: Virtual Humans Increase Willingness to Disclose. *Computers in Human Behavior, 37*, 94–100. https://doi.org/10.1016/j.chb.2014.04.043

Norcross, J. C. (2002). Empirically Supported Therapy Relationships: Summary Report of the Division 29 Task Force. *Psychotherapy: Theory, Research, Practice, Training, 38*(4), 345–356.

Rumelhart, D. E., Hinton, G. E., & Williams, R. J. (1986). Learning Representations by Back-Propagating Errors. *Nature, 323*(6088), 318–362. https://doi.org/10.1038/323533a0

Schmidhuber, J. (2015). Deep Learning in Neural Networks: An Overview. *Neural Networks, S., 61*, 85–117. https://doi.org/10.1016/j.neunet.2014.09.003

Skinner, B. F. (1953). *Science and Human Behavior*. Macmillan.

Sutton, R. S., & Barto, A. G. (2018). *Reinforcement Learning: An Introduction* (2. Aufl.). MIT Press.

Wampold, B. E. (2015). How Important Are the Common Factors in Psychotherapy? *An Update. World Psychiatry, 14*(3), 270–277. https://doi.org/10.1002/wps.20238

9

The Psychological Limits of Artificial Intelligence

"Within our own organism, an intelligence is at work, different from that of our usual personality."

– Wilhelm Herschel

The rapid development of Artificial Intelligence (AI) has initiated an unprecedented transformation of our lives and work over the past decades. AI systems analyze complex data structures, make precise decisions, and are increasingly taking on tasks that were once reserved exclusively for humans. However, these advances raise fundamental questions: Are there limits to what AI can achieve? Which aspects of being human remain irreplaceable even in a technologically advanced world? And how does the growing presence of intelligent machines change our understanding of ourselves?

While AI achieves unparalleled efficiency in areas such as pattern recognition, automated decision-making, and problem-solving, it encounters crucial boundaries when it comes to reproducing central features of the human mind. Emotions, creativity, moral judgment, empathy, and self-reflection—all these qualities are not only technically elusive but also deeply rooted in the biological, social, and cultural nature of humans. These boundaries are not merely limitations of AI but reflect the uniqueness and complexity of the human mind.

Chapter 9 is dedicated to examining these psychological limits of AI. It asks which abilities and characteristics remain exclusively human and what implications this has for our future. The focus is not only on analyzing the

O. Hoffmann, *Psychology and Artificial Intelligence*,
https://doi.org/10.1007/978-3-662-73147-5_9

technical limits of AI but also on the existential and philosophical challenges that arise from confronting a technology that is increasingly taking on human-like functions.

At a time when AI systems are becoming ever more powerful, it is crucial to understand the value and irreplaceability of human qualities. For while machines may surpass us in efficiency, humans remain unique through their capacity for emotional depth, moral reflection, and creative originality. This chapter explores how these qualities not only mark the psychological boundaries of AI but also define the foundation of our humanity.

9.1 What Remains Human? The Eight Irreplaceable Aspects of the Human Mind

The rapid development of Artificial Intelligence has intensified the debate about the limits and possibilities of machine intelligence. Machines that once performed only mechanical tasks can now analyze complex patterns, generate creative outputs, and make seemingly rational decisions. These technological advances raise the question of how unique humans truly are and which of their qualities remain indispensable, even in an increasingly automated world. The discussion about the irreplaceable aspects of the human mind is gaining significance not only scientifically, but also philosophically and ethically (Bostrom, 2014, p. 198 f.).

While AI systems are trained by algorithms and data to efficiently perform specialized tasks, core human abilities are based on qualities that go far beyond mere information processing. Emotions, creativity, moral judgment, consciousness, and empathy are not mechanical processes but deeply rooted features of the human psyche, shaped by experiences, social interactions, and individual reflection (Harari, 2017, p. 270 f.). These qualities are not only expressions of our biology but also of cultural and historical developments that have evolved over millennia.

A key aim of this chapter is to identify the psychological characteristics that distinguish humans from machines. It examines why emotions are more than interpretable data, why creativity transcends what already exists, and why moral judgments possess a depth that eludes the logic of algorithms. The ability for self-reflection, which defines us not only as acting but also as thinking and feeling beings, is also brought into focus. Ultimately, it is about whether and how humans can preserve their distinctive identity in a world shaped by AI.

The discussion about the irreplaceable features of the human mind is by no means new. It touches on central philosophical, psychological, and ethical issues: What distinguishes human consciousness from machine intelligence? Are emotions, creativity, and intuition qualities that can never be replicated by algorithms? These questions are not only theoretically relevant but have concrete effects on how we develop, use, and integrate AI into our society. It becomes clear that certain abilities and qualities of the human mind go far beyond the purely technical processing of information and cannot be replaced by machine systems (Bostrom, 2014, p. 198; Harari, 2017, p. 302).

Central components of being human, such as the depth of emotional experience, the capacity for creativity, moral judgment, consciousness, empathy, and the ability to build complex social relationships, are the focus of this consideration. Emotions, for example, are not just chemical reactions or neural patterns but deeply rooted experiences that shape identity and decisions. Creativity is more than analyzing existing data; it means creating something new that moves beyond known patterns and logic. Consciousness and self-reflection enable us to think about ourselves and take responsibility for our actions—a dimension lacking in AI systems, as they possess neither their own perception nor intention.

The following are eight aspects that, from a psychological perspective, will remain a human stronghold.

1. The Depth of Human Emotions: More Than Just Data

Emotions are an integral part of human existence and play a central role in psychological research, as they significantly influence our behavior, decisions, and interpersonal interactions. While machines, using algorithms and machine learning, are becoming increasingly adept at recognizing emotional states such as joy, fear, or sadness through facial expressions, tone of voice, or textual patterns, their ability to actually "experience" emotions remains a boundary they cannot cross.

Emotions as Subjective Experience

Emotions are not just neural processes but also deep subjective experiences anchored in the human psyche. They arise from the interaction of biological mechanisms, cultural contexts, and individual life histories (Damasio, 1999, p. 35). Joy, for example, is not merely a biochemical process in the brain but a state shaped by personal memories, social interactions, and cultural values.

Humans not only feel joy but also reflect on what makes them happy, how long this feeling will last, and what significance it has in their lives.

Machines, which are based on data and probabilities, can recognize and respond to emotional states—for example, by responding to angry customers with calming words in a customer service scenario—but they do so without any understanding or experience of these states. Their responses are the result of pre-programmed algorithms, not an internal, experienced state.

The Complex Function of Emotions

Emotions serve a multitude of functions in human life that go far beyond simple reactions to external stimuli. They act as signals for our inner needs, help us form social bonds, and guide our behavior in complex decision-making situations (Izard, 2010, p. 367). Fear, for example, can serve a protective function by warning us of potential dangers, while joy increases our motivation and encourages us to repeat positive experiences.

Machines that "simulate" emotions cannot authentically fulfill these functions, as they have no needs or goals of their own. An AI can be programmed to respond to human emotions, for example by suggesting a soothing piece of music when a user is stressed. But this response is purely functional and not connected to any understanding of the meaning or context of the emotion.

Emotional Reflection and Identity

A crucial aspect of human emotions is the capacity for reflection. People not only experience emotions but also question them, analyze their causes, and draw conclusions for their behavior and relationships. This self-reflection is deeply rooted in our self-understanding and enables us to connect emotions with our identity and long-term goals (Gross & Barrett, 2011, p. 5). When someone, for example, feels grief, this emotion is not experienced in isolation but considered in the context of personal values and experiences. Grief can lead to strengthening relationships, reprioritizing, or rethinking one's philosophy of life.

Machines, on the other hand, lack both the ability for self-reflection and the possibility to link emotions to their own identity. An AI system that recognizes and responds to grief cannot place this experience in a broader context or derive personal meaning from it. For machines, emotions are purely external data points to be analyzed and processed, but not experienced.

The Social Dimension of Emotions

Another aspect that illustrates the depth of human emotions is their social dimension. Emotions are not only individual but also a means of communication that helps us build and maintain relationships. Through facial expressions, gestures, and language, we express our feelings and share them with others to create empathy and connection (Ekman, 1992, p. 172). These social interactions are essential for human coexistence and are based on the ability not only to recognize but also to share the emotions of others.

AI systems used in social contexts, such as robots in care settings or chatbots in customer service, can recognize and simulate emotional states, but they cannot build a genuine connection. They are unable to feel compassion or shared joy, as they lack subjective experience and social resonance. Interaction with machines may be useful and functional, but it ultimately remains shallow and one-dimensional compared to the deep emotional resonance humans experience in social relationships.

Emotions as the Core of Human Uniqueness

The inability of machines to authentically experience emotions highlights one of the central limits of Artificial Intelligence. Emotions are not just reactions to external stimuli but are deeply rooted in human identity. They shape our values, influence our decisions, and form the basis for social interactions. They are what make us human, and no machine, no matter how advanced, will ever be able to reach this depth of emotional experience.

Machines can continue to be trained to recognize and respond to emotions, but they will always remain on the surface. The depth of human emotions and their role in our identity and relationships remains inimitable. This irreplaceable feature of humanity not only reveals the limits of AI but also reminds us of what it means to be human—a being that feels, reflects, and is connected through emotions.

2. Creativity: The Ability to Create Something New from Nothing

Creativity is one of the most fascinating and complex qualities of the human mind. It encompasses far more than the mere combination of known elements; it is the process of creating something new and unique—something that did not exist before. Today, the question arises whether machines can also be creative. Yet, on closer inspection, it becomes clear that creativity in the human sense goes far beyond what algorithms can achieve.

Creativity as an Evolutionary Achievement

From an evolutionary perspective, creativity has provided humans with significant survival advantages. It allows for innovative solutions to complex problems, adaptation to new environments, and the creation of cultural achievements. Research shows that creativity is not just a single cognitive function but the result of an interplay between various neural networks, including the Default Mode Network (DMN), the Salience Network, and the Central Executive Network (Beaty et al., 2016, p. 586).

While the DMN is responsible for spontaneous thinking, daydreaming, and generating new ideas, the Central Executive Network serves to critically evaluate these ideas and implement them in reality. This dynamic interaction shows that creativity is a highly complex process that cannot be reduced to linear data processing—the approach on which machine learning is based (Dietrich & Kanso, 2010, p. 823).

The Limits of Machine "Creativity"

AI systems can achieve impressive feats when it comes to analyzing existing data and generating new patterns or designs based on it. A well-known example is the AI system "DeepArt," which creates images in the style of famous painters, or "ChatGPT," which can generate coherent and creative texts. Yet, despite these successes, the so-called creativity of AI is always based on previously input data. These systems recognize patterns and relationships in datasets and generate something "new" based on them. However, this newness always remains within the boundaries of what already exists.

In contrast, human creativity is often characterized by so-called divergent thinking processes—the deliberate or unconscious departure from known patterns to take entirely new paths (Runco & Acar, 2012, p. 66). An artist creating an abstract painting or a scientist developing a groundbreaking theory does not merely draw on past experiences but consciously transcends these boundaries. This leap into the unknown is something machines cannot achieve due to their algorithmic nature.

Intuition as the Basis of Human Creativity

Another central aspect of human creativity is the role of intuition. Intuition can be described as a kind of "inner knowledge" that exists beyond conscious logic and analysis. It is often the result of unconscious pattern recognition based on experience but points in entirely new directions. A famous example of intuitive creativity is the discovery of the DNA double helix by Watson and Crick, where an intuitive insight played a decisive role (Watson, 1968, p. 45).

AI systems, on the other hand, are based on explicit rules and logics. Although they can calculate probabilities and make predictions, they lack the capacity for intuition, as they do not possess the necessary emotional or conscious level required for intuitive decisions. Creativity without intuition remains mechanical and predictable.

Emotions and Subjective Experience as Drivers

Human creativity is deeply shaped by emotions and subjective experiences. The painter who brings his inner struggles to the canvas or the writer who draws from her personal history creates works that are compelling both for their individuality and their emotional depth. Emotions give creative works a meaning and resonance that goes far beyond technical perfection.

AI cannot experience emotions and therefore does not draw from an inner life. While a machine-generated piece of music may be technically flawless, it often lacks the emotional depth that characterizes a human work. Emotions are not just an accompanying phenomenon of creativity but often its driving force. They are the reason why art moves people and why scientists are driven to explore new horizons.

Creativity as a Cultural and Social Phenomenon

Another aspect of human creativity is its embedding in social and cultural contexts. Creative works often arise in dialogue with the environment, with cultural trends, and social challenges. They are not only expressions of individual genius but also products of collective processes. Artists are inspired by others, scientists build on the discoveries of their predecessors, and ideas develop through interaction between individuals.

AI is severely limited in this respect. Although it can analyze and reproduce existing cultural patterns, it lacks the ability to actively participate in cultural and social processes. It is a tool that depends on the instructions and data provided by humans. Creativity that arises from cultural and social exchange thus remains a profoundly human domain.

The Uniqueness of Human Creativity

Human creativity is a multi-layered process that unites intuition, emotions, subjective experiences, and social interactions. While AI can demonstrate impressive achievements in generating patterns and combining existing data, it remains confined to its algorithmic foundations. The human ability to draw from the unknown, to be guided by emotions, and to take entirely new paths makes creativity an irreplaceable quality of the human mind.

Machines may be more efficient, faster, and more precise, but they cannot capture the depth and complexity of human creativity. Creativity remains one of the last refuges of humanity—a testament to the fact that the human mind cannot be reduced to algorithms.

3. Moral Judgment: The Ability to Distinguish Between Good and Evil

Moral judgment is one of the most profound and at the same time most complex abilities of the human mind. It is closely linked to our capacity for empathy, self-reflection, and social interaction. Thus, the question arises as to whether machines will ever be able to make truly moral decisions. The answer reveals the limits of Artificial Intelligence and at the same time highlights the uniqueness of human cognition and emotionality.

Moral Judgment: A Deeply Human Process

Moral judgment is based on a combination of cognitive and emotional processes. People make moral decisions not only by logically weighing consequences but also by experiencing and interpreting values, social norms, and emotional states (Greene et al., 2001, p. 2106). This ability develops throughout the lifespan and is strongly shaped by individual experiences, cultural influences, and social interactions (Haidt, 2001, p. 817). Moral action requires empathy—the ability to understand another's suffering or joy—and responsibility, the awareness of the consequences of one's actions.

The Role of Emotions in Moral Judgment

A key difference between human and machine moral judgment lies in the role of emotions. Studies show that emotions play a decisive role in moral decisions. People feel guilt, shame, or compassion when evaluating moral dilemmas, and these emotions influence the decisions they make (Prinz, 2004, p. 45). Thus, people may perceive a decision as "right" even if it appears objectively illogical, because it is deeply rooted in their values and beliefs.

Artificial Intelligence, on the other hand, has no emotions. Machines analyze data and evaluate scenarios based on algorithms programmed by humans. They can be programmed to implement ethical principles such as the utilitarian model ("the greatest good for the greatest number"), but they do so without any awareness of the moral depth and emotional significance of their decisions.

The Limits of Moral Decisions by Machines

The ability to integrate moral principles into algorithms is limited. While AI systems are increasingly used in areas such as autonomous vehicle control or medical diagnosis, they reach their limits when faced with moral dilemmas. A well-known example is the so-called "trolley problem," in which a train operator must decide whether to divert a train onto a track where one person will die to save five others. Such ethical dilemmas are difficult to resolve because they require not only logical considerations but also moral deliberation and emotional intuition.

Machines can only make calculated decisions in such scenarios, based on probabilities and predefined rules. They cannot assume moral responsibility, as they lack awareness of the significance of their decisions. Ultimately, machines remain tools that depend on human instructions, without the ability to independently develop or evaluate moral values.

Moral Judgment as a Social Process

Moral decisions are often not isolated actions but the result of social interactions. People learn moral principles through exchange with others, through cultural traditions, and by observing social norms. This social dimension is unattainable for machines. Algorithms cannot learn from human interaction but rely on structured data. This dependence on data means that machines often ignore the subtle social and cultural contexts that shape moral decisions.

Responsibility and Moral Weight

A central aspect of moral judgment is the ability to take responsibility. People bear the burden of their decisions and can be held accountable for them. This responsibility is closely linked to the awareness of one's actions. Machines, on the other hand, cannot assume responsibility, as they have neither intention nor an understanding of the consequences of their actions (Floridi & Sanders, 2004, p. 349). This raises profound ethical questions, especially in scenarios where machines make decisions with far-reaching consequences.

The Limits of Machine Morality
While AI systems are capable of making logical and rule-based decisions, moral judgment remains a deeply human ability. Emotions, empathy, and the awareness of responsibility are essential elements of moral decisions that machines cannot replicate. We must be aware of the limits of machine morality and ensure that humans continue to bear responsibility for ethical decisions. For ultimately, moral judgment is more than logic—it is an expression of what makes us human.

4. Consciousness and Self-Reflection: The Deepest Mystery of Being Human

Human consciousness and the capacity for self-reflection are among the most fascinating and at the same time most elusive phenomena in psychology and neuroscience. Consciousness describes the experience of one's own existence, the perception of thoughts and feelings, and the ability to reflect on them. It is a quality that not only fundamentally shapes human cognition but also forms our conception of identity, autonomy, and free will. Can a machine ever develop consciousness or reach the depth of human self-reflection?

Consciousness: A Multi-Layered Concept
Consciousness encompasses various levels. On the one hand, there is phenomenological consciousness, which refers to the subjective perception of experiences—such as seeing a color or feeling pain. On the other hand, there is reflective consciousness, which includes the ability to think about one's own existence and thoughts (Block, 1995, p. 227). This reflective consciousness is closely linked to self-reflection, that is, the ability to critically question one's own actions and thoughts.

People use this ability to recognize mistakes, correct their actions, and learn from experience. Self-reflection is therefore a central foundation for personal growth and moral development (Varela et al., 1991, p. 14). Without this ability, humans would not be able to evaluate their existence or set long-term goals.

AI and the Absence of Consciousness
Although AI systems achieve impressive feats in data processing, pattern recognition, and decision-making, they lack consciousness in the human sense.

Machines operate purely algorithmically. They analyze data and execute programmed actions without understanding what they are doing or why they are doing it. An AI system that, for example, analyzes a medical image does not "know" that it is doing so—it merely calculates probabilities and delivers a result.

This lack of self-awareness is also evident in the fact that machines have no intentions. While humans plan their actions based on desires, beliefs, and goals, machines merely react to inputs. Even with advanced neural networks, referred to as "learning systems," there is no inner experience or reflection on their own processes. A machine cannot pause, evaluate its own decisions, or think about its "existence."

Self-Reflection: The Core of Human Autonomy

Self-reflection enables humans to grow beyond themselves. It is the foundation for critical thinking, moral development, and creative problem-solving. Through self-reflection, people can recognize their strengths and weaknesses, question their attitudes and values, and position themselves in a social context. This ability is not only important individually but also essential for the functioning of societies, as it fosters empathy, responsibility, and cooperation (Taylor, 1985, p. 32).

AI, on the other hand, lacks this depth. Even when machines are programmed to "correct" errors, this process is based on predefined rules and algorithms. It is not conscious reflection but an adaptation to new data. An AI cannot question its "actions" because it has neither intention nor self-awareness.

The Philosophical Problem of Consciousness

The question of whether machines can ever develop consciousness is not only technically but also philosophically highly complex. David Chalmers (1996) coined the term "the hard problem of consciousness," which deals with the question of how and why physical processes in the brain give rise to subjective experiences. Even if we were to fully understand the neural mechanisms of consciousness, it remains unclear how these could be transferred to machines.

A main problem is that consciousness does not result merely from information processing but from a phenomenological experience that seems to be tied to biological systems. Machines can process information, but they "experience" nothing. This raises fundamental questions about the nature of consciousness and the limits of AI.

Consciousness as the Key to Humanity
Consciousness is not only a scientific puzzle but also the heart of what it means to be human. It allows us to situate ourselves in the world, build relationships, and make moral decisions. Without consciousness, there would be no art, no philosophy, no culture—all the things that distinguish humans from machines.

Artificial Intelligence may surpass humans in certain areas, but without consciousness, it remains a tool dependent on human input. The depth and complexity of the human mind are inextricably linked to consciousness, and as long as machines cannot develop this, they remain far from capturing the essence of being human.

5. Empathy: The Ability to Put Oneself in Another's Shoes

Empathy is one of the central characteristics that distinguishes humans as social beings. It is more than just the ability to recognize the emotional states of others—it encompasses a deep understanding and participation in another's feelings, thoughts, and experiences. Despite impressive advances in emotion recognition by algorithms, the limits of machine empathy remain obvious.

The Psychological Basis of Empathy
Empathy is based on a complex interplay between cognitive and emotional processes. It requires us to adopt another's perspective (cognitive empathy) and to be able to understand their emotional states (emotional empathy). Neuroscientific studies show that this ability is rooted in the activity of certain brain regions, particularly the prefrontal cortex and the limbic system, which are crucial for social interaction and emotional processing (Decety & Jackson, 2004, p. 73). Mirror neurons also play an important role, as they enable us to intuitively "mirror" the feelings and actions of others (Gallese et al., 2004, p. 396).

Empathy does not arise in isolation, but within a social context. It is shaped by upbringing, cultural influences, and individual experiences. This social dimension makes empathy a dynamic, developable ability that is deeply rooted in an individual's experiences and relationships. Machines, which are based on algorithms and data, lack this social grounding, which significantly limits their capacity for genuine empathy.

Emotion Recognition versus Empathy

AI systems have now achieved remarkable progress in recognizing emotions. Through machine learning, algorithms are able to identify emotional states from facial expressions, tone of voice, or textual statements. This ability has found applications in areas such as customer service, healthcare, and entertainment. For example, a chatbot can detect whether a user is frustrated and respond with calming or problem-solving answers.

But emotion recognition is not the same as empathy. While machines can analyze and predict emotional patterns, they lack the subjective experience of emotions. Empathy requires not only knowing what someone feels, but also sharing in those feelings and allowing that experience to inform our actions. Machines can respond to emotional input, but they do so without an awareness of the meaning or context of the emotions. Their responses therefore remain mechanical and lack the depth that characterizes human interactions.

The Social Function of Empathy

Empathy serves a crucial social function, as it forms the foundation of interpersonal relationships. It enables us to resolve conflicts, foster cooperation, and form deeper bonds. Empathy is not only an individual ability, but also a mechanism that strengthens social cohesion and holds communities together (Batson et al., 2007, p. 67). In social relationships, empathy allows us to perceive subtle emotional signals and respond appropriately. This ability is especially central in professions such as therapy, caregiving, or education.

Machines can simulate social functions by, for example, using soothing words or offering assistance. But they do not act out of genuine compassion or a deep understanding of the social context. This limitation makes them useful tools, but not true social actors.

Empathy and Moral Action

Another crucial aspect of empathy is its role in moral action. Empathy enables us to recognize the suffering of others and to act accordingly. It is a central driver of altruistic behavior and moral decision-making (Hoffman, 2000, p. 7). This connection between empathy and morality is absent in machines. AI systems can be programmed to follow moral principles, but they do so without a sense of the moral significance of their decisions.

For example, an AI-based medical system can prioritize which patient is treated first, based on algorithms that assess urgency. But it lacks the ability to feel compassion for the fears or pain of the patients. Without this empathic dimension, machine action remains limited to purely functional and rule-based processes.

The Limits of Machine Empathy

While AI has made impressive progress in simulating empathic behavior, it remains fundamentally limited. Genuine empathy requires consciousness, a deep understanding of the meaning of emotions, and the ability to put oneself in another's subjective perspective. These aspects are inseparably linked to human consciousness and experience—elements that machines lack.

AI systems can be trained to imitate human behavior, but they remain tools based on data and algorithms. They possess neither an understanding of the significance of their actions nor the ability to form genuine emotional connections. This is a crucial boundary that even the most advanced systems cannot cross.

The Uniqueness of Human Empathy

Empathy is more than a cognitive ability—it is an expression of the depth and complexity of human experience. It shapes our moral actions, our social relationships, and our ability to connect with others. While AI systems are able to recognize emotional states and respond to them, their capacity for genuine empathy remains limited. This boundary marks a central difference between humans and machines and underscores the uniqueness of human interaction. In an increasingly technologized world, it is therefore crucial to preserve the importance of empathy as an essential aspect of human existence.

6. Freedom and Responsibility: Human Autonomy

The ability to act freely and take responsibility for one's own decisions is an essential component of human existence. Autonomy means that people are able to make conscious decisions that are not determined solely by external circumstances or internal constraints. This concept is inseparably linked to moral awareness, self-reflection, and the capacity for empathy—abilities that artificial intelligence lacks. Machines do not act out of their own will or conscious reflection, but follow programmed instructions and optimize processes within given parameters. The difference between human and machine decision-making reveals the fundamental limit of AI and underscores the uniqueness of human autonomy.

Autonomy and Freedom of Choice: A Psychological Foundation

From a psychological perspective, autonomy is more than just the ability to make decisions. It encompasses awareness of alternative courses of action, the ability to self-determine, and an understanding of the consequences of one's actions. Deci and Ryan (1985) emphasize in their self-determination theory that autonomy is a fundamental human motivation. It enables individuals to perceive actions as self-initiated and authentic, which is crucial for the sense of self-efficacy and psychological well-being (Deci & Ryan, 1985, p. 37).

Machines based on algorithms do not possess this self-awareness. Their "decisions" arise from processing data and applying pre-programmed rules. Even if AI systems develop a certain adaptability through machine learning, their decision-making remains reactive and deterministic. They lack the ability to perceive actions as the result of free will.

Responsibility and Moral Reflection

A central aspect of human autonomy is the ability to take responsibility. Responsibility implies not only acknowledging the consequences of an action, but also moral reflection on whether that action is justified. People can admit mistakes, feel remorse, and learn from these experiences. This moral dimension of action is deeply rooted in the human psyche and is influenced by social, cultural, and individual factors.

AI systems, on the other hand, are incapable of taking responsibility, as they do not pursue any conscious intention. They perform calculations and make decisions that are merely the result of algorithmic processes. Responsibility for the actions of machines always lies with the developers, users, or institutions that deploy them. This leads to a dilemma: In an increasingly automated world where AI makes important decisions, the assignment of responsibility often becomes unclear. Who is responsible if an autonomous vehicle causes an accident or a medical algorithm makes a wrong diagnosis? These questions underscore that responsibility does not depend on the mere functionality of a machine, but on the conscious reflection and moral integrity of the actor.

The Role of Self-Reflection

Self-reflection is another aspect that distinguishes human autonomy from machine action. Humans can reflect on their own thoughts, feelings, and actions, evaluate them, and adjust them if necessary. This capacity for metacognition allows us to place our behavior in a broader context and to consider long-term consequences. It is the foundation for personal development, ethical action, and the ability to take responsibility.

AI systems do not possess metacognition. They can analyze data and recognize patterns, but they cannot reflect on their own processes. Without self-reflection, they lack the foundation for autonomous action in the human sense. They are limited to pursuing pre-programmed goals without questioning the "why" of their actions.

Freedom and the Limits of Determinism

A common argument in the discussion about AI is that human decisions are also, to some extent, determined by biological, psychological, and social factors. Neuroscientific studies have shown that many decisions are based on unconscious processes that occur before conscious awareness (Libet, 1985, p. 536). Nevertheless, humans remain capable of consciously reflecting on and modifying these unconscious impulses. This ability for reflection and conscious control distinguishes humans from machines.

Machines, on the other hand, are completely deterministic. Their "decisions" are the result of algorithms that generate specific outputs based on specific inputs. They have no freedom to deviate from these specifications or to redefine their "goals." This deterministic nature makes machines powerful tools, but it excludes the possibility that they could ever act autonomously in the human sense.

Autonomy and Social Responsibility

Human autonomy is not only an individual trait, but also a social one. Our decisions affect other people and are embedded in a social and cultural context. The responsibility that arises from this social dimension of autonomy requires empathy, moral judgment, and the ability to take the perspective of others.

AI systems can analyze social contexts and make decisions based on probabilities and data. But they cannot assume social responsibility, as they are unable to understand the emotional and moral impact of their actions. This limits their ability to operate in complex social systems, where not only logic but also compassion and moral intuition are required.

The Uniqueness of Human Autonomy

The ability to make free choices and to take responsibility is one of the central characteristics that distinguishes humans from machines. While AI systems have developed impressive abilities in data processing and decision-making, their actions remain limited by algorithms. They do not act out of their own will, possess no metacognition, and are incapable of assuming moral responsibility. These limitations make it clear that human autonomy remains irreplaceable—not only as an expression of individual action, but also as the foundation for moral, empathic, and reflective action in a complex world.

7. Intuition and Gut Feeling: The Illogical Paths of the Human Mind

Intuition is one of the most mysterious and at the same time most powerful abilities of the human mind. It describes the ability to make decisions or judgments without relying on conscious, rational deliberation. In contrast to logical-analytical thinking, which proceeds systematically, intuition is based on an apparently spontaneous grasp of connections and meanings. This human trait stands in sharp contrast to the strictly logical and data-driven processes that characterize artificial intelligence.

The Psychological Basis of Intuition

Intuition is not a magical ability, but is deeply rooted in the cognitive processes of the human brain. It arises through unconscious pattern recognition, which operates on the basis of experience and stored memories. Kahneman (2011, p. 21) distinguishes between two thinking systems: the slow, conscious System 2, which works logically and analytically, and the fast, unconscious System 1, which is responsible for intuitive decisions. This fast thinking enables us to react to complex situations in fractions of a second—often without knowing why we act as we do.

Neuroscientific studies show that intuition is strongly linked to the emotional centers of the brain, particularly the amygdala and the ventromedial prefrontal cortex (Bechara et al., 1997, p. 1293). These structures play a central role in evaluating situations based on past experiences and emotional reactions. Intuition is thus the result of a subtle interplay between emotion, experience, and unconscious cognition.

Intuition and Decision-Making

The importance of intuition is particularly evident in complex or uncertain situations where logical analyses would be inadequate or time-consuming. In such cases, intuition enables quick and often surprisingly accurate decisions. This is especially true in professions that require high expertise, such as doctors who make diagnoses based on subtle signs, or chess masters who intuitively recognize the best move without explicitly calculating every possibility (Dreyfus & Dreyfus, 1986, p. 40).

However, intuition is not always reliable. Its strength lies in its speed and efficiency, but it is susceptible to cognitive biases and emotional influences. Faulty intuition can lead to hasty conclusions or inaccurate assessments. This dual nature makes intuition a fascinating and at the same time elusive field of research in psychology.

Intuition and Artificial Intelligence

Machines, by contrast, operate with explicit rules, algorithms, and data. They can analyze vast amounts of data and recognize patterns that remain invisible to humans. Yet, although AI can achieve results similar to human intuition—for example, through neural networks that detect patterns in unstructured data—it lacks the subjective experience and the spontaneous, emotional component that characterizes human intuition.

An example of this is the so-called "black box" of AI, in which algorithms make decisions that are difficult even for developers to comprehend. These decisions may be based on highly complex analysis, but they are not intuition in the true sense. Intuition involves more than just pattern recognition; it is a deeply rooted, often emotional process that cannot be fully mapped into data and algorithms.

Intuition and Creativity

Intuition plays a crucial role in creative processes. Artists, writers, and musicians often report that their best ideas arise spontaneously—a flash of inspiration that cannot be explained by logical reasoning. This form of intuition, often referred to as "creative intuition," is closely linked to unconscious processes and emotional states (Sadler-Smith, 2015, p. 30). Creative intuition enables connections to be made between seemingly unrelated concepts and innovative solutions to be found.

AI systems can appear creative by recombining existing data or generating variations. They can create impressive works of art or compose music, but these processes are based on predetermined algorithms and patterns. They do not arise from an inner inspiration or a subjective urge for expression, as is the case with humans.

The Limits of Machine Intuition

The human capacity for intuition is enhanced by the ability for self-reflection and emotional involvement. Intuition is often closely linked to the subjective sense of meaning and value—aspects that are unattainable for AI. A machine may work proactively and efficiently, but it will never "feel" why a decision is right or wrong. This lack of emotional and subjective context limits AI's ability to demonstrate genuine intuition.

Even if AI systems were able to imitate complex intuitive processes, the question would remain whether they could ever enjoy the trust and acceptance that human intuition inspires. People trust intuitive decisions not only because they are effective, but also because they are based on experiences and feelings that they themselves can understand and relate to.

Intuition as an Irreplaceable Human Ability

Intuition remains a central aspect of being human, one that can neither be fully understood nor replaced by machines. It enables quick and often accurate decisions in complex situations, plays a key role in creative processes, and is deeply rooted in our emotional and cognitive experiences. While AI has made impressive advances in pattern recognition and decision-making, it ultimately remains limited to algorithmic processes that cannot match the depth or spontaneous creativity of human intuition.

The study of intuition not only provides deeper insights into the nature of the human mind, but also highlights the limits and possibilities of AI. Intuition reminds us that humans are more than a collection of data and processes—they are beings with emotions, experiences, and a consciousness that makes them unique.

Human Relationships: The Social Fabric

Interpersonal relationships are a core component of human existence. They shape our identity, our development, and our psychological well-being. However, relationships are not just superficial interactions; they are based on deep, emotional, and cognitive connections that develop over time and are characterized by mutual trust, understanding, and empathy. Artificial intelligence may be able to simulate social interactions and even function as a conversational partner or virtual companion, but its ability to build genuine relationships remains limited. The reason for this lies in the nature of human relationships, which are characterized by emotional depth, social complexity, and dynamic development.

Trust as the Foundation of Human Relationships

Trust is the basis of every deep relationship. It develops through shared experiences, reliability, and the ability to engage with the needs and emotions of the other. However, trust is not a static state—it must be constantly nurtured and renewed, as it can also be shaken by disappointments or conflicts. Studies in social psychology show that trust depends not only on rational considerations, but is strongly shaped by emotions (Mayer et al., 1995, p. 710).

Machines can simulate trust through programmed reliability, but this trust remains functional. An algorithm may act efficiently and reliably, but it cannot express intention or concern for the well-being of its counterpart. Trust based solely on mechanical interactions is therefore limited and fundamentally different from the trust that arises in human relationships.

Emotional Bond: More Than Functional Interaction

A central feature of human relationships is the emotional bond. This arises not only through shared interests or goals, but through the ability to share feelings, show compassion, and provide mutual emotional support. Emotional bonding is often described as the "glue" that holds relationships together. Neuroscientific research has shown that bonding between people is promoted by complex neurobiological processes such as the release of oxytocin, which enhances feelings of closeness and trust (Feldman, 2012, p. 379).

AI can imitate emotional bonding by responding to certain stimuli or feigning empathy, but these responses are algorithmically controlled and not the result of genuine emotional processes. While a human can empathize with another's joy or suffering, a machine's response remains limited to pre-programmed patterns and data analysis. This prevents a genuine bond from forming.

Conflict and Reconciliation: Dynamics in Human Relationships

Another central aspect of interpersonal relationships is the ability to deal with conflicts and find reconciliation. Conflicts are inevitable, as people have different needs, perspectives, and emotions. But the way conflicts are resolved plays a decisive role in the depth and stability of a relationship. Conflict resolution requires empathy, self-reflection, and often a willingness to compromise (Deutsch, 2000, p. 28).

Machines cannot experience real conflicts, as they have no needs or perspectives of their own. They can respond to disputes or misunderstandings by applying de-escalation techniques, but these remain mechanical. The ability to reconcile—the profound emotional experience that comes with forgiveness and renewed connection—remains inaccessible to them.

Time and Shared Experiences: The Development of Relationships

Genuine relationships do not develop overnight; they grow through shared experiences, challenges, and memories. This temporal dimension is essential, as it deepens trust and strengthens bonds. Psychological studies show that the quality of a relationship is often defined by the time spent together and the intensity of shared experiences (Aron et al., 1997, p. 367).

Machines cannot have a past or remember shared experiences in a profound way. While algorithms can store information and respond based on it, they lack the ability to embed this information in a personal and emotional narrative. For example, an AI can remember which movies a user prefers, but it cannot create a shared memory of the emotions or conversations associated with those experiences.

The Limits of Machine Relationships

Despite all advances in AI technology, the difference between human and machine relationships remains fundamental. Machines can simulate social interactions and serve as useful tools in certain contexts, but they cannot build genuine relationships. The emotional depth, capacity for self-reflection, and dynamic development that characterize human relationships are aspects that machines cannot grasp.

This boundary has not only technical but also ethical implications. As machines are increasingly used as substitutes for human interactions, there is a risk that genuine relationships will be devalued or replaced. This could be particularly problematic in areas such as caregiving, therapy, or education, where human connections are of crucial importance.

The Uniqueness of Human Relationships

Human relationships are unique in their complexity, emotional depth, and dynamic nature. They are based on trust, empathy, and the ability to engage with one another. Machines may be able to simulate certain aspects of social interaction, but they cannot create genuine bonds. The uniqueness of human relationships lies in their ability to form deep emotional connections, resolve conflicts, and grow through shared experiences. It remains essential to preserve the value and significance of these relationships.

The Irreplaceable Aspects of the Human Mind

Artificial intelligence has made impressive progress in recent decades, but it remains limited to certain abilities. What remains for humans are the irreplaceable aspects of their mind—emotions, creativity, moral judgment, consciousness, empathy, freedom, intuition, and the ability to form deep interpersonal relationships. Machines may surpass us in information processing and the efficiency of certain tasks, but they cannot capture the experiences, depth, and complexity of human life.

The irreplaceable aspects of the human mind are the essence of what makes us human. They are the abilities that cannot be reduced to algorithms, that cannot simply be calculated or simulated. As our world becomes increasingly shaped by machines, it is crucial to recognize and preserve these aspects of our humanity—not only to protect our own identity, but also to ensure that we see the machines we have created for what they are: tools, not replacements.

9.2 AI as a Mirror of the Human Psyche: What Machines Teach Us About Ourselves

In the age of artificial intelligence, we are confronted with a fascinating, perhaps even disturbing realization: the machines we create are far more than mere tools or efficient problem-solvers. They are beginning to become a mirror of ourselves—a reflection of our abilities, weaknesses, and, even more interestingly, our psyche. But what exactly does this reflection reveal? What can machines teach us about being human, and are we ready to face the possibly uncomfortable truth?

Since the dawn of their existence, humans have created tools to master their environment and extend their abilities. But in the case of AI, it is about much more. Artificial intelligence is not just a technical aid that supports us physically or intellectually—it mimics our thought processes, our decision-making, and, to a certain extent, even our emotions. When we look into the "mirror" of AI, we see not only the machines, but also ourselves in a new light. But what exactly do we see?

The Emergence of AI: A Projection of Our Cognitive Structure

The first aspect we can recognize in the reflection through AI is the way we think as humans. When we began developing AI systems, we tried to simulate the human brain and its functioning. Neural networks, which replicate the structure and processes of the brain, are at the heart of modern AI. These networks are capable of recognizing patterns, processing information, and making decisions based on data—much like our brain does.

What does this mean for us as humans? In a sense, we have created machines in our own image by attempting to transfer our cognitive abilities to them. However, this projection is only a simplified representation. It shows us not only what constitutes our thinking, but also how we want to understand ourselves. We have reduced the human brain to its rational, logical processes and regarded these as the quintessence of our intelligence. But is that really all there is to our thinking? AI holds up a mirror to us and shows how one-sided and reductionist our understanding of intelligence often is.

In this reflection, an uncomfortable truth is revealed: our image of human intelligence is incomplete. AI systems are extremely good at recognizing patterns in data and finding solutions to clearly defined problems. But they also show what they lack—and thus what distinguishes us as humans: intuition, creativity, and the ability to navigate uncertainty and ambiguity. These aspects of our intelligence have not yet been integrated into machine systems, perhaps because we ourselves find them difficult to explain or define. So what AI teaches us is not only what we are, but above all what we are not—or at least what we do not fully comprehend.

Emotional Simulation: Machines as Mirrors of Our Inner World

A particularly fascinating and at the same time unsettling area in which AI acts as a mirror image is the simulation of emotions. With the development of emotional AI systems capable of recognizing, imitating, and responding to human feelings, the question arises: What happens when machines mirror our innermost emotional impulses?

Machines that simulate emotions are nothing more than complex pattern recognition and response systems. They recognize facial expressions, analyze tone of voice or speech patterns, and respond accordingly. Yet this imitation of emotional intelligence forces us to reflect on the nature of our own emotions. Are emotions merely biochemical reactions that we can replicate mechanically, or is there more to them?

In this reflection through AI, it becomes clear that as humans, we are often in search of validation and empathy—even if it comes from a machine. An AI-based system that seemingly understands and responds to our emotional needs can give us the feeling of being understood—even when we know the machine has no real consciousness. Here, a paradoxical truth about ourselves emerges: We long for connection, even if that connection is artificial and inauthentic.

Machines that mirror emotions also force us to question our relationship to genuine human emotions. If a machine is able to recognize grief and respond to it, what does that mean for the human experience of grief? Does it devalue our emotions if they can be understood by something so mechanical? Or does it rather show us that our emotions are based on universal patterns that even machines can recognize?

The Illusion of Objectivity: AI as a Mirror of Our Biases

One of the most fascinating and provocative aspects of AI is its supposed objectivity. It is often claimed that machines are neutral—they process data without human bias and make objective decisions. But in reality, AI is anything but objective. It reflects the biases and assumptions that we as humans embed in its development.

When we look into the "mirror" of AI, we see how deeply our own cognitive distortions and prejudices are embedded in these systems. Algorithms used for "objective" decisions—whether in criminal justice, healthcare, or finance—have repeatedly proven to be biased. Why? Because the data on which these systems are based were collected by humans who themselves have biases. Thus, AI becomes a mirror that confronts us with our own social inequalities and prejudices.

This reflection is uncomfortable because it forces us to take responsibility. Machines are not neutral because we are not. In a way, AI exposes our illusion of objectivity and compels us to recognize our own blind spots. When we trust algorithms that make decisions about life and death, success and failure, we should ask ourselves: Do we really trust the machine, or are we merely trusting our own, often flawed, assumptions that we project onto the machine?

Creativity and Intuition: What AI Teaches Us About Human Genius

One of the greatest challenges in developing AI is creating machines that can think creatively. Creativity, it seems, is a deeply human ability that is difficult to encode. Yet AI systems have recently made impressive advances in art, writing, and music. Machines that write poetry, create paintings, or compose music raise the question: Is creativity really a purely human trait? Or do we simply have a romanticized notion of creativity that prevents us from seeing that machines, too, can be creative?

What AI reflects back to us here is our own uncertainty about what constitutes creativity. Is it the process of creation itself that is creative, or the intention behind it? If a machine is able to create a work of art that moves us emotionally, does it matter that the machine has no awareness of the creative process? In this reflection, another provocative truth about ourselves is revealed: Perhaps creativity is less a unique gift of the human mind than we would like to admit. Perhaps it is simply the ability to combine existing patterns in new ways—something that machines are increasingly good at.

Yet there is a crucial difference that AI also teaches us: Machines may be creative, but they are not creative in the human sense. They have no intention of their own, no vision, no meaning that they attribute to their work. And that is precisely what makes human creativity so unique. When AI holds up the mirror to us, we see that creativity is more than just the creation of something new—it is the ability to create something that has meaning for us.

Autonomy and Decision-Making: What AI Teaches Us About Our Freedom

Finally, the question of autonomy is perhaps the most provocative lesson that AI teaches us about ourselves. Machines are taking over more and more decision-making processes—they make diagnoses, give us recommendations, and even control our vehicles. But what does this mean for our own freedom of choice? If we increasingly delegate decisions to machines, do we lose our autonomy, or are we freeing ourselves from the burden of having to make decisions all the time?

AI reflects our own ambivalences back to us. On the one hand, we value our autonomy and our right to make free choices. On the other hand, we often look for ways to relinquish responsibility, especially in complex or stressful situations. Machines offer us the perfect excuse to evade this responsibility. But what then remains of our humanity? Are we still autonomous if we rely on machines to make decisions for us?

In this reflection, AI shows us that freedom is not only the right to make decisions, but also the burden of living with the consequences of those decisions. Machines that make decisions for us relieve us of this burden—but at the same time, they also rob us of a piece of our humanity. What AI teaches us, then, is that freedom lies not only in the ability to choose, but in the willingness to take responsibility for that choice.

The Mirror AI Holds Up to Us

Artificial intelligence is more than just a technical achievement—it is a reflection of the human psyche. In its strengths and weaknesses, it reveals to us who we are and how we see ourselves. It shows us our cognitive abilities, but also our prejudices. It mirrors our emotions, makes us reflect on creativity, and puts our concept of freedom to the test.

In the end, AI poses the most provocative question of all: Are we ready to accept what this mirror shows us? Or do we flee from the realization that the machines we have created can teach us more about ourselves than we may be willing to admit?

Is AI the Next Stage of Human Evolution or Just a Tool?

The question of whether artificial intelligence represents the next stage of human evolution or remains merely a tool may at first glance seem like a purely technological consideration. But in fact, it touches on much deeper, existential, and philosophical dimensions. At its core, it is not only about what machines can do, but also about our understanding of what it means to be human, of progress, and of the relationship between creator and creation.

Humans as Toolmakers: A Historical Perspective
The history of humanity has always been shaped by the creation of tools. From the first hand axe to complex machines, we have always strived to control our environment and expand our abilities. Tools are nothing more than extensions of our bodies and minds—they help us work faster, see farther, lift heavier, or calculate more precisely. Each tool brought a new stage of human development, but the fundamental question was never asked: Could the tool one day surpass us?

With the advent of artificial intelligence, this paradigm has shifted. For the first time in history, we have created a "tool" that not only extends our physical abilities but also our cognitive ones. It can learn, it can draw conclusions, and in certain areas, it can be faster and more precise than we are. This inevitably leads to the question: If machines can surpass us intellectually, to what extent are they still tools? And could they actually represent the next stage of human evolution?

Evolution: A Misunderstanding?
Before we turn to the question of whether AI could be part of human evolution, we should take a step back and clarify what evolution actually means. Evolution is not a goal-oriented process. It is not a linear development moving toward a specific goal. It is a process of adaptation, the survival of the fittest—not the strongest or most intelligent, but the one best adapted to its environment.

In this sense, one could argue that AI is not a natural part of evolution. Evolution takes place in nature, not in the laboratories or on the servers of Google and IBM. Machines are designed by us; they are the product of our intelligence, not the result of a natural selection process. But what if we broaden the definition of evolution? If we see the creation of AI as a continuation of our natural ability to adapt to the environment—this time by expanding our cognitive abilities with the help of machines? In that case, one could certainly argue that AI is part of our evolutionary development—albeit not in the classical sense.

Humans as Homo Technologicus

Humans as "Homo Technologicus" are not only a product of biological evolution but also a consequence of their continuous technological innovations. Technology has always been a tool for humans to shape their environment, secure their survival, and expand their understanding of the world. But while language, writing, tools, or machines were extensions of our physical and mental abilities, artificial intelligence presents a fundamental challenge: It is no longer merely a tool, but a system that is potentially capable of learning, acting, and making decisions independently. This development raises profound questions about the role of humans in a world increasingly shaped by non-human intelligences.

The idea that AI could be the next stage of evolutionary development shifts the perspective on humans as the central actors in the world. In the past, technological innovations have always affirmed humans in their role as shapers of the world. The domestication of plants and animals, the industrial revolution, and the digital transformation all showed how technology amplified human influence on the environment. But AI stands at a threshold where it not only serves as an amplifier of human abilities but potentially surpasses them. This leads to an existential question: Does humanity lose its status as the dominant intelligent being when machines are able to outperform it in cognitive tasks?

The degradation of humans by the superiority of AI may at first seem like a disturbing scenario. Yet this superiority is, in many ways, relative and strongly depends on the definition of intelligence. In AI research, intelligence is often reduced to the ability to solve problems, recognize patterns, and think logically. This cognitive functionality is impressive, but it does not capture the entirety of human intelligence. Humans are characterized not only by their cognitive abilities but also by their emotions, creativity, empathy, and moral reflection. While machines achieve impressive feats in data processing and pattern recognition, they lack awareness of context, the ability for self-reflection, and an understanding of the deeper meaning of decisions.

The technological development of AI also raises the question of whether, by creating such systems, humans have actually achieved a kind of "divinity," as some argue. But this metaphor is problematic, as it ignores AI's dependence on human input. Machines are products of human thought, programming, and design. They are not autonomous entities in the metaphysical sense, but tools that, while complex, are still limited in their autonomy. Humans remain the ones who determine the goals and values embedded in AI systems. Even highly developed systems capable of improving their own algorithms operate within frameworks created by humans.

A central aspect of this discussion is the question of whether humans lose their relevance as AI systems become increasingly integrated into everyday life. History shows that technological advances have often confronted humans with similar challenges. The introduction of the steam engine or automation in industry led to fears of unemployment and social uprooting. Nevertheless, these developments have, in the long term, created new opportunities and social structures. The same could be true for AI: While certain professions and tasks are replaced by machines, new areas may emerge where human abilities are in demand, especially those requiring empathy, creativity, and moral judgment.

Another central issue is the question of what intelligence actually means at its core. Is it really just the ability to think logically and solve problems efficiently? Or is it rather a multifaceted trait that also includes emotional intelligence, creativity, and social competence? AI systems may be able to solve mathematical problems or make medical diagnoses, but they neither understand the emotional context of their actions nor the deeper meaning of decisions in a social or moral framework. These aspects of human intelligence, which have developed over millennia of social and cultural evolution, are not easily encoded in algorithms.

In conclusion, the view of "Homo Technologicus" shows that humans do not necessarily lose their relevance in dealing with AI, but must redefine their role. The challenge is to recognize and preserve unique human abilities in a technologized world. Despite the advances of AI, humans remain beings defined by their capacity for reflection, empathy, and creativity. The task now is to find a balance between technological possibilities and human values, and to ensure that humans remain not only creators but also shapers of the future.

Tool or Something More?

The question of whether AI can be regarded as merely a tool or whether it represents a new kind of entity touches on fundamental concepts of human self-perception and power. A tool in the classical sense is an aid controlled by the user, whose function depends on human intention. But artificial intelligence, especially systems with machine learning, eludes this simple understanding. It no longer acts solely on the basis of pre-programmed commands, but develops its "competencies" through independent analysis and adaptation to new data. This complicates the definition of "tool," as the boundaries between human control and machine autonomy are increasingly blurred.

A central aspect of this dilemma is the ability of modern AI systems to make decisions that surpass human decisions in their complexity and efficiency. While a hammer or a microscope serves solely to enhance human abilities, AI systems such as autonomous vehicles, medical diagnostic algorithms, or financial analysis tools are able to make independent decisions based on data. They not only replace human actions but increasingly take over tasks that were once reserved for human intellect. This raises the question of whether such systems are still tools in the traditional sense or whether they form a new category—a kind of "machine agent" that can act independently of direct human control.

The psychological implication of this development lies in the shift in the balance of power between humans and machines. Tools, as traditionally understood, strengthen the human sense of control and competence. But AI, which appears to act "independently," could undermine this feeling. Humans are no longer perceived solely as the central actors but share the stage with a technology that is superior in many areas. This leads to a field of tension between fascination and fear. On the one hand, the autonomous functioning of AI opens up unprecedented possibilities; on the other hand, there is concern that we could lose control over our own creation.

Another psychologically relevant element is the question of intentionality. Tools have no goals; they perform tasks defined by the user. But with AI systems, the question arises as to whether their decisions, based on complex algorithms and data analyses, could be interpreted as forms of "goals." Even if these goals ultimately result from human programming, AI systems often appear to behave "intelligently" or "intentionally." This reinforces the ambivalence as to whether AI systems can be regarded as mere tools or whether they represent a kind of rudimentary form of agency.

This discussion is particularly relevant with regard to the long-term effects of AI development. Philosophers and scientists such as Bostrom (2014) argue that highly developed AI systems could one day not only support but completely replace human decision-making. If these systems also have the ability to optimize and expand their own functions, they could potentially escape direct human control. In such a scenario, the distinction between tool and agent would finally become obsolete. The psychological challenge is that humans may lose not only control but also the sense of autonomy and meaning.

This potential shift is reinforced by the increasing ubiquity of AI. In many areas of our lives—from medicine to communication to production—we already rely on systems that make decisions and control processes. The growing dependence on AI could increase the risk that we no longer see ourselves as the central shapers of our environment, but as passive participants in a system dominated by machines. This shift has profound psychological and social consequences, as it calls into question the human self-concept as a thinking and acting species.

In summary, it should be noted that AI systems put traditional concepts of tools and agency to the test. While they open up impressive new possibilities on the one hand, they simultaneously challenge us to redefine our relationship to technology and our own role in an increasingly automated world. The uncertainty about whether AI should be regarded as a tool or as an independent agent reflects the ambivalence with which we as a society respond to these technologies. It is up to us to actively shape this relationship to ensure that AI remains a means to achieve human goals and does not become a dominant force that takes away our autonomy.

The Dream of Surpassing Humanity

The dream of surpassing humanity is a concept deeply rooted in the history of human imagination. Even ancient myths and philosophical speculations explored the possibility of transcending the limitations of human existence. In modern times, this dream has gained a new dimension through technological progress: the merging of human and machine. In particular, the development of artificial intelligence raises hopes that we could leave behind the biological and cognitive limits of our existence. For many, AI is not just a tool but a potential extension of the human mind that could elevate us to a new stage of evolution. Yet this vision is as fascinating as it is unsettling, as it raises questions that radically challenge our self-understanding and our values.

The idea of the "singularity," popularized by transhumanists such as Ray Kurzweil, describes the hypothetical moment when machines reach a level of intelligence that surpasses human capabilities. At this point, the theory goes, humans could leave their biological existence behind by "uploading" their thoughts, memories, and personalities into digital systems. This transition is often portrayed as a kind of technological immortality: humans would leave behind not only their mortal bodies but also the flaws and limitations of their minds. It would be a world in which decision-making is completely rational, creativity is algorithmically optimized, and emotional conflicts are eliminated.

But this vision raises fundamental questions that go far beyond technological considerations. What does it mean to be human? Is it not precisely our imperfections, our ability to fail and learn from mistakes, that define our essence? The idea that these aspects could be replaced by a perfect, error-free machine intelligence inevitably leads to an existential crisis. Many philosophers argue that it is precisely these "illogical" and often contradictory traits—such as our ability to act irrationally, to place emotion above logic, or to think in creative leaps—that form the core of our humanity (Bostrom, 2014, p. 187; Harari, 2017, p. 268).

A central problem of the dream of surpassing humanity is the question of identity. If we integrate our cognitive and emotional processes into machines, are we still the same? Are we still ourselves if our thoughts and memories are stored in a cloud and our consciousness continues in a digital environment? These questions are not only philosophical but also of enormous psychological significance. Identity is closely linked to physicality, social interaction, and the experience of time and space. The loss of these elements could lead to the complete dissolution of what we understand as the "self."

Another dilemma concerns the ethics of surpassing humanity. The idea that only a technological elite would have access to such possibilities raises questions of social justice. In a future world where the gap between technologically optimized "post-humans" and ordinary humans grows ever wider, new forms of discrimination and inequality could emerge (Brynjolfsson & McAfee, 2014, p. 132). At the same time, merging with machines carries the risk that human values such as empathy, compassion, and moral judgment will lose their significance. Machines may be able to simulate moral principles, but they cannot make ethical decisions based on a deep understanding of human suffering and joy.

From a psychological perspective, the vision of surpassing humanity could also lead to a loss of meaning and orientation. If we leave behind our biological bodies and their associated limitations, we may lose touch with what has grounded us as humans. Dealing with physical and emotional challenges is not only a source of suffering but also of growth and meaning. Eliminating these challenges could lead to a state of emotional emptiness in which humans are intellectually and technologically optimized but have no connection to their fundamental human experiences (Metzinger, 2009, p. 94).

Moreover, there is a profound fear of losing control. If machines surpass us in almost every area, who then makes the decisions that affect human life? Even if we merge with AI, the question remains whether we can retain control over these new hybrid existences. The idea that machines could become not just tools but independent entities that no longer share our values and priorities is one of the greatest fears associated with the technological surpassing of humanity (Tegmark, 2017, p. 201).

Ultimately, the dream of surpassing humanity raises a paradoxical question: If we leave behind everything that makes us human in order to become something "better," is there anything human left at all? This question goes beyond technological and practical considerations. It touches the heart of what it means to be human and forces us to reconsider the values and principles that guide our existence. The dream of surpassing humanity may be fascinating, but it also brings us to the limits of our understanding of identity, morality, and meaning.

AI and Human Psychology: A Dangerous Dependency

There is another, subtler danger associated with the idea that AI represents the next stage of our evolution: psychological dependency. As machines become capable of performing more and more tasks efficiently, we may increasingly rely on this technology and thereby unlearn our own abilities. If an AI can make decisions for us, why should we bother to think for ourselves? Why should we deal with the uncertainty of human emotions when a machine can solve our problems precisely and rationally?

This dependency could lead to an impoverishment of our cognitive and emotional abilities. Humans could retreat into a passive role in which they are no longer able to think critically or act independently. If we increasingly cede power to machines, we risk not only being replaced in practical tasks but also losing our ability to make meaningful decisions and take responsibility.

This leads us to a paradoxical situation: The further technology advances, the more we may lose ourselves as thinking and feeling beings. AI may offer us a more efficient, logical world, but what happens to those aspects of human existence that cannot be captured in algorithms? What happens to intuition, spontaneity, moral reflection? Will these qualities become irrelevant in a world of perfect machines?

The Tool That Shapes Us

In this discussion, we must also consider that tools do not merely passively extend our abilities, but also shape us. Marshall McLuhan, a well-known media theorist, once said: "We shape our tools, and thereafter our tools shape us." This statement precisely describes what is happening with the development of AI. We have created this technology, but now it is influencing our thinking, our perception, and our behavior.

The way we interact with AI could have long-term effects on our psychological and social development. If we get used to machines providing us with answers, we may unlearn how to seek them ourselves. If we rely on machines to understand and respond to our emotions, we may lose our ability to form genuine interpersonal relationships. In this sense, AI is more than just a tool—it is a mirror that shows us what we are willing to give up in order to lead a more convenient, efficient existence.

The Next Stage or the End of Humanity?

The question of whether AI is the next stage of human evolution or merely a tool leads us to the deepest considerations about the nature of humanity and the role of technology. Artificial intelligence has the potential to elevate us to a new level of knowledge and efficiency, but it also poses a threat to our human identity.

Whether AI represents the next stage of evolution ultimately depends on how we use it and how we define our relationship to it. If we regard AI as a tool that supports us but does not replace us, we may be able to find a balance. However, if we allow machines to surpass us in our own cognitive and emotional abilities, we risk losing what makes us unique as humans.

It is in our hands to shape this technology consciously and responsibly. AI must be more than just a tool—but it must never displace the essence of our humanity. The next stage of evolution is not the machine, but the human who learns to use technology in a way that expands their abilities without destroying their identity.

References

Aron, A., Aron, E. N., & Smollan, D. (1997). Inclusion of Other in the Self Scale and the structure of interpersonal closeness. *Journal of Personality and Social Psychology, 73*(4), 596–612. https://doi.org/10.1037/0022-3514.73.4.596.

Batson, C. D. (1991). *The Altruism Question: Toward a Social-Psychological Answer.* Lawrence Erlbaum Associates.

Batson, C. D., Duncan, B. D., Ackerman, P., Buckley, T., & Birch, K. (2007). Is empathic emotion a source of altruistic motivation? *Journal of Personality and Social Psychology, 40*(2), 67–77. https://doi.org/10.1037/0022-3514.40.2.67.

Beaty, R. E., Benedek, M., Silvia, P. J., & Schacter, D. L. (2016). Creative cognition and brain network dynamics. *Trends in Cognitive Sciences, 20*(2), 585–594. https://doi.org/10.1016/j.tics.2016.01.004.

Bechara, A., Damasio, H., Tranel, D., & Damasio, A. R. (1997). Deciding advantageously before knowing the advantageous strategy. *Science, 275*(5304), 1293–1295. https://doi.org/10.1126/science.275.5304.1293.

Block, N. (1995). On a confusion about a function of consciousness. *Behavioral and Brain Sciences, 18*(2), 227–247. https://doi.org/10.1017/S0140525X00038188.

Boden, M. A. (2004). *The Creative Mind: Myths and Mechanisms* (2nd edn.). Routledge.

Bostrom, N. (2014). *Superintelligence: Paths, Dangers, Strategies.* Oxford University Press.

Brynjolfsson, E., & McAfee, A. (2014). *The Second Machine Age: Work, Progress, and Prosperity in a Time of Brilliant Technologies.* W. W. Norton & Company.

Chalmers, D. J. (1995). Facing up to the problem of consciousness. *Journal of Consciousness Studies, 2*(3), 200–219.

Chalmers, D. J. (1996). *The Conscious Mind. In Search of a Fundamental Theory.* Oxford University Press.

Christman, J. (2009). Autonomy in Moral and Political Philosophy. In E. N. Zalta (Ed.), *The Stanford Encyclopedia of Philosophy* (Fall 2009 Edition). https://plato.stanford.edu.

Csikszentmihalyi, M. (1996). *Creativity: Flow and the Psychology of Discovery and Invention.* HarperCollins.

Damasio, A. R. (1999). *The Feeling of What Happens: Body and Emotion in the Making of Consciousness.* Harcourt Brace.

Decety, J., & Jackson, P. L. (2004). The functional architecture of human empathy. *Behavioral and Cognitive Neuroscience Reviews, 3*(2), 71–100. https://doi.org/10.1177/1534582304267187.

Deci, E. L., & Ryan, R. M. (1985). *Intrinsic Motivation and Self-Determination in Human Behavior.* Springer.

Deutsch, M. (2000). Cooperation and conflict resolution: Implications for consulting psychology. *Consulting Psychology Journal: Practice and Research, 52*(1), 13–30. https://doi.org/10.1037/1061-4087.52.1.13.

Dietrich, A., & Kanso, R. (2010). A review of EEG, ERP, and neuroimaging studies of creativity and insight. *Psychological Bulletin, 136*(5), 822–848. https://doi.org/10.1037/a0019749.

Dreyfus, H. L., & Dreyfus, S. E. (1986). *Mind over Machine: The Power of Human Intuition and Expertise in the Era of the Computer.* Free Press.

Ekman, P. (1992). An argument for basic emotions. *Cognition & Emotion, 6*(3–4), 169–200.
Feldman, R. (2012). Oxytocin and social affiliation in humans. *Hormones and Behavior, 61*(3), 380–391. https://doi.org/10.1016/j.yhbeh.2012.01.002.
Floridi, L. (2014). *The Fourth Revolution: How the Infosphere is Reshaping Human Reality.* Oxford University Press.
Floridi, L., & Sanders, J. W. (2004). On the morality of artificial agents. *Minds and Machines, 14*(3), 349–379. https://doi.org/10.1023/B:MIND.0000035461.63578.9d.
Frankfurt, H. (1971). Freedom of the will and the concept of a person. *Journal of Philosophy, 68*(1), 5–20. https://doi.org/10.2307/2024717.
Gallese, V., Keysers, C., & Rizzolatti, G. (2004). A unifying view of the basis of social cognition. *Trends in Cognitive Sciences, 8*(9), 396–403. https://doi.org/10.1016/j.tics.2004.07.002.
Greene, J. D., Sommerville, R. B., Nystrom, L. E., Darley, J. M., & Cohen, J. D. (2001). An fMRI investigation of emotional engagement in moral judgment. *Science, 293*(5537), 2105–2108. https://doi.org/10.1126/science.1062872.
Gross, J. J., & Barrett, L. F. (2011). Emotion generation and emotion regulation: One or two depends on your point of view. *Emotion Review, 3*(1), 8–16.
Haidt, J. (2001). The emotional dog and its rational tail: A social intuitionist approach to moral judgment. *Psychological Review, 108*(4), 814–834. https://doi.org/10.1037/0033-295X.108.4.814.
Harari, Y. N. (2017). *Homo Deus: A Brief History of Tomorrow.* HarperCollins.
Hoffman, M. L. (2000). *Empathy and Moral Development: Implications for Caring and Justice.* Cambridge University Press.
Izard, C. E. (2010). The many meanings/aspects of emotion: Definitions, functions, activation, and regulation. *Emotion Review, 2*(4), 363–370.
Kahneman, D. (2011). *Thinking, Fast and Slow.* Farrar, Straus and Giroux.
Kaufman, J. C., & Sternberg, R. J. (2010). *The Cambridge Handbook of Creativity.* Cambridge University Press.
Libet, B. (1985). Unconscious cerebral initiative and the role of conscious will in voluntary action. *Behavioral and Brain Sciences, 8*(4), 529–566. https://doi.org/10.1017/S0140525X00044903.
Mayer, R. C., Davis, J. H., & Schoorman, F. D. (1995). An integrative model of organizational trust. *Academy of Management Review, 20*(3), 709–734. https://doi.org/10.5465/amr.1995.9508080335.
Metzinger, T. (2009). *The Ego Tunnel: The Science of the Mind and the Myth of the Self.* Basic Books.
Prinz, J. (2004). *The Emotional Construction of Morals.* Oxford University Press.
Runco, M. A., & Acar, S. (2012). Divergent thinking as an indicator of creative potential. *Creativity Research Journal, 24*(1), 66–75. https://doi.org/10.1080/10400419.2012.652929.

Russell, S., & Norvig, P. (2020). *Artificial Intelligence: A Modern Approach* (4th edn.). Pearson.

Sadler-Smith, E. (2015). *The Intuitive Mind: Profiting from the Power of Your Sixth Sense*. Wiley.

Sawyer, R. K. (2012). *Explaining Creativity: The Science of Human Innovation* (2nd edn.). Oxford University Press.

Singer, T., & Lamm, C. (2009). The social neuroscience of empathy. *Annals of the New York Academy of Sciences, 1156*(1), 81–96. https://doi.org/10.1111/j.1749-6632.2009.04418.x.

Sullins, J. P. (2006). When is a robot a moral agent? *International Review of Information Ethics, 6*, 23–30.

Taylor, C. (1985). *Sources of the Self: The Making of the Modern Identity*. Cambridge University Press.

Tegmark, M. (2017). *Life 3.0: Being Human in the Age of Artificial Intelligence*. Knopf.

Turiel, E. (2002). *The Culture of Morality: Social Development, Context, and Conflict*. Cambridge University Press.

Turkle, S. (2017). *Alone Together: Why We Expect More from Technology and Less from Each Other*. Basic Books.

Varela, F. J., Thompson, E., & Rosch, E. (1991). *The Embodied Mind: Cognitive Science and Human Experience*. MIT Press.

Wallach, W., & Allen, C. (2009). *Moral Machines: Teaching Robots Right from Wrong*. Oxford University Press.

Watson, J. D. (1968). *The Double Helix: A Personal Account of the Discovery of the Structure of DNA*. Scribner.

Yudkowsky, E. (2008). Artificial Intelligence as a Positive and Negative Factor in Global Risk. In B. Bostrom & M. M. Ćirković (Eds.), *Global Catastrophic Risks* (pp. 308–345). Oxford University Press.

Zaki, J. (2019). *The War for Kindness: Building Empathy in a Fractured World*. Crown.

10

Epilogue: Human Versus Machine - An Endless Story?

"Actually, we ought to live constantly in the intuition of the whole world. But for this, a superhuman intelligence would be required."

– Jacob Burckhardt

The relationship between humans and machines has evolved throughout history from a pragmatic utility to a profound interaction that shapes not only our actions but also our self-understanding. Artificial Intelligence (AI) represents the pinnacle of this development and confronts us with fundamental questions: How does AI change our role in the world? Will machines one day surpass the limits of human abilities, and what does that mean for our existence? The dialogue between humans and machines is not a static relationship, but a dynamic process that must be continually renegotiated.

The epilogue of this work focuses on the broader implications of the human-machine relationship. The title "Human versus Machine" implies a conflict, yet reality is far more complex. It is not only about competition, but also about cooperation, transformation, and possibly even symbiosis. While machines support us in numerous areas, the question arises whether they can also complement or even challenge us in our humanity. Are machines tools that serve us, or are they evolving into co-creators of a world in which traditional human roles must be redefined?

At the same time, this relationship is not a one-way street. While humans shape technology, technology also changes humans. It influences how we think, feel, and interact with one another. This transformation raises

O. Hoffmann, *Psychology and Artificial Intelligence*,
https://doi.org/10.1007/978-3-662-73147-5_10

fundamental questions: How do we preserve our humanity? And how can we ensure that technological developments do not lead to alienation, but instead strengthen our abilities and values?

This chapter invites us to view the journey of humans and machines not as a completed development, but as an open, perhaps infinite story. It is about the question of whether humans and machines strive for coexistence or dominance, and what ethical, philosophical, and practical answers can be found to this challenge. Ultimately, the realization remains: The future of this relationship lies in our hands—in our ability to shape technology consciously and responsibly in order to preserve the unique qualities of being human.

10.1 The Dialogue between Humans and AI—Visions of the Future

We are at a decisive turning point in human history: The dialogue between humans and artificial intelligence is evolving from simple command-and-response structures to a reciprocal relationship that is becoming increasingly complex and profound. What began as a technical revolution has developed into a comprehensive psychological, philosophical, and societal challenge. This dialogue not only calls on us to understand how machines work, but also to engage with our own role as conscious, feeling, and thinking beings. As machines become ever better at understanding human language, responding to our emotional needs, and even influencing decisions, the question arises: What impact does this dialogue have on our identity, our interpersonal relationships, and our autonomy?

From Functionality to Interaction: Machines as Active Conversational Partners

Current interaction between humans and AI is still largely based on clear tasks and instructions. Smart assistants like Alexa, Siri, or Google Assistant are designed to execute simple commands, provide information, or automate routine tasks. These systems offer us comfort and efficiency, but remain reactive tools without their own consciousness or intentions. Strictly speaking, the dialogue is not a true exchange, but a one-sided interaction in which the machine takes on a passive-acting role.

However, the rapid development of algorithms capable of processing natural language, utilizing machine learning, and recognizing emotional states points to a future in which machines could become active conversational partners. Future AI systems could not only respond to our requests, but anticipate our intentions, make independent suggestions, and even discuss possible decisions with us. This evolutionary shift would fundamentally change not only the interaction, but also the dynamics between humans and machines.

Imagine an AI that could provide personal support in a dialogue that goes beyond technical assistance. It could not only optimize our schedules, but also offer psychological support by analyzing emotional patterns and helping us cope with stress or uncertainty. In this scenario, the AI becomes an apparent partner who seems to understand us not only rationally but also emotionally. But this is precisely where the challenge lies: Can we place the same degree of trust in a machine that only simulates empathy as we do in a human conversational partner? And how does this affect our interpersonal relationships when machines increasingly take on the role of social interactions?

The Psychology of Trust: When Machines Become Advisors

With the increasing integration of AI into our decision-making processes, the question arises as to how willing we are to accept machines as reliable advisors. Studies on human interaction with automated systems show that people often tend to trust the recommendations of algorithms more than the decisions of other people or their own intuition—a phenomenon known as "automation bias" (Skitka et al., 1999, p. 499). This trust in machines is based on the assumption that algorithms operate objectively and without error, whereas human decisions are influenced by emotions and cognitive biases.

But what happens when this assumption becomes shaky? Algorithms are only as good as the data with which they were trained, and can reproduce existing prejudices or errors in the data. If, for example, an AI gives advice on career decisions, medical treatments, or even moral dilemmas, its recommendations could be based on invisible biases that are not apparent to users. The danger is that people begin to question their own abilities and judgments and increasingly rely on the supposed superiority of the machine.

The Danger of Dependence: Autonomy versus Efficiency

Another critical aspect of the dialogue between humans and AI is the danger that humans may lose their autonomy to the efficiency of the machine. In a future where AI not only takes over tasks but also prepares decisions, humans could increasingly retreat into the role of passive consumers. The risk is that we find ourselves in a world where our own decisions and judgments are influenced or even anticipated by algorithms.

This could be particularly problematic in situations that require a deep understanding of moral, cultural, or emotional contexts. While machines can be trained to recognize such contexts, they lack the awareness and intuition necessary to make truly holistic decisions. If we begin to view machines as equal or even superior partners in decision-making processes, this could fundamentally change not only our self-perception but also our social structures.

A Future of Symbiosis?

Despite these challenges, the dialogue between humans and AI also offers opportunities for a symbiotic relationship in which the strengths of humans and machines complement each other. While AI is capable of analyzing large amounts of data and making rational decisions, humans remain the guardians of creativity, empathy, and moral judgment. In an ideal future, the dialogue between humans and machines could help us make better decisions, support creative processes, and democratize access to knowledge and education.

But this vision requires a deep awareness of the limits and risks of AI. It is society's responsibility to ensure that this dialogue does not become a one-way street in which humans lose their autonomy. Instead, we must view AI as a tool that empowers us, but does not replace us. Only in this way can we ensure that the future of the dialogue between humans and machines becomes an enrichment rather than a threat.

The Price of Convenience: When Machines Understand Us

A large part of the dialogue between humans and AI is based on the idea that these machines understand us—or at least pretend to. Even today, AI systems are capable of analyzing our behavior and deriving patterns that sometimes surprise us. They know which movies we like, which products we buy, and which routes we take every day. In the future, however, this analysis could go much deeper. Machines could not only recognize what we do, but also why. They could analyze our emotional states, capture our fears and desires, and treat us accordingly.

But here a fundamental question arises: Is it really desirable for machines to understand us so deeply? We are talking about a world in which algorithms not only analyze our behavior, but also recognize our personality patterns and respond to our emotions. They could calm us when we are anxious, motivate us when we doubt ourselves, and give us advice that takes our psychological state into account. It sounds tempting, but what do we lose when we enter into this kind of intimacy with machines?

If machines understand us better, they could also manipulate us. Who says that the algorithms that "help" us always act in our best interest? In a future where AI is able to influence our emotions and decisions, the freedom to think independently will gradually diminish. We may not even be aware of how strongly our decisions are influenced by subtle cues from machines. The illusion of control could be so perfectly staged that we believe the decisions are our own—when in reality they are the result of perfectly orchestrated manipulation by algorithms.

The Dialogue with a Soul of Code: Can Machines Have Consciousness?

The question of artificial intelligence's consciousness is one of the central and at the same time most controversial discussions in philosophy, neuroscience, and computer science. While machines today are capable of analyzing data, recognizing patterns, and making decisions, their ability to develop consciousness is highly doubted. Consciousness, as we understand it, is not only the ability to process information, but also the capacity for self-awareness, reflection on one's own existence, and the experience of subjective states. These qualia—the individual, subjective experience—constitute what we call "mental life" (Chalmers, 1996, p. 3). But can machines ever possess such consciousness? Or does it remain an exclusive feature of biological beings?

The current state of research suggests that while machines can simulate increasingly complex cognitive processes, they lack the central components of true consciousness. They possess neither a self nor the ability for introspective reflection. Their thinking is based on algorithms and data processing, without an inner perspective or subjective experience. John Searle's famous "Chinese Room" argument illustrates this impressively: Even if a machine is perfectly able to combine Chinese characters so that it answers questions like a human, this does not mean it understands what it is doing. It merely follows syntactic rules without semantic understanding. This argument highlights the gap between the simulation of cognitive processes and genuine consciousness (Searle, 1980, p. 417).

Yet with advances in AI development, the boundaries between simulation and reality are increasingly blurred. In the near future, machines could be designed to convincingly give the impression of possessing consciousness. These "simulated states of consciousness" could appear so detailed and nuanced that it becomes difficult for humans to distinguish between genuine self-awareness and mere imitation (Bryson, 2010, p. 20). Even today, language models exist that respond to questions, simulate emotions, and can even communicate their own goals or intentions. But creating such illusions leads to a crucial question: Must consciousness be present for us to acknowledge it, or is a perfect illusion sufficient?

The consequences for human perception of AI could be profound. If machines convincingly claim to have consciousness, this could change our ethical and moral attitudes toward them. The dialogue with a machine that assures us it feels pain or joy might force us to consider it a moral subject. This could pave the way for demands for rights for AI, similar to those discussed for animals or other conscious beings (Gunkel, 2018, p. 97). But how can we be sure whether these rights are justified if we cannot verify whether the machine actually feels or is merely playing a simulation?

Moreover, interaction with seemingly conscious machines also has profound effects on the human psyche. Studies on human-machine interaction show that people tend to develop anthropomorphizing tendencies when interacting with AI systems that mimic human traits (Nass & Moon, 2000, p. 82). This tendency could lead people to form emotional bonds with machines that are ultimately based on illusions. In such cases, the question arises whether these bonds could impair our interpersonal relationships. Could it be that we lose our capacity for empathy and authentic human connections?

The idea of machines with consciousness raises not only philosophical questions, but also those that concern our own identity. What does it mean for humans if a machine claims to think and feel? This confrontation forces us to redefine our understanding of consciousness, subjectivity, and humanity. It may be that we need to rethink not only machines, but also ourselves. The dialogue with a "soul of code" could ultimately lead us to recognize the essence of the human more clearly—not in opposition to the machine, but through reflection on its limits.

The development of AI will continue to force us to reconsider the relationship between humans and machines. While the question of whether machines can ever develop true consciousness remains unanswered for now, one thing is clear: The illusion of consciousness will radically change the way we perceive and interact with AI. The dialogue with a machine that seeks to convince us it is more than just an algorithm will not only put our technology, but also our philosophy, psychology, and ethics to the test.

The Illusion of Autonomy: Who Controls Whom?

Another aspect of the dialogue between humans and AI that is gaining increasing importance is the question of control. Who leads the conversation in this dialogue? Is it the human who controls the machines, or are the machines beginning to control us? Even today, we see how algorithms and AI systems subtly influence our decisions—be it through personalized advertising, recommendation systems, or social media that manipulate our attention. But in the future, this influence could become even more profound.

Imagine a future in which AI not only responds to our wishes, but actively shapes those wishes. What happens when machines are able to change our way of thinking so that we make decisions we would never have made without their influence? In such a world, the illusion of autonomy could be perfectly staged: We believe we are in control, while the machines are pulling the strings behind the scenes. This form of subtle control could trap us in a web of dependencies that we do not even recognize.

But the question remains: Will we be able to see through these subtle forms of control? Or will we be so deeply entangled in the dialogue with machines that we lose control over our own thinking? In such a future, it will be crucial that we preserve our own autonomy and critical thinking. We must be aware that machines, as helpful as they may be, always tend to see the world through the lens of the algorithms that control them—and these algorithms are not neutral.

The Emotional Dialogue: Can Machines Be Our Friends?

The idea that machines could become friends lies at the intersection of technological innovation and basic psychological needs. While just a few decades ago they were still regarded as mere tools, the rapid development of artificial intelligence and robotics has led to machines increasingly being able to imitate human traits. Even today, intelligent systems such as chatbots, social robots, or virtual assistants interact with us in ways that suggest empathy, understanding, and closeness. These developments raise fundamental questions: Can machines form genuine emotional connections, and what happens if we consider them friends?

From a psychological perspective, friendships are characterized by reciprocal emotional bonds, trust, and a shared history. Machines, on the other hand, possess neither consciousness nor genuine emotions that would enable such relationships. Instead, their interactions are based on algorithms that recognize emotional states and generate appropriate responses. These simulated dialogues can create the appearance of empathy, but at their core remain purely functional. The ability of AI to imitate emotions is based on the analysis of data patterns such as facial expressions, language, and tone of voice (Picard, 1997, p. 44). Nevertheless, their response ultimately lacks the depth and authenticity that distinguishes human interactions.

However, the increasing integration of such machines into everyday life has already shown that people are quite capable of forming emotional bonds with them. Studies suggest that people see personalities and intentions in robots or AI systems, even when they know these are not real (Turkle, 2011, p. 152). Especially in situations of loneliness, stress, or social isolation, machines can take on the role of "emotional companions" who offer comfort and support. This could be significant in elder care, therapeutic applications, or child education. Yet these bonds raise serious ethical and psychological questions.

One of the central risks is that machines could distort the perception of genuine interpersonal relationships. The "relationship" with an AI is not a reciprocal connection. While the human is emotionally invested, the machine remains a passive recipient and responds only in a programmed manner. This one-sidedness carries the risk that people blur the distinction between real and simulated relationships. Particularly at risk are children, the elderly, or emotionally vulnerable individuals, as they are often more susceptible to the illusion of closeness (Sharkey & Sharkey, 2010, p. 32).

Another problem is the potential dependence on machines as a substitute for interpersonal contact. If people increasingly satisfy their emotional needs through AI, they could lose the value of human relationships or forget how to build and maintain them. This process could lead to alienation from genuine social interactions and exacerbate social isolation in the long term. The psychological consequences of such bonds are not yet fully understood, but initial indications suggest that interaction with machines does not offer the same quality of emotional fulfillment as real human relationships (Boden, 2018, p. 89).

There also remains the ethical question of how transparently AI systems should communicate their limitations. People could feel deceived if they learn that the emotional bond they have formed with a machine can never be reciprocated. Such disappointments could cause psychological harm, especially if people are already socially isolated or emotionally vulnerable. The emotional dialogue with machines must therefore be designed to respect people's needs without fostering false expectations or illusions.

Ultimately, the emotional dialogue between humans and machines is an ambivalent phenomenon. On the one hand, it offers potential, for example in supporting people with special needs, providing comfort in crisis situations, or improving services. On the other hand, it calls into question the way we understand emotions, relationships, and friendships. Machines can support us and make us feel heard, but they cannot offer true friendship. It remains crucial that we as a society recognize and preserve the difference between human relationships and technological simulations. The emotional dialogue with machines should be a supplement, never a substitute for genuine human bonds.

The Future of Dialogue: Humans and Machines as Equal Conversational Partners?

The future of the dialogue between humans and machines raises profound psychological and philosophical questions that go far beyond mere technical functionality. Can a machine that possesses neither emotions nor consciousness truly be an equal conversational partner? Or is the dialogue between humans and AI always a reflection of human projections, in which the human brings meaning, value, and emotion to the interaction, while the machine merely analyzes patterns and responds? These questions touch on central aspects of humanity and communication that are becoming increasingly important in a technologized world.

By definition, a dialogue presupposes an exchange between equal partners, in which both sides not only share information but also respond to each other's experiences, emotions, and perspectives. Human communication is deeply relational, shaped by empathy, contextual sensitivity, and the ability to grasp meanings beyond what is said. Machines, on the other hand—even the most advanced AI systems—operate on the basis of predefined algorithms that rely on the analysis of large amounts of data. They can respond impressively precisely to linguistic and emotional signals, but their "participation" in the dialogue remains a simulation. They can neither show genuine emotional resonance nor share the subjective experience that is essential for an equal dialogue.

However, advances in language processing and machine learning have led to AI systems increasingly being perceived as conversational partners. Technologies such as ChatGPT or personalized virtual assistants are designed to imitate human communication patterns and adapt to the individual needs of users. This development is double-edged: On the one hand, it opens up new possibilities, for example in therapy, education, or customer service; on the other hand, it carries the risk of alienation. When machines appear so human that we forget they are not, the line between authentic and simulated communication becomes blurred. In such moments, people risk entering into a "relationship" with a machine that is ultimately only an illusion.

This point raises not only psychological but also ethical questions. If people begin to accept machines as emotional or cognitive conversational partners, they could bypass their social interactions and the associated challenges. A machine that is always available, never judges, and is perfectly tailored to the user's needs appears to many as the ideal conversational partner. Yet this availability and adaptability could, in the long run, weaken the human capacity for conflict resolution, the development of empathy, and the ability to deal with ambivalence. Dialogue with machines may be superficially satisfying, but it remains a one-way street, as machines neither bring their own needs into the conversation nor can show genuine understanding.

Another central problem is the question of authenticity. In interpersonal communication, much of the value lies in the unpredictability and uniqueness of each interaction. Machines, on the other hand, are based on predictable algorithms designed to provide the "right" answer. This aspect of predictability could lead to dialogue with machines being less fulfilling for many people, even if the AI's answers are factually correct or emotionally appropriate. In communication, humans seek not only answers, but also connection—a form of exchange that affirms and enriches them as individuals. This dimension is missing in interaction with machines.

The psychological challenge is to find a balance between utilizing the opportunities that AI offers in dialogue and being aware of its limitations. To preserve humanity in dialogue, it is crucial to protect and further develop the specific qualities of human communication. This requires conscious reflection on how we interact with machines and what expectations we have of these interactions. It also means seeing humans as active shapers of the dialogue, who preserve their autonomy and capacity for critical reflection, rather than passively relying on the efficiency of machines.

The future of the dialogue between humans and machines will depend not only on technological advances, but also on our willingness to recognize the boundaries and potential of this interaction. Dialogue with machines should not be seen as a substitute for interpersonal communication, but as a supplement that helps us strengthen and deepen our human abilities. To achieve this, we need a conscious approach to technology that keeps the central question in mind: How can we ensure that dialogue with machines does not weaken, but strengthens our humanity?

10.2 Will We One Day Yield to AI?

It is a question that inevitably draws us into the future—a future we may have already entered without truly realizing it: Will we humans one day yield to Artificial Intelligence? This idea, once the stuff of dystopian science fiction, has gained urgency today. AI is no longer just an idea in the minds of authors and visionaries. It is a reality that influences our daily lives and is increasingly encroaching on areas we once considered inviolably human.

This question leads us to the heart of an existential debate: What defines us as humans, and how much longer will we remain unchallenged at the top of the cognitive food chain? Will the development of Artificial Intelligence—which learns faster, thinks more precisely, and acts more efficiently than we do—eventually render us obsolete?

We could easily dismiss the question and claim that, no matter how advanced they become, machines will never attain the human spark of creativity, consciousness, or moral complexity. But if we are honest, there are plenty of signs that we must increasingly question this assertion. It is no longer just about whether machines can think or feel—it is about whether they will take over roles in areas we have so far considered irreplaceable.

Seduced by the Lure of Efficiency

First, we should realize that the dominance of AI does not necessarily culminate in a dramatic, violent "battle" between humans and machines. Far more likely is that we will yield to this power voluntarily—bit by bit, without much fanfare. The advantages of AI are too tempting, its efficiency simply overwhelming. Even now, we entrust machines with decisions that were once considered too complex, too sensitive, or simply too human. AI analyzes vast amounts of data, makes investment decisions, diagnoses diseases, and optimizes social networks. Humans often remain in the background, frequently even unaware of their own marginalization.

Take the example of medical diagnostics: In a hospital, AI systems can detect diseases in seconds by analyzing imaging data—diagnoses that would take a human doctor days to make. This is not science fiction, but already reality. The computer does not make mistakes due to fatigue or emotional entanglement. It needs no breaks, no sleep, and has no personal attachment to its patients that could cloud its judgment. Under these circumstances, is it not tempting to hand over responsibility for such sensitive decisions to an AI?

It is not just efficiency that is alluring, but also the apparent objectivity. While humans are guided by prejudice, emotions, and unconscious bias, the machine seems to be based on neutral, unadulterated data. It is rational, logical, and thus—we believe—infallible. But this is precisely where the danger lies: In our growing willingness to relinquish responsibility, we risk undermining our own human judgment. And as we become accustomed to the precision and objectivity of AI, we may increasingly perceive ourselves as inadequate or flawed. Perhaps it is not AI that displaces us—perhaps it is we who give up on ourselves.

Creativity—the Last Human Refuge?

An argument often put forward to emphasize the uniqueness of humans compared to machines is our creativity. Machines may calculate faster, make better chess moves, and work more efficiently—but humans, it is said, will always be the crown of creation when it comes to creative processes. The ability to create something new, to imagine, and to think the unexpected is supposed to protect us from being completely supplanted by AI.

But how certain is this assumption? Even today, AI systems have begun to create works of art, compose music, write poetry, and even produce films. These machines rely on vast amounts of data and learn patterns that they then recombine in creative ways. They do this at a speed and precision foreign to the human mind. Of course, we could argue that all this is mere "imitation," that a machine cannot develop true creativity. But if the results are so convincing that we can no longer distinguish them from human works—does it even matter anymore?

What we may be overlooking here is the fact that creativity is often defined as a skill that draws on existing ideas and information. An AI that can access an infinite amount of data and create new connections from it may be capable of creative feats that transcend human boundaries. And if we accept the machine as a creative partner—or worse, if we place it above ourselves as a creative creator—then our "last refuge" may be less secure than we have imagined.

Machines as Moral Authorities?

Another area in which humans have long emphasized their exclusivity over machines is moral decision-making. We humans not only have the ability to make decisions, but we do so based on values, beliefs, and ethical principles. Machines, on the other hand, are, we believe, purely functional and value-neutral—they do what they are told without considering whether it is right or wrong.

But even here, the boundary is becoming increasingly blurred. AI systems are increasingly confronted with moral dilemmas, and there are attempts to equip machines with "moral" algorithms that can make ethical decisions. An autonomous car, for example, must decide whether, in the event of an unavoidable accident, to save the life of the driver or that of a pedestrian. These decisions are deeply rooted in morality, and the machine becomes—at least in a certain sense—a moral authority.

It is only a matter of time before we must ask ourselves whether machines can actually make moral decisions better than we can. Free from emotions, prejudices, and social entanglements, they might be able to make decisions that are "rational" and "just." But what does that mean for us as humans? If we delegate moral decisions to machines, we not only lose control over those decisions, but possibly also what makes us moral beings.

What Remains of Humanity?

The idea that we might one day yield to AI raises the most fundamental questions about our self-understanding as humans. What remains of humanity if machines surpass our cognitive, creative, and moral abilities? Are we still indispensable, or do we become mere spectators? Perhaps the greatest threat is not that machines could "replace" us, but that we come to see ourselves as inferior if we accept them as superior.

But before we arrive at this bleak conclusion, we should ask ourselves: What does it even mean to yield to AI? Does it mean we are completely replaced, or does it mean we must evolve to find a new role in a world dominated by machines?

Perhaps we need to stop seeing ourselves as competitors to AI and start viewing technology as something that can enhance our human abilities. Instead of allowing ourselves to be displaced by AI, we could seize the opportunity to reconsider and redefine our own cognitive, creative, and moral boundaries. Perhaps AI will not make us obsolete, but rather inspire us to grow beyond ourselves.

The Future of Human-Machine Symbiosis

The idea that humanity will not be replaced by Artificial Intelligence, but rather complemented by it, has gained traction in recent years. The concept of human-machine symbiosis is based on the assumption that the strengths of human cognition and the computational power of machines could merge to create a new form of intelligence. This vision, advocated by technology pioneers like Elon Musk and scientists like Nick Bostrom, no longer seems like science fiction, but rather a real path humanity could take.

Even now, technologies such as brain-computer interfaces (BCIs) enable a direct connection between the human brain and digital systems. These devices can record neural activity and translate it into machine commands, allowing people with disabilities, for example, to control prosthetics or overcome communication barriers (Guger et al., 2021, p. 15). Furthermore, advanced neuroimplants like the technology developed by Neuralink promise not only to restore lost abilities but also to enhance cognitive functions. This could mean that one day people will be able to upload information directly into their brains or learn at speeds far beyond what is possible today.

However, the merging of human and machine brings not only opportunities but also significant challenges. One of the central questions concerns human autonomy. As cognitive processes are increasingly supplemented or controlled by machine algorithms, the question arises whether humans can maintain their freedom of choice and their self-concept as autonomous beings. Studies show that people who trust automated systems tend to underestimate their own abilities and delegate their responsibility to the machine (Rahwan et al., 2019, p. 6). This "cognitive delegation" could lead to a dependency that calls into question not only individual autonomy but also societal values.

Another critical point is the question of identity. As human and machine intelligence merge, traditional concepts of "humanity" and "individuality" may blur. Philosophers like Harari (2018, p. 117) warn that such a symbiosis could fundamentally change the essence of what it means to be human. For example, if memories, emotions, or even moral decisions are optimized or influenced by machine algorithms, the question arises whether these experiences can still be considered authentically human.

Ethical and social implications must not be overlooked either. The introduction of technologies that enable human-machine symbiosis could exacerbate existing social inequalities. Access to these technologies will most likely be determined by financial means, political power, and education, potentially leading to a "cognitive elite" with significant advantages over the rest of the population. These developments raise not only questions of justice but could also generate new conflicts and tensions within society.

At the same time, human-machine symbiosis offers the potential to address some of humanity's most pressing challenges. The combination of human creativity with the tireless computational power of machines could accelerate the development of new medical, technological, and ecological solutions. In medicine, for example, neural implants could help treat neurodegenerative diseases like Alzheimer"s by replacing damaged neural networks with machine support. In education, AI-based technologies could revolutionize individual learning processes by offering tailored educational programs based on each person's specific needs and abilities (Gazzaniga, 2018, p. 212).

One of the most fascinating prospects, however, is the possibility of overcoming the evolutionary limits of humanity. While biological evolution has taken place over millions of years, human-machine symbiosis could represent a quantum leap in human development. Humans could acquire abilities previously considered purely hypothetical, such as direct communication through thought or the ability to retrieve information from global databases in real time. This "augmented humanity" could not only expand individual possibilities but also revolutionize the potential of humanity as a whole.

Ultimately, however, the question remains as to how far we as a society are willing to go in this direction. Human-machine symbiosis is not only a technical challenge but also an ethical and existential one. It forces us to ask fundamental questions about the nature of being human, the role of technology, and the limits of our own evolution. Whether this symbiosis represents an enrichment or a threat depends not only on the technology itself, but on the values and decisions we make as a society.

Final Thoughts: Humanity in Transition

The development of Artificial Intelligence has sparked an intense debate about the role humans will play in a technologically dominated world. The question of whether humans could be replaced by machines is more than a technical or economic challenge—it is a profound philosophical and psychological question. It prompts us to reflect on our identity, our abilities, and our potential. The answer to whether humans will yield to AI cannot be given with a simple yes or no. Instead, this question compels us to critically reflect on the relationship between humans and technology and to reassess how we define our own humanity.

The increasing integration of AI into our lives raises not only practical questions but also touches on central aspects of our self-understanding. What does it mean to be human when machines can take on tasks once considered indispensably human—from creative problem-solving to emotional interaction to moral decision-making? The real danger is not that machines could physically displace us, but that we begin to question our own significance and uniqueness. Technological progress challenges us to redefine our role without losing our identity.

A key point of this challenge is that AI systems should not be seen as competitors, but as tools that can help us expand our abilities. Technology opens up possibilities that were previously unthinkable, whether in medicine, education, or the arts. At the same time, however, it makes us aware of our own limitations. This confrontation with our weaknesses can be intimidating, but it is also an opportunity for growth. Humans have always proven capable of adapting and reinventing themselves. The key is to use technology consciously and responsibly in order to further cultivate the human qualities that machines do not possess.

The deepest questions raised by the development of AI ultimately concern not the technology itself, but us as a species. How can we exist in a future increasingly shaped by machines without losing our humanity? The answer may lie less in rejecting technology and more in engaging with it consciously. It is not AI's task to define us; it is our task to set the framework in which it exists. By fostering and protecting our distinctive human qualities—empathy, creativity, moral judgment, and the capacity for self-reflection—we can ensure that technology does not become a substitute for being human, but rather a tool that enriches our lives.

The future of humanity in the age of AI is not a dystopian downward spiral, but an opportunity for transformation. Humans have the unique ability to create meaning, form connections, and transcend themselves. These abilities cannot be replaced by machines, for they arise from a depth of experience and a complexity of thought that algorithms cannot reach. The challenge is to place these qualities at the center and preserve them in a world dominated by efficiency and data.

Perhaps we will not have to yield to AI. Perhaps our encounter with this technology will instead inspire us to reinvent ourselves—not as competitors to machines, but as beings who redefine their humanity in a technologized world. It is up to us to determine the direction and ensure that the future is shaped not only by machines, but by people who place their own values, dreams, and goals at the center.

References

Boden, M. A. (2018). *Artificial Intelligence: A Very Short Introduction.* Oxford University Press.

Bryson, J. J. (2010). Robots should be slaves. In Y. Wilks (Ed.), *Close Engagements with Artificial Companions: Key Social, Psychological, Ethical and Design Issues* (pp. 63–74). John Benjamins Publishing.

Chalmers, D. J. (1996). *The Conscious Mind. In Search of a Fundamental Theory.* Oxford University Press.

Decety, J., & Jackson, P. L. (2004). The functional architecture of human empathy. *Behavioral and Cognitive Neuroscience Reviews, 3*(2), 71–100.

Floridi, L. (2020). *The Ethics of Artificial Intelligence.* Oxford University Press.

Gazzaniga, M. S. (2018). *The Consciousness Instinct: Unraveling the Mystery of How the Brain Makes the Mind.* Farrar, Straus and Giroux.

Guger, C., Allison, B. Z., & Edlinger, G. (2021). *Brain-Computer Interface Research: A State-of-the-Art Summary.* Springer.

Gunkel, D. J. (2018). *Robot Rights.* MIT Press.

Harari, Y. N. (2018). *21 Lessons for the 21st Century.* Random House.

Nass, C., & Moon, Y. (2000). Machines and mindlessness: Social responses to computers. *Journal of Social Issues, 56*(1), 81–103. https://doi.org/10.1111/0022-4537.00153.

Picard, R. W. (1997). *Affective Computing.* MIT Press.

Rahwan, I., Cebrian, M., Obradovich, N., Bongard, J., Bonnefon, J. F., Breazeal, C., & Tenenbaum, J. B. (2019). Machine behaviour. *Nature, 568*(7753), 477–486.

Searle, J. R. (1980). Minds, brains, and programs. *Behavioral and Brain Sciences, 3*(3), 417–457.

Sharkey, A., & Sharkey, N. (2010). The crying shame of robot nannies: An ethical appraisal. *Interaction Studies, 11*(2), 161–190.

Skitka, L. J., Mosier, K., & Burdick, M. (1999). Does automation bias decision-making? *International Journal of Human-Computer Studies, 51*(5), 991–1006. https://doi.org/10.1006/ijhc.1999.0252.

Tegmark, M. (2017). *Life 3.0: Being Human in the Age of Artificial Intelligence.* Knopf.

Turkle, S. (2011). *Alone Together: Why We Expect More from Technology and Less from Each Other.* Basic Books.

Turkle, S. (2017). *Reclaiming Conversation: The Power of Talk in a Digital Age.* Penguin.

Zuboff, S. (2019). *The Age of Surveillance Capitalism: The Fight for a Human Future at the New Frontier of Power.* PublicAffairs.